Mary's Heart Secrets

*But **Mary** treasured up all these things and pondered them in her heart.*
And the child grew and became strong; he was filled with wisdom, and the grace of God was
on him." **Luke 2:19** and **Luke 2:40**

By David Visser

ISBN: 1494846284
ISBN 13: 9781494846282
Library of Congress Control Number: 2013923811
CreateSpace Independent Publishing Platform
North Charleston, South Carolina

Dedicated to
Les Feldick, who for the past twenty years
taught me each weekday morning, the Word of God.
Les and Iris, his help mate and wife,
gave their lives to the teaching of the Word of
God to gatherings homes to Bible studies
and then to teaching the nations. I also
thank Robert H. Bailey who edited
this book to make it what it is.

Notes: Les can be seen on Ion TV each weekday morning or on your
local Christian TV Station.
All scriptures are in italic.

Introduction

God did not talk to his people, Israel, for four hundred years. All was quiet for all these years between God and Israel. But now is was time for the Son of God to come to his people Israel. The Bible tells us, *"But Mary kept all these things, and pondered them in her heart."* What were all these things Mary kept hidden deep within her heart? It all started in the **temple on Mount Zion, in Jerusalem of Judah. It was the beginning of a two thousand year march back to Zion.** It was Zechariah's, a priest of the lineage of Aaron, time to burn incense in the temple of the Lord. While in the temple the Angel Gabriel appeared to Zechariah. The appearance of Gabriel broke the four years of silence from Israel hearing from the Lord. Following the appearance of Gabriel, there were many other appearances of angels, visions and dreams which foreshadowed the coming of the Messiah. All these things Mary kept in her heart and she told her young child these stories over and over so that after his Bar Mitzvah at the age of twelve he sat in the temple for three days answering the questions of the learned Rabbis of Israel. His parents were amazed and sorrowful because he was not with them on the way back to Nazareth but then found the young man in the **temple on Mount Zion in Jerusalem of Judah.** *"How is it that ye sought me? Were you not that I must be about my* **Father's** *business?"* These words are the first red letter words in the Bible. He was not answering questions about the work of a carpenter. He was there answering the Rabbis' questions about His Heavenly Father. At this time at the age of twelve he, the son of man, the son of Mary, knew he was **THE SON OF GOD.** This faith that he was the the son of man and also **THE SON OF GOD** enabled him to make the blind see, the deaf hear, dead to come alive, and preach the gospel of the kingdom to the poor.

Being without sin and having his faith that he was the Son of God, enabled Christ to face Satan's temptations to take the easy way to be the King of Israel vi | David Visser

and ruler of the world. Unlike Adam who fell into sin the first time he was tempted, Jesus, the second Adam, had to face three mass temptations. He did not fail because of his faith that he was the Son of God, He knew that his mission was not to reign Israel and rule the world, but to take on the wrath of God, on the cross to redeem the world of the sting of sin and death.

He lived a sinless life fulfilling the Law of Moses which no other could do. Before the cross Jesus went to the Garden of Gethsemane to pray to God the Father knowing what was to happen, *"O my Father, if it be possible, let this cup pass from me: nevertheless not as I will, but as thou wilt."* As the son of man he asked that if it were possible to avert the cross, but knowing he was the Son of God, there was no other way to redeem man.

He died on that cross. The God the Father, forsook God the Son and let him die on the cross, to be buried, so that God the Spirit could raise him from death and hell. He was forsaken. He was buried and laid dead for three days. But he arose again from the dead conquering death for all who would believe. He was the first to be resurrected from the dead. Ten days after his ascension into heaven on the day of Pentecost, the Holy Spirit came to dwell in the bodies of the believers. In the **temple on Mount Zion** the news of the risen Messiah was preached to Israel. Like Israel had forty years in the wilderness to turn to the Law of Moses the Jews had forty years to recognize that Jesus was the Messiah. After the forty years the temple, Jerusalem, and Judah were destroyed. The temple mount was totally removed from Mount Zion, and filled with dirt and planted with vegetation. The city of Jerusalem was rubble. The cities of Judah were destroyed. The people whose lives were spared were removed from Judah and put in diaspora. (Diaspora is the scattering of the Jews to all the nations of the world).

For nineteen hundred years the people of Israel were scattered throughout the world. There was not a major city in the world that did not have a community of Jews in diaspora. They came to all the cities of the world poor and needy. They would build a synagogue, buy a cemetery, and start businesses. But in the later years of the nineteenth century and at the beginning of the twentieth century the Jews began to return to what was then Palestine and in 1948 they again became a nation. The nation of Israel named after their father Jacob.

Mount Zion is now theirs. It is still trodden down by the Gentiles. But soon their Messiah will return to this earth with his feet touching the Mount of Olives. A temple will have to be built again on Mount Zion in Jerusalem of Judah. God, the God of their fathers Abraham, Isaac, and Jacob shall rule Israel and all the world from **Mount Zion in Jerusalem.**

one

God Ends 400 Years of Silence

"In the beginning God created the heavens and the earth." This statement starts the written Word of God in Genesis 1:1. It also was the beginning of a segment of eternity called time. This segment of eternity will end when God again creates a new heaven and earth where only righteousness dwells. The apostle John starts his gospel with the same theme. *"In the beginning was the Word, and the Word was with God, and the Word was God. He was with God in the beginning. Through him all things were made; without him nothing was made that has been made."* **John 1:1-3** Here John is writing about the second person of the Trinity the Lord Jesus Christ.

The Lord Jesus Christ, just what does this title mean? John tells us that this person of the trinity, the Lord Jesus Christ, was the person who created all things and has authority, control, and power over all others. Jesus was the earthly name that the angel of God told Mary and Joseph to call the child. "And the angel said unto her, fear not, Mary: for thou has found favor with God. And behold, thou shall conceive in thy womb and bring forth a son, and shall call his name **JESUS**." **Luke 1:30-31** An angel also appeared to Joseph saying, "And she shall bring forth a son, and thou shalt call his name **JESUS**; for he shall save his people from their sins." **Matthew 1:21**. The name in Hebrew means "Yahweh is Salvation" or Yehoshau **"Jehovah Saves."** The word Christ means the promised one of Israel, the Messiah, the Son of God. Putting all these meanings together we find He is the one with authority, control, power, who saves his people from their sins, and is the promised Messiah of the Old Testament. John called him the Word in the opening verses of his gospel. If we put the name of the Lord Jesus Christ in John's opening verses the meaning comes more alive.

"In the beginning was the Lord Jesus Christ, and the Lord Jesus Christ was with God, and the Lord Jesus Christ was God. He was with God in the beginning. Through him (The Lord Jesus Christ) all things were made; without him (the Lord Jesus Christ) nothing was made that has been made." We then realize that the Lord Jesus Christ was the person of the Trinity who spoke the universe into existence.

"The virgin will conceive and give birth to a son, and they will call him Immanuel" (which means "God with us.") **Matthew 1:23**. This was the fulfillment of **Isaiah 7:14**. "Therefore the Lord himself will give you a sign: The virgin will conceive and give birth to a son, and will call him Immanuel." The virgin who would conceive was Mary the mother of Jesus. **Luke 1:31** You will conceive and give birth to a son, and you are to call him **Jesus**. After Mary's conception by the Holy Spirit in her womb was the Son of man (Mary's part in the conception) and the Son of God (the Holy Spirit's part in the conception.) So this one person in Mary's womb was fully the Son of man and fully the Son of God.

The birth of Jesus in Bethlehem was very well know by the religious leaders in Jerusalem. When the wise men were following the star to Jerusalem they asked, *"Where is he that is born King of the Jews?"* **Matthew 2:1.** Herod the then king over the Jews, was troubled. He did not want to give up his rule over the Jews. Herod had sent for the religious leaders of the Jews demanding to know where this Christ (Messiah) would be born. They quickly told Herod the answer by quoting him *"But you, Bethlehem, though you are small among the clans of Judah, out of you will come for me one who will be ruler over Israel, whose origins are from of old, from ancient times."* **Micah 5:2**

We all know the story of the birth of Christ. We celebrate his birth every year. Mary brought forth a child in a barn and laid the child in the manger. There was no room in the inn in Bethlehem. Now, God could have had that inn completely empty. He is God, his eye is on the sparrows, and if he wanted the inn full, it would be full. Then why was Jesus born in a barn and had a manger for his bed? It is very simple. Lambs are not born in inns or houses, lambs are born in a barn. When Christ began his earthly ministry to the Jewish people, John the Baptist introduced him by saying, *"Look, the* **Lamb of God**, *who takes away the sin of the world!"* John did not introduce Jesus as the coming healer, the one who would be performing signs and wonders to the Jews. John went directly to the Cross. This was the only reason Jesus came to earth. Jesus was to be the Lamb of God who would take the sins of this world unto himself. He would die, be buried, and would be raised from the grave after three days by the power of the Holy Spirit. **His purpose was to be the Lamb slain for the sin of mankind.**

two

God Speaks

Going back to Bethlehem, a child was born who was both the Son of man and the Son of God. Could Jesus the Son of God at birth declare "I am the Son of God?" Yes, he was God. But he restricted His power as the Son of God to the maturity of the Son of man. How is this so? First, after the birth of Christ Herod made a decree that all the children under the age of two in Bethlehem be killed. An angel of the Lord appeared to Joseph in a dream saying, *"Arise and take the young child and his mother and flee to Egypt and be there until I bring you word: for Herod will seek the young child to destroy him."* **Matthew 2:13** Now when Herod was dead, behold an angel of the Lord appeared in a dream to Joseph in Egypt saying, *"Arise and take the young child and his mother, and go into the land of Israel: for they are dead which sought the young child's life."* **Matthew 2:19-20** As the Son of God Jesus would know this and could have told Joseph himself. This shows that this child, the Son of God, had limited himself to the maturity of the Son of man. Now we do not read anything about Jesus until he reaches the age of twelve. All the events up to the going back to Israel Mary held these events into her heart and as Jesus began to mature and understand she shared these things with Jesus. *"But Mary treasured up all these things and pondered them in her heart."* **Luke 2:19** The words spoken to many about this child called Jesus prior to his birth and his return to Nazareth, were hid in the heart of Mary and she treasured every word.

As the Old Testament closed and the prophets spoke no more to Israel, there was a span of approximately four hundred years of complete silence from God to the people of Israel. No one in Israel had heard from God. But one day a priest named Zechariah and his wife Elisabeth who were both righteous before God, walking in all the commandments and ordinances of the Lord blameless. They had no children. Elisabeth was barren and was beyond the age to conceive. According to the Jewish priesthood office, it was Zechariah's time to burn incense in the **temple of the Lord on Mount Zion.** As Zechariah went into the temple he saw Gabriel, the angel of the Lord standing on the right side of the altar. Gabriel told Zechariah that his wife would conceive and have a child and the child should be called John. John in the Hebrew meant "the Lord is gracious." *"This child was to be great in the sight of the Lord and* **filled with the Holy Ghost** *from birth. He will bring back many of the people of Israel to the Lord their God. And he will go on before the Lord, in the spirit and power of Elijah, to turn the hearts of the parents to their children and the disobedient to the wisdom of the righteous—to make ready a people prepared for the Lord."* God after 400 years of silence was again communicating with his people Israel. **See Luke 1:1-25**

Elisabeth conceived and after six months God sent the angel Gabriel to Nazareth to the virgin Mary who was engaged to Joseph. Joseph was from the lineage of David who would be in line to be King of Israel if Israel was a free people.

Gabriel was sent by God to Mary. The birth of Jesus foretold in the sixth month of Elizabeth's pregnancy, God sent the angel Gabriel to Nazareth, a town in Galilee, to a virgin pledged to be married to a man named Joseph, a descendant of David. The virgin's name was Mary. The angel went to her and said, *"Greetings, you who are highly favored! The Lord is with you."* Mary was greatly troubled at his words and wondered what kind of greeting this might be. But the angel said to her, *"Do not be afraid, Mary; you have found favor with God. You will conceive and give birth to a son, and* **you are to call him Jesus.** *He will be great and will be called the Son of the Most High. The Lord God will give him the throne of his father David, and he will reign over Jacob's descendants forever; his kingdom will never end." "How will this be,"* Mary asked the angel, *"since I am a virgin?"* The angel answered, *"The Holy Spirit will come on you, and the power of the Most High will overshadow you. So the holy one to be born will be called the Son of God. Even Elizabeth, your relative, is going to have a child in her old age, and she who was said to be unable to conceive is in her sixth month. For no word from God will ever fail." "I am the Lord's servant,"* Mary answered. *"May your word to me be fulfilled."* Then the angel left her. **Luke 1:26-38**

God has always had a remnant. When Elijah was running after defeating the prophets of Baal, he thought he was the only one left who served God. But God told him he had a remnant. *"Yet I reserve seven thousand in Israel—all whose knees have not bowed down to Baal and whose mouths have not kissed him."* **1 Kings 19:18** In the days of Christ's birth there was also a remnant. Like Zechariah and his wife Elisabeth were both righteous before God, walking in all the commandments and ordinances of the Lord blameless, there were also many others, including Mary and Joseph.

Mary, a young maiden, engaged to a young man called Joseph, found favor with God. Oh, may we be one of the few who God has found favor with. She was a young maiden with great faith. She was told she would conceive by the the Holy Spirit and the Most High will overshadow her. She would have a son who she was to call Jesus. He would be called the Son of the Most High, He would be given the throne of his father David and reign over the descendants of Abraham, Isaac, and Jacob. His reign would never end, it would be eternal, forever. He would be called the **Son of God.**

In the meantime Joseph knew nothing of Mary's meeting with the angel Gabriel. There he is getting his house ready for his bride and sees that she is with child. He knew for certain it was not his child in her womb. He was to be the laughing scorn of Nazareth. He decided to take Mary and put her to death privately. **But God**. These two words changed the world many times. God interfered with his plan.

But after he had considered this, an angel of the Lord appeared to him in a dream and said, "Joseph son of David, do not be afraid to take Mary home as your wife, because what is conceived in her is from the Holy Spirit. She will give birth to a son, and you are to give him the name Jesus, because he will save his people from their sins." All this took place to fulfill what the Lord had said through the prophet: *"The virgin will conceive and give birth to a son, and they will call him Immanuel"* (which means *"God with us"). When Joseph woke up, he did what the angel of the Lord had commanded him and took Mary home as his wife But he did not consummate their marriage until she gave birth to a son. And* **he gave him the name Jesus."** **Matthew 1:20-25**

After four hundred years of silence God was again looking down at His promised people Israel and was going to speak to them again, this time, by the Son of God. Gabriel had told Mary her relative, Elizabeth, in her old age that she was also going to have a child. Mary arose in haste and went to a city in Judah where Elizabeth lived. As she entered the house of Zechariah and Elizabeth, the baby John in her womb leaped with joy. He could not have leaped too far but he must have really gave a kick inside of Elizabeth! Then Elizabeth was filled with the Holy Ghost and she spake out with a loud voice saying, "Blessed are you among women, and blessed is the child you will bear! But why am I so favored, that the mother of my Lord should come to me? As soon as the sound of your greeting reached my ears, the baby in my womb leaped for joy. ***"Blessed is she who has believed that the Lord would fulfill his promises to her!"*** **Luke 1:42-45** *Mary answered, "My soul glorifies the Lord and my spirit rejoices in God my Savior, for he has been mindful of the humble state of his servant. From now on all generations will call me blessed, for the Mighty One had done great things for me – Holy is his name. His mercy extends to those who fear him from generation to generation. He has performed mighty deeds with his arm; he has scattered those who are proud in their inmost thoughts. He has brought down the rulers from their thrones but has lifted up the humble. He has filled the hungry with good things but has sent the rich away empty. He has helped this servant Israel, remembering to be merciful to Abraham and his descendants forever, just as he promised our ancestors."* **Matthew 1:42-55**

"Without faith it is impossible to please God." **Hebrews 11:6** The Holy Spirit praised the faith of Mary in believing God. This was not just a miracle. He was God the Son coming into man's world through a woman. It took great faith for Mary to believe what Gabriel had told her. As she looked and saw her belly begin to enlarge each day, it gave her faith that she would be the mother of the Son of God. Elizabeth recognized that inside of Mary was not just a child but **her Lord.** Mary in her answer to Elizabeth was to glorified God and **the Savior, the Son of God, which was inside her.** When Mary went to Elizabeth, Elizabeth was six months pregnant. She stayed with Zechariah and Elizabeth for three months. Therefore, she saw the birth of Elizabeth's child. On the eighth day it was time for the child to be circumcised and be given a name. Zechariah was still unable to speak and someone gave him a writing board to write the name of the child. But his mouth opened and his name was to be called John, meaning "Jehovah is gracious." Fear came upon all

who were present. And the news of the birth of John was told throughout all Judea. They said in their hearts, *"What manner of child shall this be! And the hand of the Lord was with him."* **Luke 1:66** Zechariah being filled with the Holy Spirit prophesied saying, *"Blessed be the Lord God of Israel; for he hath visited and redeemed his people, And hath raised up a horn of salvation for us in the house of his servant David; As he spake by the mouth of his holy prophets, which have been since the world began: That we should be saved from our enemies, and from the hand of all that hate us; To perform the mercy promised to our fathers, and to remember his holy covenant; The oath which he spoke to our father Abraham, That he would grant unto us, that we being delivered out of the hand of our enemies might serve him without fear, In holiness and righteousness before him, all the days of our life.* **And thou, child, shalt be called the prophet of the Highest:** *for thou shalt go before the face of the Lord to prepare his ways; To give knowledge of salvation unto his people by the remission of their sins, Through the tender mercy of our God; whereby the day spring from on high hath visited us,* **To give light to them that sit in darkness** *and in the shadow of death, to guide our feet into the way of peace. And the child grew, and waxed strong in spirit, and was in the deserts till the day of his shewing unto Israel."* **Luke 1:67-80**

Zechariah's prophesy covered all Israel but also the Gentile world. It is a prophesy we have yet to see fully fulfilled. Redemption was promised to many people. Salvation was promised to the house of David. God would save his people, Israel, from their enemies, and from the hand of all that hate Israel. We are living in the day where the enemy is on every side of Israel and the world is in hatred of this small nation of Israel. The prophesy confirms the promises spoken to Abraham, Isaac, and Jacob and the words spoken by the prophets of old. He shall be called the prophet of the Highest, the name used by the Gentile's for God. John would prepare the way for Jesus, the Son of God, coming to our world. This Son of God would give knowledge of salvation, and the forgiveness of sins. He would be a light in a darkened world.

three

Jesus Christ is Born

In years of Caesar Augustus issued a decree that a census should be taken of the entire Roman world. (This was the first census that took place while Quirinius was governor of Syria.) And everyone went to their own town to register. Joseph also went up from the town of Nazareth in Galilee to Judea, to Bethlehem the town of David, because he belonged to the house and blood line of David. He went there to register with Mary, who was pledged to be married to him and was expecting a child. While they were there, the time came for the baby to be born, and she gave birth to her firstborn, a son. She wrapped him in cloths and placed him in a manger, because there was no guest room available for them.

It has been important throughout the Bible that the Messiah (Jesus Christ) would come from the seed of King David. Matthew starts his gospel showing the fact that Joseph was of the lineage of David. The promise to David is that his seed will rule Israel forever. Luke chapter three traces the lineage of Joseph from Adam. In Jerusalem there was a building of records which traced every Israelite's lineage. It was destroyed during the Roman invasion of 70 AD. Jesus's lineage as a descendant of David was important because he could not be the Messiah and reign forever without being an earthly descendant of David. Even Paul makes this known in his last letter before his death to Timothy. *"**Remember that Jesus Christ of the seed of David** was raised from the dead according to my gospel: Wherein I suffer trouble, as an evil doer, even unto bonds; but the word of God is not bound."* **2 Timothy 2:8-9**

There was no room in the inn for a reason. God could easily provided a palace in Bethlehem for the birth of Jesus Christ. John the Baptist's introduction of Christ to the world called him the Lamb of God. John the Baptist saw

Jesus coming toward him and said, *"Look,* **the Lamb of God,** *who takes away the sin of the world."* Then the next day John was there with two of his disciples said, *"Look, the Lamb of God."* John went from that day to the cross where the spotless blameless Son of God would lay down His life for the sins of the world. How much more important was Jesus's death than his three years of ministry healing the sick, raising the dead, and all His other miracles. **(John 1:29-30)**

There was no room in the inn for the reason that lambs are not born in houses, motels, hotels or inns. Lambs are born in barns where the livestock are housed. Jesus, the Lamb of God, had to be born in a barn. From my personal experience living on a farm, we never had a lamb or any other livestock born in our house. They were born in the barn or out in the fields. Shepherds also knew lambs were not born in houses or palaces. It was important to God to notify shepherds that the Lamb of God was born.

And there were in the same country shepherds abiding in the field, keeping watch over their flock by night. And, lo, the angel of the Lord came upon them, and the glory of the Lord shone round about them: and they were afraid. And the angel said unto them, *"Fear not: for, behold, I bring you good tidings of great joy, which shall be to all people.* **For unto you is born this day in the city of David a Savior, which is Christ the Lord.** *And this shall be a sign unto you; Ye shall find the babe wrapped in swaddling clothes, lying in a manger."* *And suddenly there was with the angel a multitude of the heavenly host praising God, and saying, "Glory to God in the highest, and on earth peace, good will toward men."* *And it came to pass, as the angels were gone away from them into heaven, the shepherds said one to another, "Let us now go even unto Bethlehem, and see this thing which is come to pass, which* **the Lord hath made known unto us."** *And they came with haste, and found Mary, and Joseph, and the babe lying in a manger. And when they had seen it, they made known abroad the saying which was told to them concerning this child.* **Luke 2:8-17**

four

Living in Bethlehem

"And when eight days were accomplished for the circumcising of the child, his name was called **JESUS**, which was so named of the angel before he was conceived in the womb." **Luke 2:21**

While at the temple for the circumcision and naming of Jesus, there were two Israelites like Zechariah and Elizabeth who were both righteous before God, walking in all the commandments and ordinances of the Lord blameless. They were an elderly man named Simeon and an elderly woman named Anna. The Holy Ghost had revealed to Simeon that he should not die without seeing the Messiah, the Lord Jesus Christ. Seeing Jesus in the **temple on Mount Zion** he took up the child in his hands and blessed God and said, "Lord now let your servant now depart this earth in peace, according to your word. For my eyes have seen thy salvation which you have prepared before the face of all people; **a light to lighten the Gentiles,** and the **glory of your people Israel.**" Not only for the glory of Israel but He, the Lord Jesus Christ, would be a light of salvation to us Gentiles. **Praise God.** Then Simeon said to Mary, "Behold this child is set for fall and rising again of many in Israel and for a sign which shall be spoken against. Yea, a sword shall pierce through your own soul that the thoughts of many hearts may be revealed." **(See Luke 2:25-35)**

These words to Mary were sorrowful words. This child, Jesus, was born to bring deliverance, but also division and anguish. Both redemption and judgment are bound up in His advent. Mary would see much sorrow in the next thirty years. This will be discussed later.

Also in the temple that day was the prophetess Anna. She was very old and was a widow for eighty-four years. She stayed in the temple for all the eighty-four years serving God with fasting and praying night and day. She was a prophetess with much wisdom and commitment. Seeing Jesus, she gave thanks to the Lord and spake of Jesus **to all in the temple that looked for the redemption** in Jerusalem. **(See Luke 2:36-38)**

Soon after the birth of Jesus, Joseph and Mary moved from the barn into a house in Bethlehem. In the east of Jerusalem there were wise men who saw a new star in the sky. They said to one another, "Where is he that is born King of the Jews?" They traveled to Jerusalem and consulted Herod the King of Judea. They told Herod that they have seen a star in the sky and it was the star of the King of the Jews. They came to Jerusalem to worship him. Now Herod was troubled in heart with this news, for he was the King of the Jews and he did not need a rebellion. The news had gone through all the city of Jerusalem of the discovery of the wise men. Herod gathered together all the chief priests and scribes of the people. Herod demanded of them where the Christ, Messiah, would be born. They all knew the answer. Reading from **Micah 2:7** they answered Herod saying, *"And you Bethlehem in the land of Judah, are not the least among the princes of Judah: For out of you shall come a Governor, that shall rule my people Israel."*

Herod privately called the wise men and asked them when the star appeared. He sent them to Bethlehem and said, "Go and search diligently for the young child; and when you have found him, bring me word again, that I may come and worship him also." What a lie! His desire was to kill the young child before he could be the King of Israel.

The wise men followed the star to Bethlehem to the very house of Joseph, Mary and the young child. Joseph, Mary, and Jesus could have been in their home in Bethlehem for up to a year. When the wise men saw the young child with Mary, his mother, they fell down and worshiped him. Now many have wondered how many wise men there were, and who they were. To me, with the knowledge they had, I believe they were Jews or Chaldeans from as far as Persia. They opened their treasures. treasures of gold, frankincense, and myrrh. They were warned by God in a dream that they should not return to Herod, so they return another way. **(See Matthew 2:1-12)** *five*

Egypt to Nazareth

When Herod did not hear back from the wise men, he became really angry and sent men to go to Bethlehem to kill all children under the age of two. An angel of the Lord appeared to Joseph in a dream, saying, "Arise, and take the young child and his mother, and flee into Egypt and be there until I bring you word: For Herod will seek to kill the young child." Immediately that night, he arose and took Mary and the young child and departed to Egypt. The prophets had spoken a year before that *"Out of Egypt have I called by Son."* **Hosea 11:1** After Joseph and his family fled Bethlehem Herod's men slew all the children under two in Bethlehem fulfilling the prophet Jeremiah saying, *"Thus saith the Lord; A voice was heard in Ramah, lamentation, and bitter weeping; Rahel weeping for her children refused to be comforted for her children, because they were not."* **Jeremiah 31:15.**

When Herod died, an angel of the Lord appeared in a dream to Joseph in Egypt saying, *"Get up, take the child and his mother and go to the land of Israel, for those who were trying to take the child's life are dead."* Joseph took Mary and Jesus back to the land of Israel. But when he heard that Archelaus was reigning in Judea in place of his father Herod, he was afraid to go there. Having been warned in a dream, he withdrew to the district of Galilee, and he went and lived in a town called Nazareth. So, the scripture was fulfilled what was said through the prophets, that he would be called a Nazarene. **See Matthew 2:20-23** This ends the beginning of the life of Jesus. The Bible does not record the life of Jesus's until he is in the Temple discussing the things of the Old Testament scriptures with the learned Rabbi's for three days. It closes with the following verses. ***"But Mary treasured up all these things and pondered them in her heart. And the child grew and became strong; he was filled with wisdom, and the grace of God was on him."*** Luke 2:19 and Luke 2:40

All the words spoken by angels and in dreams given to Zechariah and Elizabeth; Joseph and Mary; the shepherds, and the wise men; Simeon and Anna; Mary kept in her heart and pondered them. Jesus became a little boy and grew in stature, became strong and full of wisdom and, the grace of God was upon him. What did and this mean as Mary pondered this in her heart and mind? This child was not a son of Joseph, but was conceived in Mary by of the Holy Spirit. All Israel was wanting desperately the Messiah to come and rid Israel of foreign rule and be King of Israel for ever.. But the prophets and teachers could not determine if there would be one Messiah or two Messiahs. Reading from the Old Testament, some Messiah prophesies would tell of the coming reigning Messiah yet other prophesies would tell of a suffering Messiah.

Soon after the fall of Adam and Eve, God spoke to the serpent and Eve about Satan's doom by the Messiah. *"And the LORD God said unto the woman, What is this that thou hast done? And the woman said, The serpent beguiled me, and I did eat. And the LORD God said unto the serpent, Because thou hast done this, thou art cursed above all cattle, and above every beast of the field; upon thy belly shalt thou go, and dust shalt thou eat all the days of thy life:* **And I will put enmity between thee and the woman, and between thy seed and her seed; it shall bruise thy head, and thou shalt bruise his heel."** **Genesis 3:13-15**

In Psalm 2 the writer depicts the Messiah as a conquering Messiah. *"Why do the heathen rage, and the people imagine a vain thing? The kings of the earth set themselves, and the rulers take counsel together, against the LORD, and against his anointed, saying, "Let us break their bands asunder, and cast away their cords from us." He that sitteth in the heavens shall laugh: the LORD shall have them in derision. Then shall he speak unto them in his wrath, and vex them in his sore displeasure. Yet have I set* **my king upon my holy hill of Zion.** *I will declare the decree: the LORD has said unto me, Thou art my Son; this day have I begotten thee. Ask of me, and I shall give thee the heathen for thine inheritance, and the uttermost parts of the earth for thy possession. Thou shalt break them with a rod of iron; thou shalt dash them in pieces like a potter's vessel. Be wise now therefore, O ye kings: be instructed, ye judges of the earth. Serve the LORD with fear, and rejoice with trembling. Kiss the Son, lest he be angry, and ye perish from the way, when his wrath is kindled but a little. Blessed are all they that put their trust in him."* **Psalm 2.** Today we see the heathen nations surrounding Israel in rage against Israel and want to drive Israel into the sea. Today in Israel there are approximately seven million Jews. The heathen that rage against Israel number over a billion. But God in heaven looks down at all this and laughs. He will take the enemies of Israel cause them to go into derision and cause them to kill one another.

But going forward in the Psalms we come to Psalms 22 where the writer shows the suffering Messiah. *"**My God, my God, why hast thou forsaken me?** Why art thou so far from helping me, and from the words of my roaring? O my God, I cry in the day time, but thou hears not; and in the night season, and am not silent. But thou art holy, O thou that inhabits the praises of Israel. Our fathers trusted in thee: they trusted, and thou didst deliver them. They cried unto thee, and were delivered: they trusted in thee, and were not confounded. But I am a worm, and no man; a reproach of men, and **despised of the people*** (Israel*). All they that see me laugh me* (the Messiah) *to scorn: they shoot out the lip, they shake the head, saying, "He **trusted*** (put His faith in) *on the* LORD *that he would deliver him: let him deliver him, seeing he delighted in him." But thou art he that took me out of the womb: thou didst make me hope when I was upon my mother's breasts. I was cast upon thee from the womb: thou art my God from my mother's belly. Be not far from me; for trouble is near; for there is none to help. Many bulls have compassed me: strong bulls of Bashan have beset me round. They gaped upon me with their mouths, as a ravening and a roaring lion. I am poured out like water, and all my bones are out of joint: my heart is like wax; it is melted in the midst of my bowels. My strength is dried up like a potsherd; and my tongue cleaves to my jaws; and thou hast brought me into the dust of death. For dogs have compassed me: the assembly of the wicked have inclosed me: they pierced my hands and my feet. I may tell all my bones: they look and stare upon me. They part my garments among them, and cast lots upon my vesture. But be not thou far from me, O* LORD*: O my strength, haste thee to help me. Deliver my soul from the sword; my darling from the power of the dog. Save me from the lion's mouth: for thou hast heard me from the horns of the unicorns. I will declare thy name unto my brethren: in the midst of the congregation will I praise thee. Ye that fear the* LORD*, praise him; all ye the seed of Jacob, glorify him; and fear him, all ye the seed of Israel. For he hath not despised nor abhorred the affliction of the afflicted; neither hath he hid his face from him; but when he cried unto him, he heard. My praise shall be of thee in the great congregation: I will pay my vows before them that fear him. The meek shall eat and be satisfied: they shall praise the* LORD *that seek him: your heart shall live for ever. All the ends of the world shall remember and turn unto the* LORD*: and all the people of the nations shall worship before thee. For the kingdom is the* LORD'S*: and he is the governor among the nations. All they that be fat upon earth shall eat and worship: all they that go down to the dust shall bow before him: and none can keep alive his own soul. A seed shall serve him; it* *shall be accounted to the Lord for a generation. They shall come, and shall declare his righteousness unto a people that shall be born, that he hath done this."* **Psalms 22**

Isaiah the prophet prophesied about the coming Messiah. He first describes the Messiah as the conquering King. *"For unto us a child is born, unto us a son is given: and the government shall be upon his shoulder: and his name shall be called Wonderful, Counselor, The mighty God, The everlasting Father, The Prince of Peace. Of the increase of his government and peace there shall be no end, upon the throne of David, and upon his kingdom, to order it, and to establish it with judgment and with justice from henceforth even for ever. The zeal of the LORD of hosts will perform this."* **Isaiah 9:6-7** Then later on, Isaiah describes the Messiah as the suffering Messiah. *"Who hath believed our report? And to whom is the arm of the LORD revealed? For he shall grow up before him as a tender plant, and as a root out of a dry ground: he hath no form nor comeliness; and when we shall see him, there is no beauty that we should desire him. He is despised and rejected of men; a man of sorrows, and acquainted with grief: and we hid as it were our faces from him; he was despised, and we esteemed him not. Surely he hath borne our griefs, and carried our sorrows: yet we did esteem him stricken, smitten of God, and afflicted. But he was wounded for our transgressions, he was bruised for our iniquities: the chastisement of our peace was upon him; and with his stripes we are healed. All we like sheep have gone astray; we have turned every one to his own way; and the LORD hath laid on him the iniquity of us all. He was oppressed, and he was afflicted, yet he opened not his mouth: he is brought as a lamb to the slaughter, and as a sheep before her shearers is dumb, so he opened not his mouth. He was taken from prison and from judgment: and who shall declare his generation? For he was cut off out of the land of the living: for the transgression of my people was he stricken. And he made his grave with the wicked, and with the rich in his death; because he had done no violence, neither was any deceit in his mouth.* **Yet it pleased the LORD to bruise him; he hath put him to grief: when thou shalt make his soul an offering for sin, he shall see his seed, he shall prolong his days, and the pleasure of the LORD shall prosper in his hand.** *He shall see of the travail of his soul, and shall be satisfied: by his knowledge shall my righteous servant justify many; for he shall bear their iniquities. Therefore will I divide him a portion with the great, and he shall divide the spoil with the strong; because he hath poured out his soul unto death: and he was numbered with the transgressors; and he bare the sin of many, and made intercession for the transgressors."* **Isaiah 53.**

How could the Rabbis of that day take these two prophesies and believe it would be both the Messiah? Who would ever believe God's chosen people,

Israel, would do such a thing? How did it please God to put the Messiah to grief, put him as an offering for sin, and put his wrath upon him?

Zachariah declared when Christ comes back to earth Israel, will see who they crucified. *"And I will pour upon the house of David, and upon the inhabitants of Jerusalem, the spirit of grace and of supplications: and they shall look upon me whom they have pierced, and they shall mourn for him, as one mourns for his only son, and shall be in bitterness for him, as one that is in bitterness for his firstborn."* **Zachariah 12:10**

The Billy Graham Evangelical Association makes the following statement on the promise of the Messiah:

"The prophesies about the Messiah were not a bunch of scattered predictions randomly placed throughout the Old Testament, but they form a unified promise-plan of God, where each promise is interrelated and connected into a grand series comprising one continuous plan of God. Thus, a unity builds as the story of God's call on Israel, and then on the house of David, progresses in each part of the Old Testament.

However, this eternal plan of God also had multiple fulfillment as it continued to unfold in the life and times of Israel. For example, every successive Davidic king was at once both a fulfillment in that day as well as a promise of what was to come when Christ, the final One in the Davidic line, arrived. Each of these successive fulfillment gave confidence that what was in the distant future would certainly happen, because God was working in the fabric of history as well. And although the promise was made to specific persons, such as Eve, Abraham, Isaac, Jacob and David, it was cosmopolitan in its inclusiveness. What God was doing through Israel and these individuals was to be a source of blessing to all the families. Some insist that the Messiah whom Christians revere is not the same one that Jewish people also look forward to meeting. Some years ago, I had an opportunity to be part of a televised debate with a rabbi who is a Jewish New Testament scholar around the question, "Is Jesus the Messiah?" The rabbi explained the Jewish point of view: "Evangelicals believe the Messiah has two comings: one at Christmas and one at His second coming. We Jews believe He will only come once, at a time of peace on earth just as the prophet Zechariah declared in Zechariah 12-14. Since we still experience wars, Messiah has not yet come."

six

Mary Ponders

If the prophets and teachers (Rabbis) of Israel were confused about the suffering Messiah and the conquering Messiah, how would Joseph and Mary deal with this? Was this child the conquering Messiah or was he the suffering Messiah? No one of Israel wanted a suffering Messiah. Freedom was the message. Let us be free. Send us a leader who would take away the bondage of Rome. Send us the conquering Messiah. Joseph and Mary are now in Nazareth and the young child is now speaking and asking questions. Mary ponders her heart. Who is the child conceived of God in my womb? He is different than other children of the city. His behavior is completely different. He causes us (Joseph and Mary) no trouble. He obeys everything we tell him. He never says "No" but always "Yes." Mary ponders.

Mary, thinking back when it all started with the angel Gabriel appearing to Zechariah. Zechariah and Elizabeth, are older relatives of Mary. It was Zechariah's time to burn incense in the temple of the Lord. This was an important event in a priest's life. As Zechariah entered the temple, Gabriel was standing on the right side of the altar. Zechariah was amazed to say the least. Gabriel told Zechariah that the child, who would be called John, would be great in the sight of the Lord and be filled with the Holy Ghost from birth. He would bring many of Israel back to their God in the power of Elijah. He would make ready people of Israel prepared for the Lord. What did it mean that John would be filled with the Holy Ghost and he would prepared Israel for the coming of the Lord?

Then Gabriel appeared to Mary herself. She would conceive and give birth to a son, and was to call him **JESUS.** He would be called the Son of the Most High. Would this child be the the Messiah and lead the people of Israel out of

Roman bondage? Would he rule as King of Israel forever? This child born to me would be called the Son of God?

Then her thoughts went to the angel who appeared to Joseph, her husband, in a dream telling Joseph not to be afraid to take Mary as his wife for what was conceived in her was from the Holy Spirit. He too was told to call the child **JESUS.**

Mary's mind goes back to the visit to Zechariah and Elizabeth and how the Holy Ghost spoke through Elizabeth in a loud voice and how the Holy Spirit called Mary blessed and the child within her womb. Then Mary answered **glorifying the Lord and rejoiced in God her Savior.** From her womb the child would perform mighty deeds, fill the hungry, and fulfill the promises given to Abraham. What did all this mean? It was too much for her to take in.

Mary remembers her experience of giving birth to Jesus in the barn. She recalls the visit of the shepherds. The shepherds told her how the angel had told them that day in Bethlehem **the Savior born that day would was Christ the Lord, the Messiah of Israel.** Then when the child was eight days old, they went to the temple for the circumcising and naming of the child. She also remembered the meeting of Simeon and Anna in the temple and how Simeon prophesied that this child would be the salvation of God, he would be a light unto the Gentiles, and the glory of Israel. Simeon said the **child was set for a fall some day and would rise again.** What did all this mean what Simeon said?

Then Mary's mind goes back when they lived in that nice house in Bethlehem, and the visit of the wise men from the East. And how they went to Herod and met with the chief priest and scribes of Israel and was told that in Bethlehem was born the **King of the Jews.** When they got to her house they worshiped the young child, and they gave treasures of gold, frankincense and myrrh. What was all this wealth for?

Then Joseph's dreams to take Mary and the child to Egypt, and after Herod's death brought them back to Nazareth. Mary shared these things with Jesus the best she could with the knowledge she had as the child began to talk and ask questions. She knew the child was special, the promised Messiah, the future King of Israel. She wondered why he was so different from all the other children his age.

Mary did not realize Jesus was the second Adam. Adam was made by God by the dust of the earth. And God said, *"Let us make man in our image, after our likeness: and let them have dominion over the fish of the sea, and over the fowl of the air, and over the cattle, and over all the earth, and over every creeping thing that creeps upon the earth. So **God created man in his own image,** in the image of God created he him; male and female created he them. And God blessed them, and God said unto them, Be fruitful, and multiply, and replenish the earth, and subdue it: and have dominion over the fish of the sea, and over the fowl of the air, and over every living thing that moves upon the earth."* **Genesis 1:26-28** Adam created in the image of God was created with only the knowledge of righteousness. Adam had no idea of what evil was until the fall. Jesus was the second Adam was made in the image of God, and was free from sin. And so it is written, *"The first man Adam was made a living soul; the last Adam was made a quickening spirit." Jesus was the last Adam. Adam lived a sinless life for a short time. Jesus lived a sinless life while on earth and from eternity to eternity. Jesus was God from eternity to eternity. Who is the image of the invisible God, the firstborn of every creature: For by him were all things created, that are in heaven, and that are in earth, visible and invisible, whether they be thrones, or dominions, or principalities, or powers: all things were created by him, and for him: And he is before all things, and by him all things consist. And he is the head of the body, the church: who is the beginning, the firstborn from the dead; that in all things he might have the preeminence.* **Colossians 1:16-18**

He was God the Son always. He was God the Son before he entered the womb of Mary and continued to be the Son of God. Never he was less that the Son of God. He was part of the Trinity. Jesus was always God. He was omnipotent, omnipresent and omniscient. These words are used in Christianity but what is the real meaning of theses words.

Omnipotent – Having the unlimited power of authority.

Omnipresent – Present everywhere at the same time.

Omniscient – Having complete unlimited knowledge, awareness, understanding, perceiving all things.

In this one person, called Jesus, was the Son of Man (Mary), and the Son of God always. As the Son of Man, he had a continued faith and knowledge that he was the Son of God. He and God the Father were one. This is hard for our human minds to understand. As we continue we will probe this duel personality.

The Bible tells us little of his life from returning to Nazareth until he appeared in the temple at the age of twelve. But we do know a few things. During this time Mary and Joseph had additional children. *"And when he was come into his own country, he taught them in their synagogue, insomuch that they were astonished, and said, Whence hath this man this wisdom, and these mighty works? Is not this the carpenter's son? is not his mother called Mary? and his brethren, James, and Joses, and Simon, and Judas? And his sisters, are they not all with us? Whence then hath this man all these things? And they were offended in him. But Jesus said unto them, A prophet is not without honor, except in his own country, and in his own house. And he did not many mighty works there because of their unbelief."* **Matthew 13:54-60** While Jesus was growing in strength and knowledge there were other children that needed the care of Joseph and Mary. There were people in Nazareth who knew him as the son of Joseph and Mary and nothing else. They were in total unbelief. Such unbelief was in the city that Jesus did not do mighty works in Nazareth during his earthly ministry. It was a busy family. But Jesus was different from the other children. He was born in the image of God, without a sin nature. All the other children of Joseph and Mary were born with a sin nature. As the earthly children of Joseph and Mary grew up I believe they got sick and tired of Mary saying, "Can't you children be like Jesus." (Sorry Mary, it was impossible).

seven

Jesus Bar Mitzvah & Teaching at the Temple

Now this is not recorded in the Bible but it had to happen, just as Jesus on the eighth day had to be circumcised. There was no getting around it. A Jewish boy goes through a Bar Mitzvah at the age of 13. But this was in Jewish terms of the age of a child. When a Jewish child is born he is one. Three hundred sixty-five days later he is two. In our English way of aging our children we do it differently. A child is not one till he has lived three hundred and sixty-five days. So, in the Jewish way of aging children Jesus would have been thirteen when he was in the temple with the Rabbis for three days. I hope we got this straight before we tell what happens when a Jewish child is Bar Mitzvah. Using the English aging system we will tell what it is to become Bar Mitzvah.

The term Bar Mitzvah literally means "son of Commandment." When a young Jewish lad comes to the age of 12 (13 in Jewish aging) he has become a "bar mitzvah" and recognized by the Jewish tradition as having the same rights as a full grown man. A boy who has become Bar Mitzvah is now morally and ethically responsible for his decisions and actions. The term "bar mitzvah" also refers to the religious ceremony that accompanies a boy becoming Bar Mitzvah. Often there is a celebration that follows the ceremony that is called a bar mitzvah.

It is important to note that the ceremony and celebration are not required by Jewish custom. Rather, a Jewish boy automatically becomes a Bar Mitzvah at the age of twelve (thirteen in Jewish aging). Although the specifics of the ceremony and celebration do vary widely, a;; depending on the families religious standing.

Joseph and Mary made a yearly pilgrimage to Jerusalem at the feast of Passover. Jesus being now twelve years old went with his parents to Jerusalem for the feast of Passover. When they had fulfilled the days of Passover they returned to Nazareth. Many kinfolk, neighbors, and acquaintances went together in a group. It was a time of worship and joy. After sometime on the journey back to Nazareth they found Jesus was not with the group. After three days they found Jesus in the **temple on Mount Zion in Jerusalem of Judah** sitting in the midst of the doctors (Rabbis) both listening to them and answering their questions. All the Rabbis that heard Jesus were astonished at his understanding and answers to their questions. Joseph and Mary when they saw him in the midst of the Rabbis were amazed, *"So when they saw Him, they were amazed; and His mother said to Him, "Son, why have You done this to us? Look, Your father and I have sought You anxiously."* **Luke 2:48**

Then Jesus said to them, *"How is it that you sought me? Know you not that I must be about my* **Father's** *business?"* **Luke 2:49** These words are the first words in the New Testament spoken by Jesus. This first statement by our Lord Jesus Christ is the subject of this book. **Jesus in the temple in the midst of the Rabbis shows to his earthly mother his FAITH that He is the Son of God.** It is a very profound statement made by this newly Bar Mitzvah Jewish young man. Here Jesus in no uncertain terms tells his mother that he is the **SON OF GOD.** He did not spend the past three days in the temple talking carpentry with the Rabbis of Israel. He was discussing with the Rabbis of Israel the things of God the Father, speaking as the **SON OF GOD.** Jesus was now a man according to the traditions of Israel. He asked his mother, *"Know you not that I must be about my* **Father's** *business?"* *"Even the righteousness of God which is by* **faith of Jesus Christ** *unto all and upon all them that believe: for there is no difference,* **for all have sinned and come short of the glory of God."** **Romans 3:22**

At that time Mary did not understand what Jesus was communicating to the Rabbis. Jesus went with Mary and Joseph back to Nazareth and was subject to them. Mary again kept all these sayings in her heart. **And Jesus increased in wisdom, and stature with in favor with God and man. Luke 3:41-52** *eight*

John the Baptist

From His appearance at the temple on **Mount Zion in Jerusalem,** at the age of twelve till his baptism by John the Baptist, we know nothing of the life of Jesus. We know that his earthly father Joseph had died. We know that his four brothers and sisters had grown up, and probably were married and had children of their own. The Bible does not record any record of his family for the eighteen years from his teaching in the temple till he was baptized by John. The Bible now turns to the work of John the Baptist. We know that Jesus and John were earthly relatives and were close to the same age. When the family would make the pilgrimages to Jerusalem for Passover, it may be assumed that the families of John and Jesus had seen one another. John the Baptist was the forerunner of Jesus. So, his ministry started before the earthly ministry of Jesus. Tiberius Caesar was in power for fifteen years when he started his reign in 14 AD. Most Bible scholars put the date of the birth of Jesus and John at 6 to 4 BC. Using these times as a guide John Began his ministry four to six years before the baptism of Jesus. At that time he began his preaching around the area of the Jordan River. John was clothed with a garment of camels hair and ate locust and wild honey. This was representative of Elijah the prophet. He preached the coming of Jesus the Messiah. John would baptize with water but he preached that Jesus would baptize men with the Holy Spirit. He preached the message of baptism of repentance for the remission of sins. Now what is the message of repentance?

Many believe that repentance is only the confessing of your sins. That is not total repentance but can be part of repentance. Gene Scott defines repentance in a few words, "to turn from to." It is turning from man's way of salvation and seeing his own sinful condition turns from his own self righteous to God's righteousness obtained by Jesus on the cross. The prophet Isaiah prophesied of John saying, *"The voice of him that cries in the wilderness,* **Prepare ye the way of the LORD,** *make straight in the desert a highway for our God. Every valley shall be exalted, and every mountain and hill shall be made low: and the crooked shall be made straight, and the rough places plain: And the glory of the LORD shall be revealed, and all flesh shall see it together: for the mouth of the LORD hath spoken it."* **Isaiah 40:3-5** John the Baptist was to prepare the people of Israel for the earthly ministry of the Lord Jesus Christ. Many Jews came from all of Israel to hear the message of John. Many repented and were baptized by John confessing their sins. But the religious leaders denied this message. John said to them, *"O generation of vipers, who hath warned you to flee from the wrath to come? Bring forth therefore fruits meet for repentance: And think not to say within yourselves, We* (Israel) *have Abraham to our father: for I say unto you, that God is able of these stones to raise up children unto Abraham. And now also the ax is laid unto the root of the trees: therefore every tree which brings not forth good fruit is cut down, and cast into the fire. I indeed baptize you with water unto repentance. but he that cometh after me is mightier than I, whose shoes I am not worthy to bear: he shall baptize you with the Holy Ghost, and with fire."* **Matthew 3:7-11**

John preached to the people of Israel with much power and might. His message turned the hearts of many of the Jewish people to God during his years of ministry. Many Jews from foreign countries when going to Jerusalem to see the temple, also came to hear the message of John and repented and were baptized. They went back to their synagogues and told of the message of John. The impact of the message of John lasted sixty years. When Apollos was at Ephesus, he met a certain man teaching fervently in the spirit. *"This man was instructed in the way of the Lord; and being fervent in the spirit, he spake and taught diligently the things of the Lord,* **knowing only the baptism of John.** *And he began to speak boldly in the synagogue: whom when Aquila and Priscilla had heard, they took him unto them, and* **expounded unto him the way of God more perfectly.** *And when he was disposed to pass into Achaia, the brethren wrote, exhorting the disciples to receive him: who, when he was come,* **helped them much which had believed through grace:** *For he mightily convinced the Jews, and that publicly, shewing by the scriptures that Jesus was Christ."* **Acts 18:25-28** God knows his own and brought Apollos to these believers of John and taught them the message of GRACE as received to the Apostle Paul by Jesus Christ in the wilderness of Arabia.

At the end of the ministry of John the Baptist, Jesus came from Galilee to Jordan to be baptized by John. John recognized Jesus coming to him and declares: *"Behold, the **Lamb of God**, which will **take away the sin of the World."* John3:29** The lamb born in the barn in Bethlehem was declared by John as **the Lamb of God** whose purpose was to take away the sin of the world. That includes yours and my sin plus all the individuals who have lived since Adam to the last person to sin against God. John declaration was stated by the Apostle John in Revelation. *"And I saw in the right hand of him that sat on the throne a book written within and on the backside, sealed with seven seals. And I saw a strong angel proclaiming with a loud voice, Who is worthy to open the book, and to loose the seals thereof? And no man in heaven, nor in earth, neither under the earth, was able to open the book, neither to look thereon.*

*And I wept much, because no man was found worthy to open and to read the book, neither to look thereon. And one of the elders saith unto me, Weep not: behold, the **Lion of the tribe of Judah, the Root of David,** hath prevailed to open the book, and to loose the seven seals thereof.*

*And I beheld, and, lo, in the midst of the throne and of the four beasts, and in the midst of the elders, **stood a Lamb as it had been slain,** having seven horns and seven eyes, which are the seven Spirits of God sent forth into all the earth. And he came and took the book out of the right hand of him that sat upon the throne.*

*And when he had taken the book, the four beasts and four and twenty elders **fell down before the Lamb,** having every one of them harps, and golden vials full of odors, which are the prayers of saints. And they sung a new song, saying,*

Thou art worthy to take the book, and to open the seals thereof: for thou wast slain, and hast redeemed us to God by thy blood out of every kindred, and tongue, and people, and nation; And hast made us unto our God kings and priests: and we shall reign on the earth.

*And I beheld, and I heard the voice of many angels round about the throne and the beasts and the elders: and the number of them was ten thousand times ten thousand, and thousands of thousands; Saying with a loud voice, **Worthy is the Lamb that was slain** to receive power, and riches, and wisdom, and strength, and honor, and glory, and blessing.*

*And every creature which is in heaven, and on the earth, and under the earth, and such as are in the sea, and all that are in them, heard I saying, **Blessing, and honor, and glory, and power, be unto him that sitteth upon the throne, and unto the***

Lamb for ever and ever. And the four beasts said, Amen. And the four and twenty elders fell down and worshiped him that lives for ever and ever. **Rev. 5.**

John first forbade Jesus when Jesus told John he needed to be baptized. Jesus said to John, *"Suffer it to be so now: For thus it becomes us to fulfill all righteousness."* **Matthew 3:15** After Jesus came out of the water the heavens opened, and the Spirit of God descended upon Jesus to sit on him. A voice from heaven said, *"This is my beloved Son, in whom I am well pleased."* **Matthew 3:18.**

Here we see the Trinity of God. We have the Son of God being baptized by John, the voice of God the Father from heaven saying, *"This is my beloved Son, in whom I am well pleased."* Then we see God the Holy Spirit descending from heaven sitting on the shoulder of Son of God. The Trinity of our one God is also brought out by the Apostle Paul, *"Looking for that blessed hope, and the glorious appearing of the great God and our Savior Jesus Christ"* **Titus 2:13** Here Paul tells believers to look for the appearing of the great God who is our Savior who is our Lord Jesus Christ.

After the baptism of Jesus, John confronted Herod for living with his brother Phillip's wife Herodias. John began to wonder. Was he wrong about Jesus being the Son of God? John sent two of his disciples to Jesus to ask of Jesus, "Art thou he that should come? or look we for another? When the men were come unto him, they said, John the Baptist hath sent us unto thee, saying, *"Art thou he that should come? or look we for another?" And in that same time Jesus healed many of their infirmities and plagues, and of evil spirits; and unto many that were blind he gave sight. Then Jesus answering said unto them," Go your way, and tell John what things ye have seen and heard; how that the blind see, the lame walk, the lepers are cleansed, the deaf hear, the dead are raised, to the poor the gospel is preached."* **Luke 7:19-22**

After these things came Jesus and his disciples into the land of Judaea; and there he tarried with them, and baptized. And John also was baptizing in Aenon near to Salim, because there was much water there: and they came, and were baptized. For John was not yet cast into prison. Then there arose a question between some of John's disciples and the Jews about purifying. And they came unto John, and said unto him, Rabbi, he that was with thee beyond Jordan, to whom thou barest witness, behold, the same baptizes and all men come to him. John answered and said, *"A man can receive nothing, except it be given him from heaven. Ye yourselves bear me witness, that I said,* **I am not the Christ,** *but that I am sent before him. He that hath the bride is the bridegroom: but the friend of the bridegroom, which* *stands and hears him, rejoices greatly because of the bridegroom's voice: this my joy therefore is fulfilled.* **He must increase, but I must decrease."** John **3:22-30** John had no idea how soon he would die and fulfill this prophesy.

Herod had laid hold on John, and bound him, and put him in prison for Herodias' sake, his brother Philip's wife. For John said unto him, "It is not lawful for thee to have her." And when he would have put him to death, he feared the multitude, because they counted him as a prophet. But when Herod's birthday was kept, the daughter of Herodias danced before them, and pleased Herod. Whereupon he promised with an oath to give her whatsoever she would ask. And she, being before instructed of her mother, said, *"Give me here John Baptist's head in a charger. And the king was sorry: nevertheless for the oath's sake, and them which sat with him at meat, he commanded it to be given her. And he sent, and beheaded John in the prison."* **Matthew 14:3-10**

nine

Just another Jews

Many portraits have been painted of the face of Jesus. The picture of Jesus we are most common seen is the picture of Jesus with a European face. If you have ever been to the Holy Land experience in Orlando, Florida, Jesus is depicted as tall with a white robe and a scarlet mantle. Each ethnic group has their own portrait of Jesus using their groups ethnic features. But the question is what did Jesus really look like? The truth is - we do not know. We like the strong facial features with the trimmed hair and beard. It is a face of a man's man. He is pictured as a charismatic leader such as George Washington, Abe Lincoln or John Kennedy. In most dramas of the passion of Christ, Jesus is portrayed as the tall leader with this white robe and scarlet mantle. When Israel wanted a king they wanted Saul who was head and shoulder above all others. This is what most all of us want as a leader.

The leaders of Israel knew that Samuel was old and his sons did not walk in the ways of their father. The elders of Israel went to Samuel and asked for a king. *"Then all the elders of Israel gathered themselves together, and came to Samuel to Ramah, and said unto him, Behold, thou art old, and thy sons walk not in thy ways: now make us a king to judge us like all the nations."* (**1 Samuel 8:4-5).** Samuel pleads with the elders saying they were not rejecting him but God. He continues in Chapter eight telling them what would happen to the nation if they had a king like other nations. At the end of the chapter Jehovah tells Samuel to give them a king. *"There was a Benjamite, a man of standing, whose name was Kish son of Abiel, the son of Zeror, the son of Bekorath, the son of Aphiah of Benjamin, Kish had a son named Saul,* **as handsome a young man as could be found anywhere in Israel, and he was a head and shoulders taller than anyone else."** **1 Samuel 9:1-2** The mighty man of power, Saul, was head and shoulder above his peers. Saul, like many of our heroes was a **head and shoulders man.**

Saul reign was as Samuel described in Chapter eight. Saul failed God and the nation of Israel. And Samuel said to Saul, *"Thou hast done foolishly: thou hast not kept the commandment of the LORD thy God, which he commanded thee: for now would the LORD have established thy kingdom upon Israel for ever. But now thy kingdom shall not continue: the LORD hath sought him a man after his own heart, and the LORD hath commanded him to be captain over his people, because thou hast not kept that which the LORD commanded thee."* **1 Samuel 13: 13-14** Saul was the peoples' man. The man the people of Israel wanted. But he was not God's choice. God's choice was David the son of Jesse. David was a ruddy man (reddish looking) with beautiful countenance and with fine looks the least of all his brothers. He was much different that Saul the **head and shoulder man. (See 1 Samuel 16:11-12)**

At his first coming Jesus came as the suffering Messiah. His outward appearance is told to us by Isaiah, *"Who has believed our report? And to whom is the arm of the LORD revealed? For He shall grow up before Him as a **tender plant,** and as a **root out of dry ground.** He has **no form or comeliness**; and when we see Him, there is **no beauty** that we should desire Him. **He is despised and rejected of men; a man of sorrows, and acquainted with grief: and we hid as it were our faces from him; he was despised, and we esteemed him not."*** **Isaiah 53:1-3** Jesus said of himself being meek and lowly. *"Take my yoke upon you, and learn of me; **for I am meek and lowly in heart:** and ye shall find rest unto your souls."* **Matthew 11:29**

Isaiah started the fifty third chapter of his book asking who would believe what he has to say and to whom would the LORD reveal this report. It is important that LORD is revealed to us as the suffering Messiah. The Jews in their synagogues would not read Isaiah fifty-three. They wanted not to hear these words.

First, Jesus is described as a tender plant. Isaiah tells us that Jesus had a soft yielding texture, easily broken, and very fragile. He was like a small weak plant which just broke out of the ground that is dry and with very little water to give it energy.

Second, Jesus had no form or comeliness. Jesus lacked any distinguishing features or pleasing appearance. Webster defines the lack of form or comeliness as "lack of pleasurably conforming to notions of good appearance, suitability, or proportion not having a pleasing appearance, homely or plain." Some dictionary define comeliness as just plain ugly.

Third, Jesus had no beauty that we should desire him. Jesus did not stand out in a crowd. He had not the beauty that children of Israel or the Gentiles would desire him. If seen him as hes appeared we would walk by without noticing him. In John chapter nine, Jesus was at the mount of Olives teaching to the people about being the light of the world and who were the true descendants of Abraham. *"Then said the Jews unto him, Now we know that thou hast a devil. Abraham is dead, and the prophets; and thou said, If a man keep my saying, he shall never taste of death. Art thou greater than our father Abraham, which is dead? and the prophets are dead: whom makes thou thyself? Jesus answered, "If I honor myself, my honor is nothing: it is my Father that honors me; of whom ye say, that he is your God: Yet ye have not known him; but I know him: and if I should say, I know him not, I shall be a liar like unto you: but I know him, and keep his saying. Your father Abraham rejoiced to see my day: and he saw it, and was glad." Then said the Jews unto him, Thou art not yet fifty years old, and hast thou seen Abraham? Jesus said unto them, "Verily, verily, I say unto you, Before Abraham was,* **I am.**" *Then took they up stones to cast at him: but* **Jesus hid himself, and went out of the temple, going through the midst of them, and so passed by."** *His appearance was so common that when the Jews wanted to stone, him he was able to hide himself among the crowd.*

Even when they came to arrest Jesus, they had to take Judas with him to identify him from among the disciples and apostles. "And when he rose up from prayer, and was come to his disciples, he found them sleeping for sorrow, And said unto them, Why sleep ye? rise and pray, lest ye enter into temptation. And while he yet spake, behold a multitude, and he that was called Judas, one of the twelve, went before them, and drew near unto Jesus to kiss him. But Jesus said unto him, "Judas, betrayest thou the Son of man with a kiss?" **Luke 14.48** The multitude had to take with them Judas because Jesus looked much like the apostle and disciples who were with him.

Jesus was far different than King Saul, the head and shoulders man that the people of Israel told Samuel they wanted as their king. It took the Holy Spirit to move the twelve apostles to follow Jesus. The apostle John tells us that the twelve were a gift of God to his Son. "I have manifested thy name **unto the men** (the twelve apostles) which thou gave me out of the world: thine they were, and **thou gave them me**; and they have kept thy word". **John 17:6**

The prophet Isaiah gave Israel a preview report of the personality and life of our Lord in the fifty-third chapter of his book. Isaiah is very descriptive of the appearance of our Lord Jesus Christ. Open up your Bible to this passage and you will see the real Jesus revealed. He was a man of sorrows who was acquainted with grief, despised, and rejected by Israel. Israel did not esteem him as the Messiah. His mission they did not understand. Israel did not recognize him as the suffering Messiah, the Lamb of God.

Joni Eareckson Tada a spinal cord injured quadriplegic, after being a skiing accident, was in her hospital bed late at night thinking of all that was wrong with her body. It was two in the morning and she saw a figure in the doorway of her room. Slowly the figure came close to her and she recognized it was one of her friend. She lowered the bed rail and climbed into the bed next to Joni. She held Joni had and whispered to Joni ear the following hymn by Philip P. Bliss.

"Man of Sorrows What A Name"

Man of Sorrows! what a name
For the Son of God, Who came
Ruined sinners to reclaim.
Hallelujah! What a Savior!
Bearing shame and scoffing rude,
In my place condemned He stood;
Sealed my pardon with His blood.
Hallelujah! What a Savior!
Guilty, vile, and helpless we;

Spotless Lamb of God was He;
Full atonement can it be?
Hallelujah! What a Savior!
Lifted up was He to die;
"It is finished!" was His cry;
Now in heaven exalted high.
Hallelujah! What a Savior!
When He comes, our glorious King,
All His ransomed home to bring,
Then anew His song we'll sing:
Hallelujah! What a Savior!

Her friend then left and so did the sorrow of Joni's heart. She knew that Jesus knew her pain.

In Isaiah fifty-three you will see the Jesus portrayed seven hundred years before his birth in Bethlehem. During his ministry on earth he was disdained by the religious leaders of the Jews. The elders, priests, scribes, Pharisees, and Sadducees had contempt, disgust, and distaste for him. In verse four to the end of the chapter Isaiah describes the cross of Christ in vivid detail. He tells how Jesus went to the cross for our benefit. He came to this earth to bare our griefs, our sorrows, to be wounded for our transgressions, bruised for our iniquities, punished for our peace, and with his stripes we are healed from the curse of our sins. Why? Because all men, like dumb sheep, have gone astray, and have turned to their own self righteousness for salvation. He died on the cross, his body of put in the grave, and his soul and spirit went to hell. Yes hell. By the power of the Holy Spirit, God after three days raised him from the death and Hell. By his righteousness he has justified all who deny self and put faith in his atonement. He didn't just die for **our** sins, he lived to give us **his** righteousness.

Paul brings out in the epistle to the Philippians the real nature of God. *"Let this mind be in you, which was also in Christ Jesus: Who,* **being in the form of God, thought it not robbery to be equal with God:** *But made himself of no reputation, and took upon him the form of a servant, and was made in the likeness of men: And being* **found in fashion as a man,** *he humbled himself, and* **became obedient**

unto death, even the death of the cross. Wherefore God also hath highly exalted him, and given him a name which is above every name: That at the name of Jesus every knee should bow, of things in heaven, and things in earth, and things under the earth; And that every tongue should confess that Jesus Christ is Lord, to the glory of God the Father."
Philippians 25-11

ten

Temptation of Jesus

After his baptism by John, Jesus was led by the Holy Spirit into the wilderness to be tempted by the devil (Satan). He was in the wilderness for forty fasting. Satan now takes advantage of the fasting and hunger of Jesus, the Son of man, questioning him as being also the Son of God. If you are the Son of God, command these stones be made bread. It was a test of the faith of the Son of Man that he was the Son of God. Jesus answered faithfully, *"It is written, Man shall not live by bread alone, but by every word that proceeds out of the mouth of God."* **Matthew 4:4** Jesus was quoting from the Old Testament, *"And he humbled thee, and suffered thee to hunger, and fed thee with manna, which thou knew not, neither did thy fathers know; that he might* **make thee know that man doth not live by bread only, but by every word that proceeds out of the mouth of the Lord** *doth man live."* **Deuteronomy 8:3** Israel had just fled from Egypt and were in the wilderness without food. The people of Israel were feeling hunger pains. God then fed them for forty years with mamma from heaven.

Then Satan took Jesus from the wilderness to Jerusalem to the highest point on the temple walls **on Mount Zion in Jerusalem.** This part of the temple wall was filled with dirt in with a foundation wall around the dirt. It is what known today as the Wailing Wall. Satan takes Jesus up to the highest point of the temple wall. Satan said unto Jesus, "If you are the Son of God, cast thyself down for it is written, For he shall give his angels charge over thee, to keep thee in all thy ways." **Psalms 91:11** Jesus said unto him, *"It is written again, Thou shalt not tempt the Lord thy God."* **Deuteronomy 6:16 & Matthew 4:7**

Satan takes the next step, and uses the Word of God again to tempt Jesus. What he said was true that was written in the Psalms. But, Jesus answered with another text from the Word of God, *"It is written again, Thou shalt not tempt the Lord thy God."* **Deuteronomy 6:16** We like Satan can find verses in the Bible to get what we want. Many false teachers and preachers use text from the Bible to back up their message of health and wealth. It is a trick used by false teachers and preachers since Satan used it. Jesus answered Satan with a higher scripture. Again he is addressing Jesus as the Son of Man to have him prove He is the Son of God by having him violate the command of God not to temp the Lord our God. Jesus knew all the Old Testament because he was the Word. He was the person of the God head that gave the words to Moses, prophets and writers of the Old Testament. He gave them each word letter by letter, and he as the Son of God knew what each scripture said and what was the true meaning of all Scripture. Name it and claim it, is what Satan wanted the Son of Man to do. Oh yes, God gave his angels charge over his children to keep his children in all their ways. But, this verse does not give license to foolishness.

Again, the devil took Him up onto an exceeding high mountain, and showed Him all the kingdoms of the world and the glory of them, and said unto Him, "All these things will I give Thee if Thou wilt fall down and worship me." Then said Jesus unto him, *"Get thee hence, Satan! For it is written: Thou shalt worship the Lord thy God, and Him only shalt thou serve."* Then the devil left Him, and behold, angels came and ministered unto Him. **Matthew 4:8-11**

When Adam was made from the dust of the earth he was given dominion over the earth and all that was in it. When Adam and Eve fell for the temptation of Satan to eat of the tree of Good and Evil, Satan then became the power who had dominion over the earth and all that was in it. He had and still has dominion over the kingdoms of the world and the glory of the kingdoms. It was his to give away. His offer was an easy way for the Son of man to get back the dominion of all the earth. But the cost would be for God to surrender his everything to Satan. Then Satan would be setting in heaven as God and God would be down on earth with dominion over this earth. Righteousness would give way to total wickedness. Jesus answer was from the commandments given by God. *"Thou shalt fear the Lord thy God, and serve him, and shalt swear by his name. Thou shalt fear the Lord thy God; him shalt thou serve, and to him shalt thou cleave, and swear by his name."* **Deut 6: 13 & 10:20**

Jesus, tempted as the Son of Man overcame the temptation of Satan by the Word of God. The more we know the Word of God the easier it is to overcome the temptation. But when we fall we have an advocate in heaven, the Lord Jesus Christ, telling the Father that sin was paid for by His death on the cross.

eleven

Calling of the 12 Apostles

After the temptations by Satan, Jesus sets out to calls the twelve apostles. He first called the four fishermen. Jesus, while near the Sea of Galilee called Simon Peter and his brother Andrew. A little farther down the coast he sees the two sons of Zebedee, James and his brother John. All four fishermen dropped their nets and followed Jesus. The next day still following down the coast of Galilee, Jesus finds Philip and said, *"Follow me."* Philip did. Philip then finds Nathanael and tells Nathanael, *"We have found him, whom Moses in the law, and the prophets, did write, Jesus of Nazareth the son of Joseph."*

Now Philip knew the scriptures and about the prophesies of the coming Messiah. Nathanael has some doubt. *"Philip found Nathanael and said to him, "We have found Him of whom Moses in the law, and also the prophets, wrote—Jesus of Nazareth, the son of Joseph." And Nathanael said to him, "Can anything good come out of Nazareth?" Philip said to him, "Come and see."* **John 1:43-46** *Jesus answered him, "Behold an Israelite indeed, in whom is no guile." Nathanael answered back to Jesus, "When did you know me?" Jesus answered, "Before that Philip called you, when you were under the fig tree, I saw you." Nathanael replied,* **"Rabbi you are the Son of God, you are the King of Israel."** *It was three years before Peter said, "You are the Messiah, Son of the Living God." Here three years before Jesus ministry to Israel Nathanael saw Jesus as the Son of God and the King of Israel. Jesus closes his calling of Nathanael, "You believe because I told you I saw you under the fig tree. You will see greater things than that. Very truly I tell you, you will see 'heaven open, and the angels of God ascending and descending on the Son of man."* **John 1:35-51**

These twelve Jesus sent forth as missionaries and commanded them, saying, **"Go not into the way of the Gentiles, and into any city of the Samaritans enter ye not: But go rather to the lost sheep of the house of Israel."**

(This is an important commandment to the twelve. They were called strictly to minister to the people of Israel. Some believe that commandment included the time after the death and resurrection of Christ. They were to minister to Jews only and later God called the Apostle Paul to minister to the Gentiles.) *"**And as ye go, preach,** saying, **The kingdom of heaven is at hand.** Heal the sick, cleanse the lepers, raise the dead, cast out devils: freely ye have received, freely give. Provide neither gold, nor silver, nor brass in your purses, Nor scrip for your journey, neither two coats, neither shoes, nor yet staffs: for the workman is worthy of his meat. And into whatsoever city or town you shall enter, enquire who in it is worthy; and there abide till ye go thence. And when you come into an house, salute it. And if the house be worthy, let your peace come upon it: but if it be not worthy, let your peace return to you. And whosoever shall not receive you, nor hear your words, when you depart out of that house or city, shake off the dust of your feet.* **Verily I say unto you, It shall be more tolerable for the land of Sodom and Gomorrah in the day of judgment, than for that city."**

Warning of Persecutions

"Behold, I send you forth as **sheep in the midst of wolves***: be you therefore* **wise as serpents, and harmless as doves.** *But beware of men: for they will deliver you up to the councils, and they will scourge you in their synagogues; And you shall be brought before governors and kings for my sake, for a testimony against them and the Gentiles. But when they deliver you up, take no thought how or what you shall speak: for it shall be given you in that same hour what ye shall speak. For it is not you that speak,* **but the Spirit of your Father which will speak in you.** *And the brother shall deliver up the brother to death, and the father the child: and the children shall rise up against their parents, and cause them to be put to death. And you shall be hated of all men for my name's sake: but he that endures to the end shall be saved. But when they persecute you in this city, flee into another: for verily I say unto you, You shall not have gone over the cities of Israel, till the Son of man be come.*

Instructions of the Ministry

" The disciple is not above his master, nor the servant above his lord. It is enough for the disciple that he be as his master, and the servant as his lord. If they have called the master of the house Beelzebub, how much more shall they call them of his household? Fear them not therefore: for there is nothing covered, that shall not be revealed; and hid, that shall not be

known. What I tell you in darkness, that speak you in light: and what you hear in the ear, that preach you upon the housetops. And **fear not them which kill the body, but are not able to kill the soul: but rather fear him which is able to destroy both soul and body in hell.** *Are not two sparrows sold for a farthing? and one of them shall not fall on the ground without your Father. But the very hairs of your head are all numbered. Fear you not therefore, you are of more value than many sparrows.* **Whosoever therefore shall confess me before men, him will I confess also before my Father which is in heaven. But whosoever shall deny me before men, him will I also deny before my Father which is in heaven."**

Jesus was not to bring peace but the sword

"Think not that I am come to send peace on earth: I came not to send peace, but a sword. For I am come to set a man at variance against his father, and the daughter against her mother, and the daughter in law against her mother in law. And a man's foes shall be they of his own household. He that loves father or mother more than me is not worthy of me: and he that loves son or daughter more than me is not worthy of me. **And he that takes not his cross, and follows after me, is not worthy of me. He that finds his life shall lose it: and he that loses his life for my sake shall find it."**

Reward for service

"He that receives you receives me, and he that receives me receives him that sent me. He that receives a prophet in the name of a prophet shall receive a prophet's reward; and he that receives a righteous man in the name of a righteous man shall receive a righteous man's reward. And whosoever shall give to drink unto one of these little ones a cup of cold water only in the name of a disciple, verily I say unto you, he shall in no wise lose his reward."
Matthew 1:5-42

The Apostle Paul had his suffering during his ministry to the Gentiles. Likewise, the twelve disciples had their sufferings. They were delivered to the councils of the Jews. They were scourge in the synagogues. They were brought before governors and kings. They were hated by all who refused their message. Their message brought division between parents and children. It was not an easy life for the twelve apostles called to minister the message of Jesus being the Messiah of Israel to the Jews.

The twelve apostles were:

- **Simon** - More generally known as Peter, the brother of Andrew, a fisherman from the Sea of Galilee, and considered to be the most impulsive of the group, always ready to speak up, and swing a sword on occasion as the cutting off of a man's ear at the time of Jesus' arrest . Some traditions hold that he was eventually crucified, upside down, by the Romans.
- **Andrew** - was active in bringing people to Jesus, including his brother Peter.
- **James** - was the older brother of John, he was the first of The Twelve to be martyred.
- **John** - the younger brother of James and the one who was that was said to have loved Jesus the most.
- **Philip** - was from Bethsaida, as were Andrew and Peter.
- **Bartholomew** - was one of the disciples to whom Jesus appeared at the Sea of Tiberias after His resurrection. He was also a witness of the Ascension.
- **Thomas** - also called Didymus which is the Greek version of his name, was not easily convinced. He had the nickname "Doubting Thomas" because he wanted to actually see and touch Jesus after His Resurrection. Certainly a good witness for us today, because he wanted indisputable proof of what he was expected to report about, and he got it.
- **Matthew** - was formerly a tax-collector at Capernaum, he became one of the more prominent apostles.
- **James** - known as James the Younger, or James the Less, wrote the epistle which bears his name.
- **Thaddaeus** - also known as "Judas the brother of James;" while John probably referring to the same person, speaks of "Judas, not Iscariot."
- **Simon the Zealot** - Zealots were a nationalistic sect with very strong political views, thus offering a wide variety of personalities among the apostles.
- **Judas Iscariot** - The traitor. (Replaced by Mathias)
- **Matthias** - to bring the number back up to twelve after Judas fell away, Matthias was chosen by the remaining eleven apostles.

twelve

Beginning of Jesus Ministry

Jesus begins his ministry at this home town of Nazareth where he had been raised as a child. His custom was Jesus went into the synagogue on the sabbath day, and stood up for to read. And there was delivered unto him the book of the prophet Isaiah. And when he had opened the book, he found the place where it was written, *"The Spirit of the Lord is upon me, because he hath anointed me to preach the gospel to the poor; he hath sent me to heal the brokenhearted, to preach deliverance to the captives, and recovering of sight to the blind, to set at liberty them that are bruised,* **to** *preach the acceptable year of the Lord."* *And he closed the book, and he gave it again to the minister, and sat down. And the eyes of all them that were in the synagogue were fastened on him. And he began to say unto them,* **"This day is this scripture fulfilled in your ears."** (Jesus stopped reading in the middle passage from Isaiah. The part he had read was to do with his first coming but the rest of Isaiah forty-nine was to do with His second coming as King of Kings and Lord of Lords.) *And all bare him witness, and wondered at the gracious words which proceeded out of his mouth. And they said, "Is not this Joseph's son?"* **Luke 4:17-22**

And he said unto them, *"You will surely say unto me this proverb, Physician, heal thyself: whatsoever we have heard done in Capernaum, do also here in thy country." And he said, "Verily I say unto you, No prophet is accepted in his own country. But I tell you of a truth, many widows were in Israel in the days of Elias, when the heaven was shut up three years and six months, when great famine was throughout all the land; But unto none of them was Elias sent, save unto Sarepta, a city of Sidon, unto a woman that was a widow. And many lepers were in Israel in the time of Elijah the prophet; and none of them was cleansed, saving Naaman the Syrian."* **Luke 4:23-27**

And all they in the synagogue, when they heard these things, were filled with wrath, And rose up, and thrust him out of the city, and led him unto the brow of the hill whereon their city was built, that they might cast him down headlong. But he passing through the midst of them went his way.

Jesus gives to the people of his home town what the purpose of His mission would be:

Preach the gospel (of the kingdom) to the poor.

Heal the brokenhearted.

Preach deliverance to the captives.

Recover sight to the blind

Set at liberty them that are bruised

Preach the acceptable year of the Lord

He then tells of the time in the day of Elijah that Elijah was sent to only one city unto one of the many starving widows. The widow gave the prophet the last of her food so she could eat her last meal with her son and die. Then Elijah gave the widow a message from God, *"For thus saith the Lord God of Israel, The barrel of meal shall not waste, neither shall the cruse of oil fail, until the day that the Lord sends rain upon the earth."* **1 Kings 17:14** He also tells how the King of Syria had come to Elijah for the healing of his leprosy. He told Naaman, the Gentile Syrian, to dip seven times in the Jordan. Naaman did not want to dip in the dirty Jordan as there were clearer rivers in Syria. But he did as the prophet said and he was healed. **(see II Kings 5)**

The Jews of Nazareth were angry. Who was this Jesus, the son of Joseph and Mary? Jesus's earthly brothers and sisters were there in the city. His siblings didn't want Jesus in Nazareth anymore either. The city for Nazareth was built on and high hill. The Jews of Nazareth planned to push Jesus off the hill and kill him. But, Jesus passed through the midst of them and went his way. This again proves that Jesus **was not a head and shoulders man** with a white robe and scarlet mantle. He was dressed as any other Jew in the city and could hide himself in the midst of the people of Nazareth.

There was a marriage in Cana of Galilee and the mother of Jesus was there. Jesus and his apostles were invited also to the wedding. Mary, the mother of Jesus, now a widow, was in charge of the food and wine for the wedding. We do not know if Mary's other children were at the wedding. But, we do know when she was out on wine, they were not there to help her. Only Jesus was there. This passage shows the **faith of Mary** in her son as the Son of God with power. She was out of wine and went to Jesus saying, *"They have no wine!"*

Jesus said to her, *"Woman, what have I to do with you? Mine hour is not yet come."* Was Jesus referring to his thirst on the cross? Mary did not pay much attention to his answer, but her faith was strong. She said to the servants, *"Whatsoever he says unto you do!"* There were six empty water pots. Jesus said to the servants, *"Fill the water pots with water."* The servants filled the water pots with water. Then Jesus said to the servants, *"Draw out now, and bear unto the governor of the feast."* They did. The governor tasted what was one time water was now not only wine, but the best wine served at the wedding feast. **(See John 2:1-11)**

This was the beginning of miracles Jesus did in Cana of Galilee, and manifested forth his glory; and his disciples believed him. We are not going into the many miracles performed during the ministry of Jesus. We all know some of the miracles performed by Jesus. There were so many that John tells us in the last verse of his gospel, *"And there are also many other things which Jesus did, the which, if they should be written every one,* **I suppose that even the world itself could not contain the books that should be written.** *Amen."* **John 21:25**

thirteen

Son of Man (Son of Mary)

This child born in Bethlehem of Mary was conceived by the Holy Spirit and was born without a sin nature. He did not have the Adamic sin nature all others born on this earth have had since the fall of Adam. It is important to know we sin because we are of Adam and have a sin nature and sinning becomes automatic to all mankind. We do not have to teach our children to lie, steal, curse, or to break any of the other ten commandments, as sin comes normally as a baby learns to crawl or walk. We are not become sinners because we have sinned. We sin because we are sinners. Jesus lived a sinless life from birth to his death on the cross. When Adam fell, we do not know how long he was in the garden before he sinned, but he did eat with Eve of the forbidden fruit and became knowledgeable of good and evil. God had come to earth to be the first on earth to shed the blood of an animal to cover the sin of Adam and Eve. Their sins were only covered until the death and resurrection of Jesus where sins covered were completely removed as far as the East is from the West. They had to leave the garden not because of sin but to keep them from eating of the tree of life and live forever. Their eating of the tree of knowledge of good and evil started the dying process in their bodies.

Jesus was born the Son of man (Mary) and the Son of God. During his ministry Jesus with little exception addressed himself as the Son of man. Going through the gospels we find time and time again Jesus referred to himself as the Son of man **always knowing by faith he was the Son of God.**

Matthew 8:20

And Jesus saith unto him, The foxes have holes, and the birds of the air have nests; but the Son of man hath not where to lay his head.

Matthew 9:6

But that ye may know that the **Son of man** hath power on earth to forgive sins, (then saith he to the sick of the palsy,) Arise, take up thy bed, and go unto thine house.

Mtthew 11:19

The **Son of man** came eating and drinking, and they say, Behold a man gluttonous, and a wine bibber, a friend of publicans and sinners. But wisdom is justified of her children.

Matthew 12:8

For the **Son of man** is Lord even of the sabbath day.

Matthew 12:40

For as Jonas was three days and three nights in the whale's belly; so shall the **Son of man** be three days and three nights in the heart of the earth.

Matthew 13:37

He answered and said unto them, He that sows the good seed is the **Son of man**;

Matthew 13:41

The **Son of man** shall send forth his angels, and they shall gather out of his kingdom all things that offend, and them which do iniquity;

Matthew 16:13

When Jesus came into the coasts of Caesarea Philippi, he asked his disciples, saying, Whom do men say that I the **Son of man** am? *(Some said he was John the Baptist, others said he was Elijah, others said he was Jeremiah, and some others said one of the other prophets. It is interesting that all of those they thought he was, were already dead.)*

Matthew 16:27

For the **Son of man** shall come in the glory of his Father with his angels; and then he shall reward every man according to his works.

Matthew 16:28

Verily I say unto you, There be some standing here, which shall not taste of death, till they see the **Son of man** coming in his kingdom.

Matthew 17:9

And as they came down from the mountain, Jesus charged them, saying, Tell the vision to no man, until the **Son of man** *be risen again from the dead.*

Matthew 17:12

But I say unto you, That Elijah is come already, and they knew him not, but have done unto him whatsoever they listed. Likewise shall also the **Son of man** *suffer of them.* (Here Jesus refers to John the Baptist who was dead and likewise the Son of man would also suffer death.)

Matthew 17:22

And while they abode in Galilee, Jesus said unto them, The **Son of man** *shall be betrayed into the hands of men:* (Referring to Judas's betrayal of Christ.)

Matthew 18:11

For the **Son of man** *is come to save that which was lost.* (That is you and I.)

Matthew 19:28

And Jesus said unto them, Verily I say unto you, That ye which have followed me, in the regeneration when the **Son of man** *shall sit in the throne of his glory, ye also shall sit upon twelve thrones, judging the twelve tribes of Israel. (Promise to the twelve apostles.)*

Matthew 20:18

Behold, we go up to Jerusalem; and the **Son of man** *shall be betrayed unto the chief priests and unto the scribes, and they shall condemn him to death. (Judas would betray Jesus not to the Roman government, but to the religious leads.)*

Matthew 20:28

Even as the **Son of man** *came not to be ministered unto, but to minister, and to give his life a ransom for many. (*That includes both Jew and Gentile. You and I.)

Matthew 24:27

For as the lightning cometh out of the east, and shines even unto the west; so shall also the coming of the **Son of man** be. *(This hope was for his second coming to the Mount of Olives to Israel. We, grace age believers, are looking for the blessed hope, the rapture of the church.)*

Matthew 24:30

And then shall appear the sign of the **Son of man** *in heaven: and then shall all the tribes of the earth mourn, and they shall see the* **Son of man** *coming in the clouds of heaven with power and great glory.* (Promise to Israel of His second coming to rule from Jerusalem.)

Matthew 24:37

But as the days of Noah were, so shall also the coming of the **Son of man** *be.*

Matthew 24:39

*And knew not until the flood came, and took them all away; so shall also the coming of the **Son of man** be.*

Matthew 24:44

*Therefore be ye also ready: for in such an hour as ye think not the **Son of man** cometh.*

Matthew 25:13

*Watch therefore, for ye know neither the day nor the hour wherein the **Son of man** cometh.*

Matthew 25:31

*When the **Son of man** shall come in his glory, and all the holy angels with him, then shall he sit upon the throne of his glory.*

Matthew 26:2

*Ye know that after two days is the feast of the passover, and the **Son of man** is betrayed to be crucified.*

Matthew 26:24

*The **Son of man** goes as it is written of him: but woe unto that man by whom the **Son of man** is betrayed! it had been good for that man if he had not been born.*

Matthew 26:45

*Then cometh he to his disciples, and saith unto them, Sleep on now, and take your rest: behold, the hour is at hand, and the **Son of man** is betrayed into the hands of sinners.*

Matthew 26:64

*Jesus saith unto him, Thou hast said: nevertheless I say unto you, Hereafter shall ye see the **Son of man** sitting on the right hand of power, and coming in the clouds of heaven.*

These are all in the book of Matthew where Jesus always referred to himself as the Son of man. Jesus also referred to himself as the Son of man in the gospels of Mark, Luke and John. In the four gospels Jesus refers to himself being the son of man eighty-one times. It did not take faith to believe he was the Son of man or the son of Mary. But to call Jesus the Son of God takes faith. *"But **without faith** it is impossible to please him: for he that cometh to God **must believe** that he is, and that he is a rewarder of them that diligently seek him."* **Heb 11:6**. During the life of Christ on earth, only those who recognized Jesus as the Son of God were the people of faith and believers.

When the religious leaders of the Jews, who opposed Jesus, they always asked if He was the **Son of God. It was the Satan, his demons, and the religious leaders of Israel who questioned the fact if Jesus, the Son of man, was the Son of God.** The term "Son of God" is used eight times in the gospels by the enemies of Christ and once by Mark as he begins his gospel.

Mark 1:1

The beginning of the gospel of Jesus Christ**, the Son of God.** *(Mark puts the person of the Son of God in the first verse in his gospel.)*

Matthew 4:3

And when the tempter (Satan) came to him, he said, If you be the **Son of God,** command that these stones be made bread.

Matthew 4:6

*And said unto him, "If you be **the Son of God,** cast thyself down: for it is written, He shall give his angels charge concerning you, and in their hands they shall bear you up, lest at any time you dash your foot against a stone."* (At the temptation of as Jesus Satan asked, "If you be the Son of God." Satan wanted Jesus to obey him. If Jesus had given in to Satan and did what he asked Jesus, Satan from then on would rule the world.)

Matthew 8:28-34

*And behold they cried out, saying, "What have we to do with you, Jesus, thou **Son of God**? Are you come now to torment us before the time?" And there was a good way off from them an herd of many swine feeding. So the devils besought him, saying, "If thou cast us out, suffer us to go away into the herd of swine." And he said unto them, "Go." And when they were come out, they went into the herd of swine: and, behold, the whole herd of swine ran violently down a steep place into the sea, and perished in the waters. And they that kept them fled, and went their ways into the city, and told every thing, and what was befallen to the possessed of the devils. And, behold, the whole city came out to meet Jesus: and when they saw him, they besought him that he would depart out of their coasts."* (Jesus went to the country of the Gergesenes where he met with two men possessed with devils. The devils knew and recognized that Jesus was the Son of God. At one time they were angels of God. But they chose to follow Lucifer. They knew then at end of time they would be tormented for eternity.)

Matthew 14:33

*Then they that were in the ship came and worshiped him saying, "Of a truth you are the **Son of God**."* (Now Jesus was on a mountain praying and his disciples were on a ship in the Sea of Galilee. Jesus came to them walking on the water. Peter went to Jesus walking on the water and but the wind boisterously hard caused Peter to be afraid and he began to sink crying out, *"Lord, Save me."* Jesus reached out and caught him before he drowned. When Jesus and Peter entered the ship, the boisterously wind ceased. The disciples were amazed with Christ's power over the winds and said, *"Of a truth **you are the Son of God.**"*)

Matthew 26:63

*But Jesus held his peace, and the high priest answered and said to Jesus, "I adjure you by the living God, that you tell us whether you be the Christ (Messiah), the **Son of God**."* (The high priest used his office to adjure Jesus to answer him. To adjure is to charge or command earnestly and solemnly, often under oath or the threat of a penalty.)

Matthew 27:40

And (Jesus) s*aid, "You that destroyed the temple, and build it in three days, save yourself. If you be the **Son of God,** come down from the cross."* (Again the religious leaders hated Jesus because he was not the conquering Savior who would deliver them from the power of Rome. A suffering Savior is not what they wanted. They did not want even to read Isaiah Fifty-three about the suffering Savior. They wanted that part of the Old Testament out of their minds.)

Matthew 27:43

He trusted God, let him deliver him now, if he (God) *will have him: for he said, "**I am the Son of God.**"* (Jesus answered the leaders who tried him during his trial with the religious leader for saying that he was the *"I am."* That is the name God told Moses to use when asked by Israel who had sent him. He was the answer *"I am sent me."*)

Matthew 27:54

Now when the centurion, and they that were with him, watching Jesus, saw the earthquake, and those thing that were done, they feared greatly, saying, "Truly this was the Son of God." (Jesus had died. Salvation and the curse of sin was paid for. Only the grave stood in the way for believers to have eternal life.. The religious Jews had done with Jesus what they wanted. They wanted him gone. The Jews wanted Jesus, the Son of God, out of their lives, and religion gone forever. It would not happen. Hell could not hold the Son of God, and three days later he arose from the grave and conquered sin and Satan. At Calvary, it was a the thief on the cross and a Roman soldier, who realized Jesus was the Son of God.)

Jesus expressed his being the Son of God by using the title that Moses was given to answer the children of Israel who he was. When Moses asked God who had sent him to Israel, God answered, *"I AM THAT I AM, thus shall you say to the children of Israel, I AM has sent me."* **Exodus 3:14.** Jesus the Son of man expressed His being the Son of God by using the term **"I AM."** The gospel of John is where the **"I AM's"** are recorded. In the gospel of John Jesus said:

I AM the bread of life which came down from heave.

I AM the living bread.

I AM am from the Father.

I AM the light of the world.

I AM from above.

I AM am not of this world.

I AM the door.

I AM come that they might have life, and that they might have it more abundantly.

I AM the good shepherd and I know my sheep, and my sheep know that they are mine And I give unto them eternal life; and they shall never perish, neither shall any man pluck them out of my hand. My Father, which gave them me, is greater than all; and no man is able to pluck them out of my Father's hand. **(see John 10)**

I and the Father are ONE.

I AM the Son of God.

I AM the resurrection, and the life: he that believeth in me, though he were dead, yet shall he live:

I AM Master and Lord.

I AM with you.

Where I AM, there you will be also.

I AM the way, the truth, and the life: no man cometh unto the Father, but by me.

I AM in the Father, and the Father in me? The words that I speak unto you I speak not of myself: but the Father that dwells in me, he does the works.

I AM in my Father, and ye in me, and I in you.

I AM the vine, ye are the branches: He that abideth in me, and I in him, the same bring forth much fruit: for without me ye can do nothing.

I AM not alone, because the Father is with me.

Jesus is the great I AM that God told Moses from the burning bush. The religious leaders wanted nothing to do with the suffering Messiah. They wanted freedom from Rome not freedom from sin.

Jesus said of the Jews, "Then said they unto him, Where is thy Father? Jesus answered, Ye neither know me, nor my Father: if ye had known me, ye should have known my Father also." **John 8:19**

Jesus said, I said therefore unto you, that ye shall die in your sins: for if ye believe not that I AM he, ye shall die in your sins. **John 8:24**

Then said Jesus unto them, When ye have lifted up the Son of man, then shall ye know that I AM he, and that I do nothing of myself; but as my Father hath taught me, I speak these things. **John 8:28**

Father, I will that they also, whom thou hast given me, be with me where I AM; that they may behold my glory, which thou hast given me: for thou loved me before the foundation of the world. **John 17:24**

Then said the chief priests of the Jews to Pilate, Write not, The King of the Jews; but that he said, I AM King of the Jews. **John 19.21**

The question of the ages has to be answered, Was Jesus the Son of God, the great **I AM?**

fourteen

The Passion of Christ

Were you there when they crucified our Lord? No, but we can from the Old and New Testaments to get a true picture of the Passion of Christ. Only four people were at the cross of Christ during the crucifixion - the apostle John, his mother and two other women. Other women stood afar off because they could not endure the site. We often minimize the suffering of Christ just to the cross. But it went much further than the cross. In the words of an old unknown spiritual hymn the question is asked.

Were You There ?

Were you there when they crucified my Lord?
Were you there when they crucified my Lord?
Oh, sometimes it causes me to tremble, tremble, tremble.
Were you there when they crucified my Lord?
Were you there when they nailed him to the tree?
Were you there when they nailed him to the tree?
Oh, sometimes it causes me to tremble, tremble, tremble.
Were you there when they nailed him to the tree?
Were you there when they laid him in the tomb?
Were you there when they laid him in the tomb?
Oh, sometimes it causes me to tremble, tremble, tremble.
Were you there when they laid him in the tomb?
Were you there when God raised him from the tomb?
Were you there when God raised him from the tomb?

Oh, sometimes it causes me to tremble, tremble, tremble.

Were you there when God raised him from the tomb?

No one knows who penned these Questions. It caused the writer to tremble, tremble, tremble as he surveyed the price that was paid for the sins of mankind. The life that was lived without sin to give us the righteousness of God. The cost of redemption to buy man back from Satan. To give man eternal life. Only God could be able to pay the price. Before the foundation of the earth was created God's plan to redeem fallen man was in place. We will start with a birth in Bethlehem and will end with a risen Christ seated at the right hand of God the Father.

Jesus began his earthly ministry by being baptized by John. John tells us: *The next day John saw Jesus coming unto him, and saith,* **"Behold the Lamb of God,** *which takes away the sin of the world." This is he of whom I said, "After me cometh a man which is preferred before me: for he was before me. I knew him not: but that he should be made manifest to Israel, therefore am I come baptizing with water. John bare record, saying, I saw the Spirit descending from heaven like a dove, and it abode upon him. I knew him not: but he that sent me to baptize with water, the same said unto me, Upon whom thou shalt see the Spirit descending, and remaining on him, the same is he which baptizes with the Holy Ghost. I saw, and bare record that this is the Son of God. Again the next day after John stood, and two of his disciples; And looking upon Jesus as he walked, he saith,* **Behold the Lamb of God!"** John 1:29-36

Before John or the creation of the earth **God had planned the Son of God to be the Lamb slain for the sins of mankind.** *"And all that dwell upon the earth shall worship him, whose names are not written in the book of life of the Lamb slain from the foundation of the world."* **Revelation 13:8**

Jesus's mission was to make atonement for the sins of the world. He healed the sick, raised the dead, did many miracles to show to Israel he was the Messiah. "But though he had done so many miracles before them, yet they believed not on him." **John 12:37**. Israel as a people did not believe that he was the Messiah. They were looking for a **head and shoulder Messiah, the Lion of Judah,** that would lead a revolt against the Roman government and set Israel free. The day is coming when their desire for a ruling reigning Messiah will be fulfilled.

The twelve apostles were told of the crucifixion, death, and resurrection of Christ but they did not understand. Going to Jerusalem to be crucified Jesus said, *"Behold, we go up to Jerusalem, and all things that are written by the prophets concerning the Son of man shall be accomplished.* **For he shall be delivered unto the Gentiles, and shall be mocked, and spitefully entreated, and spitted on: And they shall scourge him, and put him to death: and the third day he shall rise again."** *And* **they understood none of these things: and this saying was hid from them,** *neither knew they the things which were spoken.* **Luke 18:31-34** Jesus told the apostles very clearly that he would be delivered to the Roman government, be mocked, spitefully treated, scourged, put to death, and on the third day he would rise again. But God hid these clear words from them, so they did not understand what he said, until after the resurrection.

The Passover supper and Gethsemane:

It was time for the Jewish Passover. Jesus sent into the city the disciples to make ready the table for the Passover supper. Jesus was there in the room with the twelve. As they sat and ate the Passover supper with Jesus he told the twelve that one of them would betray him. The twelve in sorrow asked Jesus, "Lord is it I?" All twelve realized that they were sinful and capable of being a betrayer. Their response was from men who knew their unrighteous nature. Judas asked, "**Master** is it I?" Jesus was not his Lord but only his **master.** Judas saw Jesus as a teacher or a religious leader. Jesus was not his Lord. *"Then **entered Satan into Judas.**"* **Luke 22:3** When the saints are raptured into heaven to be with Christ a man again will be entered by Satan and will deceive the world. This man will be the Antichrist. After the Passover supper they sang a hymn together and went to the Mount of Olives.

There Jesus told the eleven (Judas had left) that they would be offended with resentment, trouble and irritated that night. The next day they would leave Jesus and be scattered like sheep. Peter said, *"Not me Lord."* Jesus told Peter, *"Verily I say unto thee, that this day, even in this night, before the cock crow twice, thou shalt deny me thrice."* **Mark 14:30** He told them he would die and rise again.

At the Mount of Olives the eleven went with Jesus to pray in the Garden of Gethsemane. Jesus took Peter, James and John with him to the garden. Jesus prayed, *"O my Father, if it be possible, let this **cup** pass from me: nevertheless not as I will, but as thou wilt."* **Matt 26:39** The **cup was the WRATH of God** to be poured out on Jesus for all the sins of the world. The Father could not change His word. Jesus must suffer for the sin of man. He went back to the disciples and they were all asleep. Jesus a second time went back to pray: *"O my Father, if this **cup** may not pass away from me, except I drink it, thy will be done."* **Matt 26:42** This cup of God's wrath for sin would not pass from our Savior. There would be no salvation unless the will of the Father be done. So, many today profess there are other ways. But Jesus, the Son of God, God in the flesh, proclaimed to Israel and the world: *"I am the way, the truth and the life no man* **(NO MAN – Jew or Gentile)** *can come to the Father* **but by me."** **John 14:6** The way of the cross leads home.

The betrayal and arrest of Jesus

While the eleven slept Judas came with a great multitude armed with swords and spears sent from the chief priests and elders of the people. Corruption always starts from the top down. It was not the people who were fed with loaves and fish on the mountain side who wanted Jesus dead. It was the religious leaders of Israel. After Judas left the Passover supper he went to the chief priests to betray Jesus. He told them that he was one of the twelve apostles Jesus had chosen. The chief priests, scribes, elders, Pharisees and Sadducees rejoiced over Judas's betrayal. They offered him thirty pieces of silver to take them to Jesus. They worked up the people into a mob. As they reached Jesus, Judas goes straight to Jesus and said, "**Master, master,**" and kissed him. The mob laid their hands on Jesus, and took him. Peter standing by, drew his sword and cut off the ear of the servant of the high priest. Jesus took the ear and healed the servant. Jesus started his miracle ministry by turning water into wine now ended his miracle ministry by healing one of the mob who were there to arrest him. And when they that had laid hold on Jesus, led him away to Caiaphas the high priest, where the scribes and the elders were assembled. Then his disciples forsook Jesus and fled for their lives. But Peter **followed him afar off** unto the high priest's palace, and went in, and sat with the servants.

Peter being one of the last to flee followed **afar off** as the chief priests and all the council assembled themselves. **Looking from afar** is where Christians are most comfortable. With our fleshly Adamic nature we do not want to get too close to Him. Being close to him is where we find refuge and comfort. While before the chief priests many false witness stood up and falsely accused Jesus saying, "We heard him say, I will destroy this temple that is made with hands, and within three days I will build another made without hands." Jesus stood mute and did not answer. Then the high priest asked Jesus, "Art thou the Christ (the Messiah), the Son of the Blessed? Jesus answered, *"I am: and you shall see the Son of man sitting of the right hand of power, and coming in the clouds of heaven."* Mark 14:62

Throughout Jesus ministry he never referred to himself as the Son of God. He always used the term the Son of man. In the gospels the question, "art thou the Son of God," was given to Jesus by those who were against him including Satan during his temptation. Jesus would never answer them. When Moses was called by God in the burning bush, he asked God, *"Who shall I say that sent me?"* And *God said unto Moses,* *"I AM THAT I AM:"* *and he said, "Thus shalt thou say unto the children of Israel, I AM hath sent me unto you."* Exodus 3:14 During Jesus's ministry on earth Jesus used this same name to refer to his being.

Jesus was the one who talked to Moses from the bush. Jesus is the great **I AM.** During his ministry he used the term many times referring to himself. He said, *"I AM – the blessed son whom God was well pleased – the one who came to fulfill the law and the prophets – the one who will bring peace to the earth - meek and lowly – the God of Abraham – the living bread – the one who gives living water – the light of the world – the one who bear witness of himself – the one from above – the one who would die for your sins – the one who is lifted up – the door of the sheepfold – the true vine – the King of the Jews." Jesus asked the apostles, "But whom say ye that I am?" Peter answering said,* **"The Christ (Messiah) of God!"** Luke 9:20 *The high priest asked him, and said unto him, "Art thou the Christ, the Son of the Blessed?" And Jesus said,* **"I AM:** *and ye shall see the Son of man sitting on the right hand of power, and coming in the clouds of heaven."* Luke 9:62 After this **"I AM"** the high priest ripped his clothes saying Jesus was a blasphemer and all his accusers condemned him to be guilty of death. After the announcement by his accusers were enraged with **wrath** and began to spit on Jesus, covered his face, striking his face with powerful bruising force, and asking him to prophesy who had smote him. This fulfilled the prophecy of Isaiah 53:10 *Yet it pleased the LORD to bruise him.*

This was the beginning of the marring and bruising of our Lord's face. The Jewish leaders who were doing the marring and bruising of our Lord were instruments of GOD to pour His **wrath** upon Christ for our sins. Isaiah foretold this in Isaiah 52:14 *"As many were astonished at thee; his* **visage (face)** *was* **so marred (spoiled or destroyed) more than any man,** *and* **his form** *more* *than the sons of men:"* Do we understand this? Our Lord's face and body was **destroyed more than any man on** earth. To look at his face we, like the many women who knew Jesus, one would have to **look from afar.** We could not have been able to be under his cross as his mother and John.

Peter's denial

And as Peter was beneath in the palace, there came one of the maids of the high priest: And when she saw Peter warming himself, she looked upon him, and said, And thou also was with Jesus of Nazareth. But he denied, saying, "I know not, neither understand I what thou said." And he went out into the porch, and the cock crew. And a maid saw him again, and began to say to them that stood by, "This is one of them." And he denied it again. And a little after, they that stood by said again to Peter, "Surely thou art one of them: for thou art a Galilean, and thy speech agrees thereto." But he began to curse and to swear, saying, "I know not this man of whom ye speak." And the second time the cock crew. And Peter called to mind the word that Jesus said unto him, "Before the cock crow twice, thou shalt deny me thrice." And when he thought thereon, he wept. **Mark 14:66-72** This same Peter when asked by Jesus, *"But whom say ye that **I am?"** Peter answering said, **"The Christ of God"** was now denying he ever knew him. **Luke 9:20** We as believer's worship in our church with high praise to our Lord and Savior. But soon after we leave and are on the freeway hurrying to get home for that nice Sunday dinner, find ourselves cursing at that slow driver in front of us who is driving us to anger. Jesus knew how Peter felt as he wept. We do not know the agony that Peter felt as his Lord was being crucified. But we know our Lord's love for Peter. After arising from the tomb Jesus tells the women there to go tell the disciples, **and Peter.** Do you see the Love of God in those two words **"And Peter."** After Pentecost, Peter being filled with the Holy Spirit was the one who appeared before the Jews without fear declaring the resurrection of our Lord.

Jesus before the Roman Government

Then early the next morning came the chief priests, scribes and elders counseled together to put Jesus to death. They led Jesus bound from Caiaphas to the hall of judgment to Pilate the governor. Pilate then went out unto them, and said, *"What accusation bring ye against this man"?* They answered and said unto him, "If he were not a malefactor, we would not have delivered him up unto thee." Then said Pilate unto them, *"Take ye him, and judge him according to your law."* The Jews therefore said unto him, "It is not lawful for us to put any man to death." And they began to accuse him, saying, *"We found this fellow perverting the nation, and forbidding to give tribute to Caesar, saying that he himself is Christ a King."* Standing bound before Pilate, Pilate asked Jesus if he was **King of the Jews**. Jesus answered him, ***"Thou said it."*** Then said Pilate to the chief priests and to the people, I find no fault in this man. The chief priest again accused Jesus of many other things before Pilate. And they were the more fierce, saying, *"He stirs up the people, teaching throughout all Israel, beginning from Galilee to this place."* **(See Mark 15)**

After Pilate heard that Jesus was from Galilee he knowing that he belonged unto Herod's jurisdiction, he sent him to Herod, who himself also was at Jerusalem at that time. And when Herod saw Jesus, he was exceeding glad: for he was desirous to see him of a long season, because he had heard many things of him; and he hoped to have seen some miracle done by him. Then he questioned with him in many words; but he answered him nothing. And the chief priests and scribes stood and vehemently accused him before Herod. Jesus refused to answer the accusations against him. Herod with his men of war set him at naught, and mocked him, and arrayed him in a gorgeous robe, and sent him in to Pilate. **(See Luke 23:11)** The soldiers with iron meshed gloves braided a crown of thorns making sure the thorns were pointed toward the scalp so the thorns would cut his scalp and pin the crown of thorns to Jesus's head. When they had platted a crown of thorns, they put it upon Jesus's head, and a scepter reed in his right hand: and they bowed the knee before him, and mocked him, saying, ***"Hail, King of the Jews!"* Matt 27:29** Then Herod sent him back to Pilate. It was passover time in Jerusalem and each passover the governor would offer to free a prisoner whoever the people chose.. Pilate not wanting to put Jesus to death went to the people gathered before him said unto them, *"Whom will ye that I release unto you, Barabbas, or Jesus which is called Christ* (the Messiah)?" Barabbas had been charged with the crime of treason, and murder against Rome. Pilate wanted to wash his hand of Jesus and release him. But the chief priests stirred up the people to release Barabbas and crucify Jesus. They cried out, ***"Crucify him." Mark 15:13*** *When Pilate sat down on the judgment seat, his* *wife sent a message to him, saying, "Have thou nothing to do with that just man: for I have suffered many things this day in a dream because of him." An unwilling Pilate called again to the people, "What shall I do, then, with the one you call the* **King of the Jews?"** *Pilate asked them again and they cried out , "**Crucify him.**" Pilate saith unto them, "What shall I do then with Jesus which is called* **Christ (the Messiah)?"** *They all said to him, "**Let him be crucified.**" And the governor said, "Why, what evil hath he done"? But they cried out the more, saying,* **"Let him be crucified".** *When Pilate saw that he could prevail nothing, but that rather a tumult was made, he took water, and washed his hands before the multitude, saying, "I am innocent of the blood of this just person: see ye to it." But they cried out,* **"Away with him, away with him, crucify him".** *Pilate saith unto them, "Shall I crucify your King"? The chief priests answered,* **"We have no king but Caesar."** *Then answered all the people, and said,* **"His blood be on us, and on our children."** *Pilate ordered the release of Barabbas and delivered Jesus to leader of the Roman soldiers. Pilate therefore said unto him,* **"Art thou a king then?"** *Jesus answered, "Thou says that* **I am a king. To this end was I born,** *and for this cause came I into the world, that I should bear witness unto the truth. Every one that is of the truth hears my voice."* **John 18:37** After Pilate turned Jesus to the Roman soldiers lashed Jesus with thirty-nine stripes. Many men had died from a lashing of the thirty-nine stripes but Jesus was able to bare the beating. Then the soldiers violently plucked off his beard from his face. The crimson red blood from the crown of thorns and plucked beard covered his swollen bruised face with blood dripping down his chin unto his naked torso. On his back the blood flowed down his legs unto the ground which he created. During this time Christ did not hide his face which was set like a flint toward Calvary and death. **Isaiah 50:6-9**

Pilate sent Jesus and two malefactors to Calvary to be crucified. Jesus, unlike the two malefactors was so weak from the beatings by the Jewish leaders and Roman Soldiers could not carry his cross. The soldiers put the cross of Jesus on a man from Cyrene in Africa to carry the cross for him. And there followed him a **great company of people, and of women, which also bewailed and lamented him.** But Jesus turning unto them said, *"Daughters of Jerusalem, weep not for me, but weep for yourselves, and for your children. For, behold, the days are coming, in the which they shall say, Blessed are the barren, and the wombs that never bare, and the paps which never gave suck. Then shall they begin to say to the mountains, Fall on us; and to the hills, Cover us."* **Luke 23:27-30**

They reached Calvary, also called Golgotha, the place of the skull. The soldiers ripped off the clothes from those to be crucified. But they parted Jesus's garments, the soldiers cast lots to decided who would own His garments. With iron nails the soldiers nailed the three to their crosses. On the center cross was our Lord and Savior, Jesus, and a superscription was written over him in letters of Greek, and Latin, and Hebrew, **Luke 23:38** The soldiers raised the crosses. Three wooden crosses stood holding two malefactors and the Son of God the creator of the trees from which the crosses were hewed and set in the ground he created. **(See John 1:1-3)**

The chief priests and elders along with the mob they assembled, stood beholding the site on Calvary's hill. And the rulers derided him, saying, *"He saved others; let him save himself, if he be Christ, the chosen of God." After this, Jesus, knowing that all things were now accomplished, that the Scripture might be fulfilled, said, "I thirst!" His throat was dry and he asked for water. He thirst, the one who gave Moses the water from the rock for the thirsty children of Israel in the wilderness. He thirst, the one who made springs in the desert. He thirst, the one who who made bubbling streams and winding rivers. He thirst, the one who gave living water to the women at the well. He thirst, the one who gives living water to all that call on him. But all he was offered was bitter vinegar. The soldiers also mocked him, coming to him, and offering him vinegar saying, "If thou be the king of the Jews, save thyself." He could have called ten thousands angels but he opened not his mouth. One of the malefactors which were hung with Jesus railed on him, saying, "If thou be Christ(the Messiah), save thyself and us." But the other answering rebuked him, saying, "Do you not fear God, seeing thou art in the same condemnation? We indeed justly; for we receive the due reward of our deeds: but this man hath done nothing amiss." He said unto Jesus, "Lord, remember me when thou come into thy kingdom." Jesus said unto him, "Verily I say unto thee, Today shalt thou be with me in paradise."* **Luke 23:35-43** The crowd watched as the three slowly were dying. Jesus looked down and could see the one disciple who loved him most, John. With John at the cross of Jesus was Mary His mother, and His mother's sister, Mary the wife of Clopas, and Mary Magdalene.

When Jesus therefore saw His mother, and the disciple whom He loved standing by, He said to His mother, "Woman, behold your son!" **John 19:25-26** Jesus's siblings James, Jude, Joses, and Simon along with his sisters had all **forsaken** their elder brother and mother. Jesus assigned his elder son responsibility to take care of his mother to John. It must have been hard for the younger siblings of Jesus to follow after a sinless older brother. Jesus, the Son of God, was born without a sin nature. After the birth of Jesus, Mary and Joseph had many other children that were born with the same sinful nature we all have. How could they walk in the path of Jesus? **Impossible!** So, they gave up and went their own way rejecting their elder brother and their widowed mother. After the resurrection we know that two of Jesus's brothers, James and Jude, believed that Jesus was the Messiah and became leaders in the church.

Jesus's naked body, being weaken by the bruising blows of the Jewish religious leaders and Roman soldiers, gave up the fight for life. His bones were out of joint, his heart was like wax melted in the midst of his bowels. His strength dried up like potsherds (broken pieces of pottery), and his tongue cleaved to his jaws. **(See Psalms 22:11-14)** With his bones out of joint, his torso fell limp, and forward stretching out his arms and legs. His unrecognizable naked body was held only by the nails in his hands and feet, was near death. Dried blood covered his naked body. It was the sixth hour and Jesus was ready to die. Pitch black darkness filled the earth for the next three hours. His face was marred beyond recognition. In the temple, the veil between God and man was rent in twain from the top to the bottom; and the earth did quake, and the rocks rent; and the graves were opened; and many bodies of the saints which slept arose, then came out of the graves after his resurrection, and went into the holy city, and appeared unto many. **(See Matt 27:53)**

"The darkness ended on the ninth hour. At about that ninth hour Jesus cried with a loud voice, saying, "Eli, Eli, lama sabachthani," that is to say, "My God, my God, why hast thou **forsaken me?"** *Some of them that stood there, when they heard that, said, This man calls for Elias."* **Matt 27:46** He was not calling for Elias but was crying out to the Father who had turned His face from him. One of the greatest punishments for those who died without faith in Jesus Christ will be to lose all hope being forsaken by God for ever.

Many of us do not know what it is to be abandoned. I was having lunch with my friend, Tom. Tom was abandoned at birth by this birth mother. He was later adopted by a couple in their mid thirties. Soon after the couple adopted Tom his new father died leaving him in the care of a uneducated mother. She had to go to work as a waitress to support Tom and herself. She worked many hours to provide for herself and Tom. To work more hours she put Tom in military school for five years. She could only see him on Tuesdays, her day off.

Tom knows what it is to be forsaken and abandoned. With tears in his eyes he said, "Being forsaken by God is the worse thing that could happen to a man!" For the unbeliever the worse thing they will face is to have no hope being forsaken by God eternally. Like the Gentile nations were before the cross, *"That at that time ye were* **without** *Christ, being* **aliens** *from the commonwealth of Israel, and strangers from the covenants of promise,* **having no hope, and without God in the world:** Eph 2:12

Jesus being forsaken by the Father cried with a loud voice, he said, *"Father, into thy hands I commend my spirit:" and having said thus, he gave up the ghost* (he died). **Luke 23:46** The earth quaked. When the centurion, and they that were with him, watching Jesus, saw the earthquake, and those things that were done, they feared greatly, saying, ***"Truly this was the Son of God."*** Matthew 27:54

Looking from Afar

The dead unrecognizable body of Jesus hung naked, limp, covered with crimson blood upon the cross. Mary Magdalene and others could not bare the gruesome sight beneath the cross. They left their place beneath the cross of Jesus and went with the other women who were there **beholding afar off.** They had followed Jesus from Galilee, ministering unto him: Among which was Mary Magdalene, and Mary the mother of James and Joses, Salome, the mother of James and John and many other women who came up with Him to Jerusalem. **(See Matt 50:55-56, and Mark 15:40-41)** Today we also do not want to be too close to the gruesome sight of the cross. **We want to see it from afar.** We do not want to visualize our savior with his face and form that was marred more than any man hanging naked, limp, and bloody on the cross. We want a head and shoulder man. We want a strong man grabbing with strength the nails holding himself up having a loin cloth covering his nakedness. We do not want to visualize him during his earth ministry as meek and lowly without form or comeliness. But that is what the scriptures tell us. He was a man of sorrow, despised, regarded with contempt, without form or comeliness (without charisma - ugly), and we would not desire him. We would walk away from him. But God's Holy Spirit blinds us to his appearance but to the cross. As many were astonished at thee; **his visage was so marred more than any man, and his form more than the sons of men: Isaiah 52:14**

The Holy Spirit leads us to the grace of God to be our redeemer. We will never find Christ while looking for a head and shoulder leader. For by **grace** are ye **saved** through **faith**; and that not of yourselves: it is the gift of God: **Ephesians 2:8** The grace of God was shown to us by his virgin birth in Bethlehem, to the betrayal kiss of Judas, to the quaking of the earth when Jesus the Messiah gave up his spirit and died, to his body laying dead in the tomb for three days, to his resurrection from the dead, and to his ascension into heaven to sit at the right hand of the Father. Only by putting faith in this saving grace as payment for sins can man be saved. During the time of the Son of God on earth, God's grace was shown to all. The Jewish religious leaders, the mob, and the Roman government were only the instruments used by God to **pour His wrath on His Son for the sins of mankind**. The wrath of God for my sins, your sins and and sins of the whole world was poured out on his Son so we could have our sins forgiven and be redeemed from the power of Satan. Much more then, being now justified by his blood, we shall be saved from **wrath** through him. **Roman 5:9** Yet it **PLEASED** the LORD to **bruise him**; he hath **put him to grief:** when thou shalt **make his soul an offering for sin,** he shall see his seed, he shall prolong his days, and the pleasure of the LORD shall prosper in his hand. **Isaiah 53:10** During this time of grace being displayed to the world the curse of sin was gone. Sin's curse was paid for and man was redeemed from the power of Satan. But did it give man eternal life? Paul tells us in Corinthians, *"For if the dead rise not, **then is not Christ raised: if Christ be not raised, your faith is vain; ye are yet in your sins.** Then they also which are fallen asleep in Christ are perished"*. **1Cor 15:16-18.** Jesus must be raised from the dead.

Jesus's side pierced and His burial

The Jews therefore, because it was the preparation, that the bodies should not remain upon the cross on the sabbath day, (for that sabbath day was a high day,) besought Pilate that their legs might be broken, and that they might be taken away. Then came the soldiers to break the legs of those crucified. But when they came to Jesus, and saw that he was dead already, they brake not his legs: But one of the soldiers with a spear pierced his side, and forthwith came there out blood and water. And he that saw it bare record, and his record is true: and he knoweth that he saith true, that ye might believe. For these things were done, that the scripture should be fulfilled, A bone of him shall not be broken. And again another scripture saith, They shall look on him whom they pierced. **John 19:31-37**

When the evening was come, there came a rich man of Arimathaea, named Joseph, who also himself was Jesus' disciple: He went to Pilate, and begged the body of Jesus. Then Pilate commanded the body to be delivered. Then came also Nicodemus, which at the first came to Jesus by night, and brought a mixture of myrrh and aloes, about a hundred pound weight. Then took they the body of Jesus, and wound it in linen clothes with the spices, as the manner of the Jews is to bury. Now in the place where he was crucified there was a garden; and in the garden a new sepulcher, wherein was never man yet laid. There laid they Jesus therefore because of the Jews' preparation day; for the sepulcher was nigh at hand. And when Joseph had taken the body, he wrapped it in a clean linen cloth, laid it in his own new tomb, which he had hewed out in the rock: and he rolled a great stone to the door of the sepulcher, and departed. And there was Mary Magdalene, and the other Mary, sitting over against the sepulcher. Now the next day, that followed the day of the preparation, the chief priests and Pharisees came together unto Pilate, saying, "Sir, we remember that that deceiver said, while he was yet alive, *"After three days I will rise again."* Command therefore that the sepulcher be made sure until the third day, lest his disciples come by night, and steal him away, and say unto the people, *"He is risen from the dead: so the last error shall be worse than the first."* Pilate said unto them, *"Ye have a watch: go your way, make it as sure as ye can."* So they went, and made the sepulcher sure, sealing the stone, and setting a watch. **(See Matthew 27:57-66, John 19:39-42)**

The Resurrection

When the sabbath was past, Mary Magdalene, and Mary the mother of James, and Salome, had bought sweet spices, that they might come and anoint him. Very early in the morning the first day of the week, they came unto the sepulcher at the rising of the sun. They found the stone rolled away from the sepulcher. They entered in, and found not the body of the Lord Jesus. They said among themselves, *"Who shall roll away the stone from the door of the sepulcher?"* They looked, they saw that the stone was rolled away: for it was very great. Entering into the sepulcher, they saw a young man sitting on the right side, clothed in a long white garment; and they were frighted. Jesus said unto her, *"Woman, why weep thou? whom do you seek?"* She, supposing him to be the gardener, saith unto him, *"Sir, if thou have borne him hence, tell me where thou hast laid him, and I will take him away." Jesus said unto her, "Mary." She turned herself, and saith unto him, "Master." Jesus said unto her, "Touch me not;* **for I am not yet ascended to my Father:** *but go to my brethren, and say unto them, I ascend unto my Father, and your Father; and to my God, and your God." He said to them, "Be not frighted: Ye seek Jesus of Nazareth, which was crucified: he is risen; he is not here: behold the place where they laid him. But go your way, tell his disciples* **and Peter** *that he goes before you into Galilee: there shall ye see him, as he said unto you." They then remembered his words, "The Son of man must be delivered into the hands of sinful men, and be crucified, and the third day rise again."* They went out quickly, and fled from the sepulcher; for they trembled and were amazed: neither said they any thing to any man; for they were afraid. Returning from the sepulcher, they told all these things unto the eleven, and to all the rest. It was Mary Magdalene and Joanna, and Mary the mother of James, and other women that were with them, which told these things unto the apostles. **And their words seemed to them as idle tales, and they believed them not.** Peter and John ran both together: and John out ran Peter, and came first to the sepulcher. John stooping down, and looking in, saw the linen clothes lying; yet went he not in. Then came Simon Peter following him, and went into the sepulcher, and sees the linen clothes lie, and the napkin, that was about his head, not lying with the linen clothes, but wrapped together in a place by itself. Then went in also that other disciple, which came first to the sepulcher, and he saw, **and believed. For as yet they knew not the scripture,** that he must rise again from the dead. Then the disciples went away again unto their own home. **(See Mark 16:1-8, Luke 24:2-12, John 20:4-17)**

Jesus told Mary not to touch him because he had not ascended to the Father. When he went to the room where the eleven were meeting, Jesus came through a wall the apostles thought that it was a spirit. *But Jesus said to them, "Behold my hands and my feet, that it is I myself: handle me, and see; for a spirit hath not* **flesh and bones,** *as you see me have."* **Luke 24:39** Then Jesus went to Thomas and told Thomas to put his fingers into the holes in his hands. Why could not Mary touch Jesus then Jesus tells Thomas to touch him? The answer is that between the time he met Mary and the time he met with Thomas and the apostles, Jesus ascended into heaven and presented his incorruptible blood on the mercy seat before God the Father. When Jesus met with the eleven, he told them he had flesh and bone but did not say he had blood because his blood was in heaven setting on the mercy seat before God the Father. As Peter said in his first epistles *"For as much as ye know that ye were not redeemed with* **corruptible things, as silver and gold,** *from your vain conversation received by tradition from your fathers;* **but with the precious blood of Christ,** *as of a lamb without blemish and without spot".* **1 Peter 1:18-19** Iron rust, and aluminum corrodes in a few years but the corrosion of silver and gold takes centuries. But the body and blood of Jesus did not see corruption. As his body laid for three days in the tomb not one cell of his body changed. Jesus was conceived by the Holy Spirit and his body did not contain the corruptible seed of Adam. His body was like the bodies of Adam and Eve before the fall. Jesus had an eternal body. The Psalmist said hundreds of years before: *"For thou wilt not leave my soul in hell; neither wilt thou suffer thine Holy One to see* **corruption."** **Psalm 16:10**

That he should still live for ever, and **not see corruption Psalm 49:9** Without a resurrected Christ, there would be no hope for mankind. Our belief in the cross would be in vain if Christ did not rise from the dead. There is no salvation for those who do not believe in the resurrection. Paul said: **"If Christ be not raised, your faith is vain; ye are yet in your sins.** *Then they also which are fallen asleep in Christ are perished. If in this life only we have hope in Christ, we are of all men most miserable. But now is* **Christ risen from the dead,** *and become the first fruits of them that slept.* For **since by man came death, by man came also the resurrection of the dead. For as in Adam all die, even so in Christ shall all be made alive."** **1 Corinthians 15:17-24** God the Holy Spirit was the one that raised Christ from the dead. It is the same Spirit that dwells in each believer. In Romans Paul tells us: *"But if the* **Spirit of him that raised up Jesus from the dead dwell in you,** *he that raised up Christ from the dead shall also quicken your mortal bodies by his Spirit that dwells in you."* **Romans 8:11** Our bodies are tabernacles of the Holy Spirit. In the wilderness God dwelt in the tabernacle planned by God and built by Moses. Moses received the plans for the tabernacle on Mt. Sinai. There God gave him the plan from the least part to the greatest part of the structure. It was the dwelling place of God for his people, Israel. The tabernacle was a tent. God sent Paul to the Gentiles. Paul was a tent maker for his earthly occupation. His heavenly occupation was to call the Gentiles to God so that our bodies could be a tent for the Holy Spirit to dwell in.

The Lion of Judah

We started this writing with the suffering Messiah and the Lamb of God. When Jesus comes again, he will come as the reigning Messiah and the Lion of Judah. He will come as a head and shoulder leader. The Jews are looking forward to his second coming. We, as grace age believers, are *"Looking for that blessed hope* (the rapture of the church), *and the glorious appearing of the great God and our Savior Jesus Christ."* **Titus 2:13** His second coming will be with power and great glory. He will be coming as the conquering Messiah. He will be coming as the **King of kings and Lord of lords.** He is coming to rule and reign with a rod of iron. *"The government shall be upon his shoulder: and his name shall be called Wonderful, Counselor, The mighty God, The everlasting Father, The Prince of Peace."* **Isaiah 9:6** He will be *"clothed in a robe reaching down to his feet and with a golden sash around his chest. The hair on his head was white like wool, as white as snow, and his eyes were like blazing fire. His feet were like bronze glowing in a furnace, and his voice was like the sound of rushing waters."* **Revelation 1:13-15**

As we look for the soon appearing of our Savior to met us in the air, let us keep in mind what the apostle Paul said to the believers in Philippi: *"If there be therefore any consolation in Christ, if any comfort of love, if any fellowship of the Spirit, if any bowels and mercies, fulfill ye my joy, that ye be like minded, having the same love, being of one accord, of one mind. Let nothing be done through strife or vainglory; but in lowliness of mind let each esteem other better than themselves. Look not every man on his own things, but every man also on the things of others.* **Let this mind be in you, which was also in Christ Jesus: Who, being in the form of God, thought it not robbery to be equal with God: But made himself of no reputation, and took upon him the form of a servant, and was made in the likeness of men: Being found in fashion as a man, he humbled himself, and became obedient unto death, even the death of the cross.** *Wherefore God also hath highly exalted him, and given him a name which is above every name:* **That at the name of Jesus every knee should bow, of things in heaven, and things in earth, and things under the earth; and that every tongue should confess that Jesus Christ is Lord, to the glory of God the Father."* **Philippians 2:1-11**

The book of John closes the four gospels. The four gospels were a record of the Son of God's visit to earth to redeem man from the curse of sin. After the ascension of Christ into heaven forty days later was the feast of Pentecost.

The believers met in the upper room . The Son of Man had faith from the time he announced to his earthly parents, that he about his **Father's** business. This was his first declaration that he was the Son of God and not the son of Joseph. From that time onward Jesus had complete faith always that **he was the Son of God.** He never doubted or wavered that he was not the Son of God.

His faith was continually based on being the Son of God. *"Even the righteousness of God which is by* **faith of Jesus Christ** *unto all and upon all them that believe: for there is no difference, for all have sinned and come short of the glory of God."* **Romans 3:22**

"Knowing that a man is not justified by the works of the law, but by **the faith of Jesus Christ,** *even we have believed in Jesus Christ, that we might be justified by the* **faith of Christ,** *and not by the works of the law: for by the works of the law shall no flesh be justified."* **Galatians 2:16**

"But the scripture hath concluded all under sin, that the promise by **faith of Jesus Christ** *might be given to them that believe."* **Galatians 3:22**

"And be found in him, not having mine own righteousness, which is of the law, but that which is through the **faith of Christ,** *the righteousness which is of God by faith:"* **Philippians 3:9**

"Here is the patience of the saints: here are they that keep the commandments of God, and the **faith of Jesus."** **Revelation 14:12**

Even the Son of man had to have faith. *"But* **without faith** *it is impossible to please him: for he that cometh to God must believe that he is, and that he is a rewarder of them that diligently seek him."* **Hebrews 11:6** In our daily lives the believer has to live by faith. We have to live by faith when sickness, disease, death of a family member, and in all things we must have faith that this is God's will in our lives. Three times in Paul's epistles Paul tell the churches that, **"The just shall live by faith." (See Romans 1:17, Galatians 3:11 Hebrews 10:38)**

fourteen

The Gospel of the Kingdom

The Gospel of the Kingdom is the gospel that John the Baptist preached and that Jesus taught in most of his Parables. In the book of Matthew the term "Kingdom of Heaven" is used thirty-two times in the gospels whereas the term "Kingdom of God" is used fifty-four times in the four gospels. It used six times in the book of Acts, and nine times in the epistles of Paul.

Knowing the difference between the "Kingdom of Heaven" and the "Kingdom of God" is important to understand the time line in the Biblical history of times past, the present, and the future. The Kingdom of God consist of the (1) Jewish promised Kingdom of Heaven, (2) the Age of Grace believers, and (3) the whole universe. It is very important to understand that the Kingdom of Heaven, the Millennium Age, is part of God's covenant with Israel and NOT part of the grace age church. The Kingdom Heaven is what the Jews have waited for, a kingdom the reaches from the River Euphrates, to the River of Egypt with the Messiah ruling from **Zion in Jerusalem of Judah.**

John the Baptist came preaching the Kingdom of heaven was at hand. "Now after that John was put in prison, Jesus came into Galilee, preaching the gospel of the kingdom of God." **Mark 1:14** *Nicodemus came to Jesus and asked, "Rabbi we know that thou art a teacher come from God: for no man can do these miracles that thou does, except God be with him." Jesus answered and said unto him, "Verily, verily, I say unto thee,* **Except a man be born again, he cannot see the kingdom of God."** *Nicodemus said unto him, "How can a man be born when he is old? can he enter the second time into his mother's womb, and be born?" Jesus answered, Verily, verily, I say unto thee, "Except a man be* **born of water and of the Spirit, he cannot enter into the kingdom of God."** *John 3:1-5*

Then Pilate entered into the judgment hall again, and called Jesus, and said unto him, "Are you the King of the Jews?" Jesus answered him, "Say thou this thing of thyself, or did others tell it thee of me?" Pilate answered, "Am I a Jew? Thine own nation and the chief priests have delivered thee unto me: what hast thou done?" Jesus answered, **"My kingdom is not of this world:** *if my kingdom were of this world, then would my servants fight, that I should not be delivered to the Jews: but now is my kingdom not from hence."* **John 18:33-36**

Jesus was telling Pilate **NOW** he was not speaking about the spiritual kingdom within man but of a literal political kingdom yet to come on Earth.

Israel was not looking for a suffering Messiah. They rejected their Messiah, the Lord Jesus Christ. They were looking for a political king who make Israel the world ruling kingdom spoken by their prophets. They wanted a earthly Messiah that would bring deliverance from the Roman government that ruled over them. Even the twelve Apostles were looking for a conquering Messiah. *"Then came to him the mother of Zebedee's children with her sons, worshiping him, and desiring a certain thing of him. And he said unto her, What wilt thou? She saith unto him, Grant that these my two sons may sit, the one on thy right hand, and the other on the left,* **in thy kingdom."** **Matthew 20:20-21** After the arrest of Jesus they all fled and did not understand that there was more to come. Jesus told them what was to happen yet they did not understand because God hid it from their comprehension.

The Gospel of the Kingdom was the message preached by John the Baptist and Jesus. It was the message to the people of Israel. John the Baptist, the forerunner of Jesus cried out to the people of Israel *"Repent for the Kingdom of Heaven is at Hand."* John the Baptist was to prepare the people of Israel for the earthly ministry of the Lord Jesus Christ. Many Jews came out all of Israel to hear the message of John. Many repented and were baptized by John confessing their sins. But the religious leaders denied this message. John called them a generation of vipers. He said, *"Bring forth therefore fruits meet for repentance: And think not to say within yourselves, We have Abraham to our father: for I say unto you, that God is able of these stones to raise up children unto Abraham." I indeed baptize you with water unto repentance. but he that cometh after me is mightier than I, whose shoes I am not worthy to bear: he shall baptize you with the Holy Ghost, and with fire:"* **(See Matt 3:7-11)**

John preached to the people of Israel with much power and might. His message turned the hearts of many of the Jewish people during his years of ministry. Many Jews from foreign countries when going to Jerusalem to see the temple, also came to hear the message of John and repented and were baptized. They went back to their synagogues and told of the message of John.

Jesus also taught the Kingdom of Heaven or the Kingdom of God. From that time Jesus began to preach, and to say, *"Repent: for the* **kingdom of heaven** *is at hand."* **Matthew 4:17** Jesus ministry to the Jews was the Kingdom of Heaven. Jesus said to the Jews, *"But seek you first the kingdom of God, and his righteousness; and all theses things shall be added unto you."* **Matthew 6:33** It was the message to Israel only. Jesus told the twelve, *"***Go not into the way of the Gentiles,** *and into any city of the Samaritans enter ye not: But go rather to the lost sheep of the house of Israel. And as ye go, preach, saying,* **The kingdom of heaven is at hand."** Matthew 10:5-7

Job with pain running throughout his body cried out, *"For I know that my redeemer lives, and that he shall stand at the latter day upon the earth: And though after my skin worms destroy this body, yet in my flesh shall I see God:* **Whom I shall see for myself, and mine eyes shall behold,** *and not another; though my reins be consumed within me."* **Job 19:25-27** Job here was looking beyond his death and the grave to a time when the Redeemer would bring the Kingdom of Heaven down to earth and that time his body would be resurrected and he would see God reigning on earth. What a faith Job had.

John the Baptist told Israel to repent confessing their sins and be baptized. Repentance was to turn from their wicked ways, and turn to living and walking in all the commandments and ordinances of the Lord their God blameless. This was also the message of the Kingdom of God was repentance and turning to living and walking in all the commandments and ordinances of God.

Then he took unto him the twelve, and said unto them, Behold, we go up to Jerusalem, and all things that are written by the prophets concerning the Son of man shall be accomplished. **For he shall be delivered unto the Gentiles, and shall be mocked, and spitefully entreated, and spitted on: And they shall scourge him, and put him to death: and the third day he shall rise again. Luke 18:31-33**

Could not this be any clearer? Jesus was to be delivered to the Gentile Roman government, be mocked, spitefully entreated, spitted on, scourged, and put to death. Then on the third day he would rise from the death. But it was not God's will that at that time they should understand what Jesus said. *And* **they** *understood none of these things: and this saying was hid from them, nei-ther knew they the things which were spoken.* **Luke 18:34** *After the resurrection the disciples asked Jesus asked about the Kingdom saying, "Lord, wilt thou at this time* **restore again the kingdom to Israel** *(or the Kingdom of Heaven)?" And he said unto them, "It is not for you to know the times or the seasons, which the Father hath put in his own power. But ye shall receive power, after that the Holy Ghost is come upon you: and ye shall be witnesses unto me both in Jerusalem, and in all Judaea, and in Samaria, and unto the uttermost part of the earth."* **Acts1:6-8**

This is one of the most disputed question that has been with the church since the early church fathers declared that the church has replaced Israel and all the promises God made to Abraham, Isaac, and Jacob. Today eighty percent or more in Christendom believe the church has replaced Israel. God has no interest at all in the nation Israel or the Jewish people. The world does not want the Lord Jesus Christ to return and rule over them. That is why the Jews killed their King the first time he came. Here is what their King will say about that when he returns: *"But those mine enemies, which would not that I should reign over them, bring hither, and slay them before me."* **Luke 19:27**

There will be a big attitude difference between the Lord's first coming as the suffering Messiah and his second coming as the conquering warrior King, the Lion of Judah:

"And I saw heaven opened, and behold a white horse; and he that sat upon him was called Faithful and True, and in righteousness **he doth judge and make war.** *His eyes were as a flame of fire, and on his head were many crowns; and he had a name written, that no man knew, but he himself. And he was clothed with a vesture dipped in blood: and his name is called The Word of God."* **Rev 19:11-13**

The Jews did not receive Jesus when he came to earth as the suffering Messiah. They refused to believe he was the Son of God, the Messiah, God temporarily blinded their eyes, and stopped their ears to the message of salvation. He then called the Apostle Paul to bring the message of grace to the Gentiles, kings, and a few Jews that believed Jesus was the Messiah. After God has called all those that are his during this Age of Grace, God will again turn his attention to the salvation of the Jews. He will return as King of kings and Lord of lords. He will bring the Kingdom of Heaven down to earth and rule from Jerusalem for one thousand years and then forever. The children of Israel will have all the earthly and spiritual blessings promised to Abraham, Isaac, and

Jacob. The believing Jews will be resurrected and the nation of Israel will be from the river Euphrates to the river of Egypt. The land will be so rich that the reapers cannot keep up with the plowers. It will be a land of milk and honey. This will be the Kingdom of Heaven that will come to earth. All the promises to the Jews of the kingdom will be fulfilled.

It is important that the Jews never looked forward to heaven after death. They were always looking forward to the Kingdom of Heaven coming down to earth and Israel. At that time God would rule Israel and the world from Jerusalem. Job said of his faith, *"For I know that my redeemer lives, and that* **he shall stand at the latter day upon the earth:"**

We as believers in the cross of Jesus look forward to going to heaven after death. As Paul had said, *"We are confident, I say, and willing rather to be absent from the body, and to be present with the Lord."* **II Corinthians 5:8**

fifteen

Jesus and the Law of Moses

The time from Adam to Noah was a time that man did what was right in his own mind. There was a remnant that served God with blood sacrifices for their sins. But as it came closer to the flood only eight, Noah and his family, served God. *"And God saw that the wickedness of man was great in the earth, and that every imagination of the thoughts of his heart was only evil continually."* **Genesis 6:5.** When Noah left the ark the first thing he did was build an altar and gave a blood sacrifice to God for his sin and that of his family. This was the only offering God would accept to cover the sins of man. And almost all things are by the law purged with blood; *"Without the shedding of blood is not remission of sin."* **Hebrews 9:22** The book of Job, the oldest written book in the Bible starts with Job making sacrifices for his family. Satan was about to bring tribulation on to Job. It started with the death of all this children. How wonderful was God to Job to have him make sacrifices for his children before Satan took their lives.

When God called Abraham, Abraham offered blood sacrifices to covering the sins of his family. There was no written law at that time but **those of faith** offering blood sacrifices to cover their sin. Before Israel left Egypt each family had to kill and lamb and put the blood on their door post. They ate the meat of the lamb standing up with their shoes on to be ready to leave Egypt. At that time the people of Israel had little knowledge of the God of Abraham, Isaac, and Jacob. After leaving, God had his remnant but they were few.

Three months after the children of Israel had left Egypt, they were in the wilderness. And Moses went up unto God, and the LORD called unto him out of the mountain, saying, *"Thus shalt thou say to the house of Jacob, and tell the children of Israel; You have seen what I did unto the Egyptians, and how I bare you on eagles' wings, and brought you unto myself.* **Now therefore, if you will obey my voice indeed,**

and keep my covenant, then ye shall be a peculiar treasure unto me above
all people: for all the earth is mine: And ye shall be unto me a kingdom of priests, and an
holy nation. These are the words which thou shalt speak unto the children of Israel." And
Moses came and called for the elders of the people, and laid before their faces all these words
which the LORD commanded him. And all the people answered together, and said, "All that
the LORD hath spoken we will do." *And Moses returned the words of the people*
unto the LORD." **Exodus 19:3-8**

At this time Moses went up to Mount Sinai, and God gave to Moses the
Ten Commandments. Then on Mount Sinai God gave Moses the Leviticus
Laws, and the plans for the ark of the Covenant, the table of show bread, the
golden candlestick, the tabernacle, the altar of burnt offering, the court of
the tabernacle, the tending of the lamp, and the garments of the priest. The
Leviticus laws are said to number up to six hundred thirteen separate laws and
ordinances. God gave Moses the plans of every item of the tabernacle, down
to the type of tent stake to the thread for the cloth used. God gave Moses the
required seven feasts of Israel. Everything in and of the tabernacle was to
point to the Lord Jesus Christ. There was nothing there that did not point to
our Lord Jesus. Dr. M. R. DeHaan's book on the tabernacle tells about every
item used in the tabernacle and how it pointed to the sacrifice of Jesus on the
cross. The book drips with the blood of Jesus.

Moses established a new way of approaching God. The head of the household was no longer required to make blood sacrifices for his family. All animal
sacrifices were to be made by a priest inside the tabernacle area. It took forty
years in the wilderness to take Egypt out of the children of Israel. When they
entered the promised land, the old generation had died in the wilderness and a
new generation which were brought up under the Law of Moses would enter
the land.

This was the first time there was a written law for the children of Israel to
follow. The tribe of Levi was to be responsible for all the things of the tabernacle. Aaron's family were the appointed priesthood. The other twelve tribes were
given specific portions of land. The tribe of Levi would not have a portion of
land ascribed to them. They would live by the tabernacle and live off the tithes
of the people. The Laws of Moses would be in effect until the destruction of
the second temple in seventy AD. As John and Jesus ministered to the Jews,
they were under the Law of Moses. Jesus would fulfill the Law of Moses as

required. Jesus lived under the Laws of Moses. He fulfilled each tenant of the Law. Jesus did not break one of the tenants of the Law of Moses. The Laws of Moses were very difficult to live by. Every Jew failed to keep the law, and the tabernacle system was the only way a Jew could have their sins covered.

sixteen

An Introduction To The Book of Acts

The book of Acts is the book of transition from the Gospel of the Kingdom of Heaven to the Gospel of Grace. The book of Acts was written by Luke to Theophilus to record what happen after Christ's resurrection. He states that, *"Jesus began both to do and teach, until the day in which he was taken up, after that he through the Holy Ghost had given commandments unto the apostles whom he had chosen: To whom also he showed himself alive after his passion by many infallible proofs, being seen of them forty days, and speaking of the things pertaining to the kingdom of God: And, being assembled together with them, commanded them that they should not depart from Jerusalem, but wait for the promise of the Father, which, saith he, "ye have heard of me. For John truly baptized with water; but ye shall be* **baptized with the Holy Ghost** *not many days hence."* **Acts 1:1-5**

When the apostles and believers came together after the resurrection, they asked Jesus when he would restore the Kingdom of Israel as a free nation or when would be the Kingdom of Heaven brought to earth. *Jesus answered, "It is not for you to know the times or the seasons."* **Acts 1:7** But they were told of the promise of the **Holy Spirit** that they would be witnesses in Jerusalem, all Judah, Samaria and to the far ends of the earth. They would be witnesses to the Jewish people starting in the city of Jerusalem, to the tribe of Judah, to Samaria (which were half Jew and half Gentile) and then to the Jews in the far ends of the earth.

We have seen that the disciples in Jerusalem were to be baptized by the Holy Spirit. Jesus told the apostles that the power of the Holy Spirit would to the the uttermost parts of the earth. *"But ye shall receive power, after that the* **Holy Ghost is come upon you:** *and ye shall be witnesses unto me both in Jerusalem, and in all Judaea, and in Samaria, and unto the uttermost part of the earth."* **Acts 1:8**

Then we saw the Holy Spirit baptized believers in Samaria. *"But when they believed Philip preaching the things concerning the kingdom of God, and the name of Jesus Christ, they were baptized, both men and women. Then Simon himself believed also: and when he was baptized, he continued with Philip, and wondered, beholding the miracles and signs which were done. Now when the apostles which were at Jerusalem heard that Samaria had received the word of God, they sent unto them Peter and John: Who, when they were come down, **prayed for them, that they might receive the Holy Ghost:** For as yet he was fallen upon none of them: only they were baptized in the name of the Lord Jesus. Then laid they their hands on them, and they received the Holy Ghost."* **Acts 8:12-17**

Later on, Peter had a vision about a sheep coming down from heaven. It contained animal both clean and unclean by Jewish law. Peter was perplexed about the vision. Then a voice from heaven said to Peter, *"What God has cleansed, that call not common."* Then came three men to the house where Peter was abiding. They were from Caesarea to ask Peter to go with them to a the house of Cornelius, who was a Gentle. The Spirit bade Peter to go with the men. *"Then Peter went down to the men which were sent unto him from Cornelius; and said, Behold, I am he whom ye seek: what is the cause wherefore ye are come? And they said, "Cornelius the centurion, a just man, and one that feareth God, and of good report among all the nation of the Jews, was warned from God by an holy angel to send for thee into his house, and to hear words of thee."* **Acts 10:21-22**

Then called he them in, and lodged them. And on the morrow Peter went away with them, and certain brethren from Joppa accompanied him. And the morrow after they entered into Caesarea. And Cornelius waited for them, and he had called together his kinsmen and near friends. And as Peter was coming in, Cornelius met him, and fell down at his feet, and worshiped him. But Peter took him up, saying, "Stand up; I myself also am a man." And as he talked with him, he went in, and found many that were come together. And he said unto them, "Ye know how that it is an unlawful thing for a man that is a Jew to keep company, or come unto one of another nation; but God hath shewed me that I should not call any man common or unclean. Therefore came I unto you without gainsaying, as soon as I was sent for: I ask therefore for what intent ye have sent for me?" **Acts 10:23-29**

"And Cornelius said, Four days ago I was fasting until this hour; and at the ninth hour I prayed in my house, and, behold, a man stood before me in bright clothing, And said, Cornelius, thy prayer is heard, and thine alms are had in remembrance in the sight of God. Send therefore to Joppa, and call hither Simon, whose surname is Peter; he is lodged in the house of one Simon a tanner by the sea side: who, when he cometh, shall speak unto

thee. Immediately therefore I sent to thee; and thou hast well done that thou art come. Now therefore are we all here present before God, to hear all things that are commanded thee of God. Then Peter opened his mouth, and said, Of a truth I perceive that God is no respecter of persons: But in every nation he that feareth him, and worketh righteousness, is accepted with him." **Acts 10:30-35**

"Then Peter opened his mouth and said: "In truth I perceive that God shows no partiality. But in every nation whoever fears Him and works righteousness is accepted by Him. The word which God sent to the children of Israel, preaching peace through Jesus Christ—He is Lord of all— hat word you know, which was proclaimed throughout all Judea, and began from Galilee after the baptism which John preached: how God anointed Jesus of Nazareth with the Holy Spirit and with power, who went about doing good and healing all who were oppressed by the devil, for God was with Him. And we are witnesses of all things which He did both in the land of the Jews and in Jerusalem, whom they killed by hanging on a tree. Him God raised up on the third day, and showed Him openly, not to all the people, but to witnesses chosen before by God, even to us who ate and drank with Him after He arose from the dead. And He commanded us to preach to the people, and to testify that it is He who was ordained by God to be Judge of the living and the dead. To Him all the prophets witness that, through His name, whoever believes in Him will receive remission of sins." **Acts 10:33-43**

We see the progression of the message of salvation starting with the Jews. Ten days after the ascension of Jesus, the Holy Spirit fell upon the Jews in in the upper room in Jerusalem. Then Philip preached salvation to the Samaritans. Then Peter went to the house of Cornelius, a Gentile, and spoke words of salvation to all who were in the house of Cornelius. The one thing different was that the **Holy Spirit fell upon the Gentile immediately** after they believed without the laying on of hands.

Paul had to remind the saints in Rome that the Holy Spirit dwelt in their bodies. *"But ye are not in the flesh, but in the Spirit, if so be **that the Spirit of God dwell in you**. Now if any man have not the Spirit of Christ, he is none of his."* **Romans 8:9** Today many believers forget that the Spirit of God, God himself, dwells in our bodies as believers. With the rise of the Pentecostal Church and the Charismatic Movement with its emphases on present day healing, speaking in tongues, and health and wealth preaching, many believers in non-pentecostal churches have put little emphasis on the fact that the Holy Spirit dwells in their bodies.

After spending forty days on earth after his resurrection, it was time for Christ's ascension into heaven. During the forty days Jesus was seen by the eleven apostles and after that he was seen by over five hundred brethren at once. Just before the feast of Pentecost about one hundred twenty of Christ's disciples were gathered together in an upper room. Among the one hundred twenty were the eleven apostles, Mary the mother of Jesus, and his brethren. Peter was the leader and he wanted to find a replacement of Judas who betrayed Jesus. The eleven apostles cast lots and the lot fell on Matthias. and he was numbered among the twelve apostles. On the day of Pentecost the disciples were gathered together in the upper room and suddenly came a sound from heaven like a mighty wind, and it filled all the house where they were meeting. And there appeared unto them cloven tongues like as of fire, and it sat upon each of them. And they were all filled with the Holy Ghost, and began to speak with other tongues, as the Spirit gave them utterance. **(See Acts 2:2-4)**

*"And there were **dwelling at Jerusalem Jews, devout men, out of every nation under heaven.** Now when this was noised abroad, the multitude came together, and were confounded, because that every man heard them speak in his own language. And they were all amazed and marveled, saying one to another, "Behold, are not all these which speak Galileans? And how hear we every man in our own tongue, wherein we were born?" And they were all amazed, and were in doubt, saying one to another," "What means this?"* **Acts 2: 5-12**

At the time of Christ the Jerusalem temple was the most beautiful building in the then know world. The temple area covered about thirty-seven acres. King Herod, who was the ruler over Israel, wanted to please the Jews by redoing the temple area. For approximately forty to sixty years men were working on the temple area remodeling and redoing the temple site. The Jewish people were scattered throughout the world from the time of the Assyrians taking the ten tribes of Israel and scattering them through out the then known world. After the seventy years of captivity in Babylon many of the Jews stayed in Babylon. At the time of Christ there were more Jews living outside of Israel than in Israel itself. It was the desire of every Jew in a foreign country to make a pilgrimage to Jerusalem to see the temple and worship God there. At the time of the Passover. there would be thousands of foreign Jewish visitors in Jerusalem.

After hearing the believers speaking in their foreign tongue, they were amazed. Peter, standing up with the eleven, lifted up his voice, and said unto them, "*Ye men of Judaea, and all ye that dwell at Jerusalem, be this known unto you, and hearken to my words: For these are not drunken, as ye suppose, seeing it is but the third hour of the day. But this is that which was spoken by the prophet Joel; And it shall come to pass in the last days, saith God,* **I will pour out of my Spirit** *upon all flesh: and your sons and your daughters shall prophesy, and your young men shall see visions, and your old men shall dream dreams: And on my servants and on my handmaidens I will pour out in those days of my Spirit; and they shall prophesy:* (This is the end of the prophesy of the coming of the Holy Spirit, the remaining prophesy by Joel pertained to the time of Jacob trouble) *And I will shew wonders in heaven above, and signs in the earth beneath; blood, and fire, and vapor of smoke: The sun shall be turned into darkness, and the moon into blood, before the great and notable day of the Lord come: And it shall come to pass, that whosoever shall call on the name of the Lord shall be saved.* (This is the end the prophesy of Joel.) **Acts 2:14-21**

Ye men of Israel, hear these words; **Jesus of Nazareth, a man approved of God among you by miracles and wonders and signs, which God did by him in the midst of you, as ye yourselves also know: Him, being delivered by the determinate counsel and foreknowledge of God, ye have taken, and by wicked hands have crucified and slain: Whom God hath raised up, having loosed the pains of death: because it was not possible that he should be holden of it.** *For David spoke concerning him, I foresaw the Lord always before my face, for he is on my right hand, that I should not be moved: Therefore did my heart rejoice, and my tongue was glad; moreover also my flesh shall rest in hope: Because thou wilt not leave my soul in hell, neither wilt thou suffer thine Holy One to see corruption. Thou hast made known to me the ways of life; thou shalt make me full of joy with thy countenance. Men and brethren, let me freely speak unto you of the patriarch David, that he is both dead and buried, and his sepulcher is with us unto this day. Therefore being a prophet, and knowing that God had sworn with an oath to him, that of the fruit of his loins, according to the flesh, he would raise up Christ to sit on his throne; He seeing this before spake of the resurrection of Christ, that his soul was not left in hell, neither his flesh did see corruption. This Jesus hath God raised up, whereof we all are witnesses. Therefore being by the right hand of God exalted, and having received of the Father the promise of the Holy Ghost, he hath shed forth this, which ye now see and hear. For David is not ascended into the heavens: but he saith himself, The Lord said unto my Lord, sit thou on my right hand, until I make thy foes thy footstool.* **Therefore let all the house of Israel know assuredly, that God hath made the same Jesus, whom ye have crucified, both Lord and**

Christ." Now when they heard this, they were pricked in their heart, and said unto Peter and to the rest of the apostles, "Men and brethren, what shall we do?"

Then Peter said unto them, **"Repent, and be baptized every one of you in the name of Jesus Christ for the remission of sins, and ye shall receive the gift of the Holy Ghost. For the promise is unto you, and to your children, and to all that are afar off, even as many as the LORD our God shall call."** And with many other words did he testify and exhort, saying, "Save yourselves from this untoward generation." **Then they that gladly received his word were baptized: and the same day there were added unto them about three thousand souls.** And they continued steadfastly in the apostles' doctrine and fellowship, and in breaking of bread, and in prayers. **Acts 2:14-42**

This messages by Peter in the days after Pentecost to the thousands who were at the temple pricked the hearts of many of the Jews and thousands more were added to the believers. Many thousands of believers would go back to their own country and cities and went to their synagogues telling the message given by Peter about the Messiah had come, was crucified, died, buried and arose again on the third day from the dead.

The multitude of believers in Jerusalem were of one accord. They sold all they owned and made all things common. No one lacked for as many as were possessors of lands or house sold them and brought the prices to the apostles feet. Now, no where in the book or Acts or other scriptures tells where God or any of the twelve apostles told them to sell their land and houses. This they did believing that all Israel would believe and Christ would return and bring with him the Kingdom of Heaven to Israel. Israel would be a free nation with its borders from the river Euphrates to the river of Egypt. God would rule, the twelve would be judges each over one of the tribes of Israel. But this did not happen. Although many thousands believed, many millions did not believe include most of the religious leaders of Israel. They arrested some of the apostles and commanded them not to speak or to teach in the name of Jesus. **(See Acts 4:18)** Many of the believers in Israel were forced to leave Israel because of the persecution by the religious leader. Those who stayed used up the funds from the sale of their land and houses and Paul would take offerings from the Gentile believers to help the Jerusalem Jews in their poverty.

By the hands of the apostles many signs and wonders were done. Jews from cities outside of Jerusalem would bring their sick and those with uncleaned spirits to the apostles and they were all healed. The apostles were imprisoned and then released. When the apostles were told not to teach in the name of Jesus, Peter said, *"We ought to obey God rather than men. The God of our fathers raised up Jesus, whom ye slew and hanged on a tree. Him hath God exalted with his right hand to be a Prince and a Savior, for to give repentance to Israel, and forgiveness of sins. And we are his witnesses of these things; and so is also the Holy Ghost, whom God hath given to them that obey him."* **Acts 5:29-32**

When the religious leaders heard this they were cut to the heart and took counsel to kill them. But one Pharisee, Gamaliel, a rabbi of the law, said, *"Men of Israel, take heed to yourselves what you intend to these men. Refrain from these men, and let them alone: for if this counsel or this work be of men, it will come to nothing. But if it be of God, you cannot overthrow it; lest you be found even to be fighting against God."*

"After that they called the apostles, and beat them, and commanded that they not speak in the name of Jesus and let them go. And they departed from the presence of the council, rejoicing that they were counted worthy to suffer shame for his name. And daily in the temple, and in every house, they ceased not to teach and preach Jesus Christ." (**Act 5:33-42** in part)

Stephen, a believer full of faith and power, did great miracles and wonders among the people. The religious leaders accused Stephen of speaking blasphemous word again Moses. They stirred up the people and the leaders arrested Stephen and brought him to the counsel. They set up false witnesses against him. Then the high priest asked Stephen if these things were true. Stephen answered with a long discourse starting with the call of Abraham to Moses, to the building of the temple by Solomon.

Stephen ends his long discourse with saying to the counsel, "You stiff necked and uncircumcised in heart and ears, ye do always resist the Holy Ghost: as your fathers did, so do ye. Which of the prophets have not your fathers persecuted? and they have slain them which shewed before of the coming of the Just One; of whom ye have been now the betrayers and murderers: Who have received the law by the disposition of angels, and have not kept it." **Act 7:51-53**

"When they heard these things, they were cut to the heart, and they gnashed on him with their teeth. But he, being full of the Holy Ghost, looked up steadfastly into heaven, and saw the glory of God, and Jesus standing on the right hand of God, And said, "Behold, I see the heavens opened, and the Son of man standing on the right hand of God." Then they cried out with a loud voice, and stopped their ears, and ran upon him with one accord, And cast him out of the city, and stoned him: and **the witnesses laid down their clothes at a young man's feet, whose name was Saul.** And they stoned Stephen, calling upon God and saying, Lord Jesus, receive my spirit. And he knelt down, and cried with a loud voice, Lord, lay not this sin to their charge. And when he had said this, he fell asleep." **Acts 7:54-60**

The slaying of Stephen was the final act by the Jews to reject Jesus as their Messiah. *"And Saul was consenting unto his death. And at that time there was a great persecution against the church which was at Jerusalem; and they were all scattered abroad throughout the regions of Judaea and Samaria, except the apostles."* **Acts 8:1** Some believers stayed in Jerusalem because of the words of Gamaliel to the Jewish religious leaders. Gamaliel said that if it was not from God it would die off by itself. But if it was of God there was nothing they could do to stop the word of the apostles. The slaying of Stephen closed the book on the Jews as a nation to understand the message of salvation through Jesus Christ. At this point in our Bibles, Saul, who later became the Apostle Paul is introduced. Up to this point in the book of Acts, God was dealing with Israel. After the slaying of Stephen the religious leaders declared all out war on Jesus believers. *"Now they* (the believers in Christ) *were scattered abroad upon the persecution that arose about Stephen traveled as far as Phenice and Cypress, and Antioch, preaching the word to non* **but unto the Jews only. Acts 11:19** The new Jewish believers in Jesus as the Messiah had no interest in preaching the gospel to the Gentiles. They still felt that salvation was only for the Jews. For the first nine years after the crucifixion the **gospel was only preached to Jews.** This was the message that was given by Peter, *"Repent, and be baptized every one of you in the name of Jesus Christ for the remission of sins, and ye shall receive the gift of the Holy Ghost."* **Act 2:38**

The Jewish believers repented (Turned for their sinful ways to walking in all the commandments and ordinances of the Lord blameless,) and were baptized and received the Holy Spirit. They still walked in the ways of the Law of Moses. They did not understand the gospel of grace. It would be the apostle Paul after he had spent three years in the Arabian wilderness with God to understand the mysteries of contained in his epistles. These mysteries of God's grace was not made know to man before this time. *"The* **secret things belong unto the Lord our God:** *but those things which are revealed belong unto us and to our children for ever, that we may do all the words of this law."* **Deuteronomy 29:29** seventeen

"And Peter"

"And Peter," are the two most precious words in the New Testament for the child of God who has gone astray. And when the sabbath was past, Mary Magdalene, and Mary the mother of James, and Salome, had brought sweet spices, that they might come and anoint him. And very early in the morning the first day of the week, they came unto the sepulcher at the rising of the sun. And they said among themselves, Who shall roll us away the stone from the door of the sepulcher? And when they looked, they saw that the stone was rolled away: for it was very great. And entering into the sepulcher, they saw a young man sitting on the right side, clothed in a long white garment; and they were frighted. *And he saith unto them, "Be not frighted: Ye seek Jesus of Nazareth, which was crucified: he is risen; he is not here: behold the place where they laid him.* **But go your way**, *tell his disciples* **and Peter** *that he goes before you into Galilee: there shall ye see him, as he said unto you." And they went out quickly, and fled from the sepulcher; for they trembled and were amazed: neither said they any thing to any man; for they were afraid.* **Mark 16:1-8**

And returned from the sepulcher, and told all these things unto the eleven, and to all the rest. It was Mary Magdalene and Joanna, and Mary the mother of James, and other women that were with them, which told these things unto the apostles. And their words seemed to them as idle tales, and they believed them not. **Then arose Peter,** and ran unto the sepulcher; and stooping down, he beheld the linen clothes laid by themselves, and departed, wondering in himself at that which was come to pass. **Luke 14:9-12**

Then she runs, and comes to **Simon Peter,** and to the other disciple, whom Jesus loved, and saith unto them, They have taken away the LORD out of the sepulcher, and we know not where they have laid him. **Peter therefore went forth**, and that other disciple, and came to the sepulcher. So they ran

95

both together: and the other disciple did outrun Peter, and came first to the sepulcher. And he stooping down, and looking in, saw the linen clothes lying; yet went he not in. **Then cometh Simon Peter following him,** and went into the sepulcher, and sees the linen clothes lie, And the napkin, that was about his head, not lying with the linen clothes, but wrapped together in a place by itself. **Then went in also that other disciple, which came first to the sepulcher, and he saw, and believed. For as yet they knew not the scripture, that he must rise again from the dead.** Then the disciples went away again unto their own home. **John 20:2-10**

Peter was the twelve apostles who was quick to speak and quick to act. From the day Jesus called him to be one of his twelve apostles, Peter was quick to answer. Peter and Andrew were casting nets into the sea of Galilee and Jesus said to them, *"Follow me and I will make you fishers of men."* **Straightway** they left their nets and followed him.

After Jesus had fed the multitude with five loaves and two fish, he sent the disciples into a ship to go before him on the other side of Galilee. While in the midst of the Sea of Galilee there came a storm with great wind and the disciples were afraid. In the night they saw Jesus walking on the water towards them. They were all scared to death. But Jesus said, *"Be of good cheer, it is I, be not afraid."* Peter answered Jesus, "If it be you, Jesus, bid me to come to you on the water." Jesus said, *"Come."* Peter stepped out of the ship and walked on the water toward Jesus. He looked down at the water under his feet and became afraid. His faith had gone he began to sink and cried out, "Lord, save me." Jesus said, *"Oh, you of little faith wherefore did you doubt?"* Of all the disciples on the ship it was only Peter who had the faith to step out on the water. The other eleven where of less courage. When Jesus taught about a rich man entering heaven Peter said, "Behold we have forsaken all and followed you, what shall we have therefore?" Jesus said to Peter, *"You that follow me, in the regeneration when the son of man shall sit on his throne* (on Mount Zion in Jerusalem of Judah) *of his glory, you also shall sit upon twelve thrones, judging the twelve tribes of Israel. But the first shall be last, and the last shall be first."*

Jesus was with his disciples at Caesarea Philippi and asked them, *"Whom do men say I am?"* They answered, *"Some say you are John the Baptist, some say you are Elijah, and others Jeremiah, or some other prophets."* Jesus said, *"but whom do you say I am?"*

Peter answered quickly, **"You are the Christ, the Son of the living God!"** Jesus blessed Peter for his quick response. But noted that man had not revealed his identity to Peter but his father in heaven. Peter was the first of the twelve to say confess with his mouth that Jesus was the Messiah, the Son of God.

From that time Jesus told them how he would go to Jerusalem, suffer many things by the elders, chief priest, and scribes. He would be killed and rise again the third day. Peter stood and rebuked Jesus and said, "Be it far from you, this shall not happen to you." This was the same Peter who just confessed Jesus as the Son of God, now is telling the Son of God that he would not die and arise again. This is so typical of man, one minute he is close to God, and a few minutes later be led by his sin nature. Jesus just told the disciples that he would go to Jerusalem and be killed and rise again on the third day. **But God hid these facts from them** and the fact of his death and resurrection until it was done.

Some time later Jesus took Peter, James and John to a high mountain. Jesus was transfigured before them. His face did shine like the sun, and his robe was as white as light. There on the mountain there appeared with Jesus were Moses and Elijah talking to him. Peter quickly said to Jesus, *"Lord, it is good for us to be here. If you will, let us make three tabernacles one for you, one for Moses, and one for Elijah."* While Peter was speaking a bright cloud overshadowed them and a voice came out of the cloud, which said, **"This is my beloved Son, in whom I am well pleased, hear you him."** Hearing this they were all afraid. Jesus touched them and said, *"Arise and be not afraid."* Jesus charged them, *"Tell the vision to no man,* **until the Son of man be risen again from the dead."** Again they were told of the resurrection and did not understand.

Jesus and the apostles were in Bethany in a room prepared by the twelve for the passover supper. As they ate, Jesus said, *"Very I say unto you, that one of you shall betray me."* The eleven said, "Is it I?" The Judas said, "Master, is it I?" Jesus said unto him, *"You have said!"*

Then Jesus took the bread and blessed it, and brake it into pieces and said, *"Take eat for this is my body which was broken for you."* Then Jesus took the cup of wine gave thanks and gave it to them saying, *"Drink you all of it, for this is my blood of the new testament, which is shed for many for the remission of sins!"* After this they sung a hymn then departed to the mount of Olives.

Speaking to the disciples on the mount of Olives Jesus said, *"All you shall be offended because of me this night, for it is written, "I will smite the shepherd (the Messiah) and the sheep (the disciples) of the flock shall be scattered." But after I am risen again, I will go before you into Galilee."*

Peter quickly answered and said, *"Though all men shall be offended because of you,* **yet will I never be offended."** Jesus said to Peter, *"Verily I say unto you, that this night, before the cock crow, you, (Peter) shall deny me thrice."* Peter said to Jesus, *"Though I should die with you, yet will I not deny you."* Likewise said all the disciples.

Peter was ready to defend Jesus to death. He was the rock. He had his sword. He was ready for action in his heart. But in a matter of hours he would be the one, who with cursing deny he knew Jesus.

Then Jesus went to Gethsemane with Peter, James, and John to pray. He said to the three to wait while he prayed. Looking at the cross which was ahead of him, Jesus was very sorrowful and heavy with grief. He prayed that the cup of suffering he was about to endure would pass from him. But not as he willed but he did the will of the Father. After going back to pray three times he went to the three apostles who were sleeping he said to Peter, *"What, could you not watch with me for one hour? Watch and pray, that you enter not into temptation for the spirit is willing but the flesh is weak. Sleep on now, and take your rest, behold the hour is at hand and the Son of man is betrayed into the hands of sinners. Rise, let us be going. Behold, he* (Judas) *is here to betray me."*

As Jesus spoke to them Judas came with a great multitude with swords and knives, from the chief priest and elders of the people. Not being able to know which one was Jesus, for his dress and countenance was the same as his disciples, they had Judas give them a sign, "a kiss." Judas came up to Jesus and kissed him saying, *"Hail Master!"* Jesus said to Judas, *"Friend, wherefore are you come?"*

They then came and took Jesus captive. Peter took his sword and cut off the ear of the high priest's servant. Jesus said to Peter, *"Put away your sword, for all them that take the sword shall die with it, think I could pray to my Father, and he shall give me more that ten legions of angels? But how then shall the scriptures be fulfilled, that this must be done?"*

At the same time Jesus said to the multitudes who were there to arrest him, *"Are you come out against a thief with with the swords and knives for to take me? I sat daily with you teaching in the temple* (On Mount Zion in Jerusalem of Judah) *and you laid not hold of me. But this is done that the scriptures of the prophets might be fulfilled."*

Jesus was then led to Caiaphas, the high priest, where the scribes and elder assembled. Peter now followed afar off. Then Peter sat without in the palace:

and a damsel came unto him, saying, "Thou also wast with Jesus of Galilee." But he denied before them all, saying, *"I know not what thou said."* And when he was gone out into the porch, another maid saw him, and said unto them that were there, "This fellow was also with Jesus of Nazareth." And again he denied with an oath, "I **do not know the man."** And after a while came unto him they that stood by, and said to Peter, "Surely thou also art one of them; for thy speech betrays thee." Then began **Peter to curse and to swear**, saying, **"I know not the man."** And immediately the cock crew. And **Peter remembered the word of Jesus,** which said unto him, Before the cock crow, thou shalt deny me thrice. And **Peter went out, and wept bitterly.**

We are not told where Peter went after this. He was not at the cross where our Lord died. He was hiding from the other ten apostles, alone weeping bitterly. Peter, the big man, the man who was always first and quick to act or speak before the other apostles, now did not know if the Kingdom of Heaven would be his. He sorrowed for the three days Jesus was in the tomb. He could not face anyone. The three days had past, and there was a knock at the door. A woman was there saying, "Peter the Lord is alive." Jesus had said, *"But go your way, tell his disciples **and Peter** that he goes before you into Galilee: there shall ye see him, as he said unto you."* Peter may had said, "Are you sure he said, *"And Peter?""* **Peter arose and ran to the tomb.**

Peter understood from the time of hearing *"And Peter"* the forgiveness, love, grace, and mercy of God. He was still Peter filled with vigor to tell the Jews that Jesus was their Messiah. Fifty days later at the Jewish feast of Pentecost he was in the upper room to receive the promise of the Holy Spirit. Soon after Peter was in the temple on Mount Zion telling the message of the cross and resurrection to the many Jews from all over the then know world. Thousand of the Jews believed and went back to their synagogues telling the wonderful story that the Messiah had come.

Of the twelve apostles it was Peter, the same Peter that denied knowing Jesus, was the one who went into the temple and preached the message of a risen Messiah. The message of Peter was for the Jews only. It was the message of the coming Kingdom of Heaven for the Jews. Peter's gospel of the kingdom was to Jews only. *"Therefore **let all the house of Israel know assuredly,** that God hath made the same Jesus, whom ye have crucified, both Lord and Christ."* Now when they heard this, they were pricked in their heart, and said unto Peter and to the rest *of the apostles, "Men and brethren, what shall we do?"* Then Peter said unto them, **"Repent, and be baptized every one of you in the name of Jesus Christ for the remission of sins, and ye shall receive the gift of the Holy Ghost. For the promise is unto you, and to your children, and to all that are afar off, even as many as the LORD our God shall call."** Acts 2:36-39 Peter told the Jews they had taken, and by wicked hand had crucified their Messiah whom God had raised from the dead. **(See Acts 2:23-24)**

Stephen, who was martyred, preached the same message to the Jews. It was a gospel for the Jews only that they were to believe that Jesus was the Messiah, that he died and rose again. They were to repent of their wicked ways to walking in all the commandments and ordinances of the Lord blamelessly. They were to be baptized and after baptism by the laying of hands receive the Holy Spirit. It was not the message of the gospel of grace Paul was to preach to the Gentiles. *"Now they which were scattered abroad upon the persecution that arose about Stephen traveled as far as Phenice, and Cyprus, and Antioch, preaching the word to none but unto the Jews only."* Act 11:19

For the next ten years the message of a risen Messiah was preached to Jews only. It would not be until approximately forty AD that Paul would start his missionary trips to the Gentiles with the gospel of grace. The difference between the two gospels helps the Gentile believer to truly understand salvation. Peter's message of the gospel of the kingdom was repentance with faith in the death and resurrection of Jesus plus baptism and the following of all the commandments and ordinances of Moses. Paul's message to the Gentiles was repentance (turning from self righteousness to Christ's righteousness) and faith in the shed blood of Jesus that paid the penalty of sin of the world (including yours and mine) and that he arose again from the dead on the third day. **It is faith plus nothing.** *"That if thou* **shalt confess with thy mouth the Lord Jesus,** *and* **shalt believe in thine heart that God hath raised him from the dead, thou shalt be saved."** Romans 10:9

It would not be Paul to be the first one to go to the Gentile with the message of Salvation. It was Peter. He was in Joppa on the housetop praying. He fell into a trance and he had a vision of a sheet filled with all matter of beast. The message was that there was no more unclean animals or man. Peter had a hard time understanding the vision, but then men came to his door telling him that a Gentile named Cornelius was asking him to go to his house. Now understanding the vision, Peter went with the men to the house of Cornelius. *"Then Peter opened his mouth, and said,* **Of a truth I perceive that God is no respecter of persons:** *But in* **every nation he that feareth him, and worketh righteousness, is accepted with him."** Acts 10:34-35

Peter told those who gathered in the house of Cornelius, *"God anointed Jesus of Nazareth with the Holy Ghost and with power: who went about doing good, and healing all that were oppressed of the devil; for God was with him. And we are witnesses of all things which he did both in the land of the Jews, and in Jerusalem;* **whom they slew and hanged on a tree: Him God raised up the third day, and shewed him openly;** *Not to all the people, but unto witnesses chosen before God, even to us, who did eat and drink with him after he rose from the dead. And he commanded us to preach unto the people, and to testify that it is he which was ordained of God to be the Judge of quick and dead. To him give all the prophets witness,* **that through his name whosoever believeth in him shall receive remission of sins."** Acts 10:38-43

"While Peter yet spake these words, **the Holy Ghost fell on all them which heard the word.** *And they of the circumcision(Jews) believed were astonished, as many as came with Peter, because that* **on the Gentiles also was poured out the gift of the Holy Ghost.** *For they heard them speak with tongues, and magnify God. Then answered Peter, Can any man forbid water, that these should not be baptized, which have received the Holy Ghost as well as we? And he commanded them to be baptized in the name of the Lord. Then prayed they him to tarry certain days."* **Acts 10:44-48**

Up to this point in Judaism, a Jew was not to enter the house of a Gentile and much less eat with them. Peter going to the Gentile Cornelius would confirm the ministry of Paul.

After Stephen was martyred we do not hear much about Peter. The scene now turns to the Apostle Paul and his missionary journeys. Sixteen years after the death of Stephen, Paul goes to Jerusalem to meet with the elders there. James, the earthly half-brother of Jesus, was the leader of the elders in Jerusalem. Paul's concern was, "There rose up certain of the sect of the Pharisees which believed, saying, *"That it was needful to circumcise them, and to command them to keep the law of Moses."* **Acts 15:5** The apostles and elder in Jerusalem met together to consider the matter. When there was much disputing, Peter rose up, and said unto them, *"Men and brethren, ye know how that a good while ago* **God made choice among us, that the Gentiles by my mouth should hear the word of the gospel, and believe.** *And God, which knoweth the hearts, bare* *them witness, giving them the Holy Ghost, even as he did unto us; And put no difference between us and them,* **purifying their hearts by faith.** *Now therefore why tempt ye God, to put a yoke upon the neck of the disciples, which neither our fathers nor we were able to bear?* **But we believe that through the grace of the LORD Jesus Christ we shall be saved, even as they."** Acts 15:7-11

Peter, the rock, was the one to stand up and verify that the Gospel of Grace is also for us Gentiles. This decision was very important to the leadership in Jerusalem and to Paul. James commanded that the decision be put in writing and to be delivered to the church by sending chosen men of Jerusalem to deliver the message to the Gentile church.

In Peter's first epistle he has a different message than the one after Pentecost to the believing Jews who were not scattered around the world. Peter says in the introduction of his first epistle, "Blessed be the God and Father of our Lord Jesus Christ, which according to his abundant mercy **hath begotten us again unto a lively hope by the resurrection of Jesus Christ from the dead,** To an inheritance incorruptible, and undefiled, and that fades not away, reserved in heaven for you, Who are kept by the power of God **through faith unto salvation** ready to be revealed in the last time." **I Peter 1:3-5** Peter does not call for repentance, baptism, and follow the Laws of Moses. It is through faith that man receives salvation. The message has changed.

In the closing of Peter's second epistles he make a final statement verifying the ministry of Paul. *"Wherefore, beloved, seeing that ye look for such things, be diligent that ye may be found of him in peace, without spot, and blameless. And account that the long suffering of our Lord is salvation;* **even as our beloved brother Paul also according to the wisdom given unto him hath written unto you; As also in all his epistles, speaking in them of these things; in which are some things hard to be understood,** *which they that are unlearned and unstable wrest, as they do also the other scriptures, unto their own destruction."* **2 Peter 3:14-16**

Peter verifies that the wise epistles of Paul, given to him by Jesus in the Arab wilderness, were hard for a Jew to understand. Peter did not have the wisdom of Paul of the Gospel of Grace as Paul had. Paul had been stopped in his tracks on the way to Damascus by the resurrected Jesus, himself, and then taken to the Arabian wilderness to be taught the Gospel of Grace. It was Peter the one who denied Christ during his trial who became the apostle who stood solid on the message of Paul.

eighteen

Saul the Jewish Terrorist

This young man, who had the clothes of those that had stoned Stephen laid at his feet, was Saul. He was to become the first terrorist in the middle east. He was a powerful young man. He studied at the feet of Gamaliel, the leading scholar of the Law of Moses and the religion of the Jews. There was none greater in Israel than Gamaliel. Gamaliel was not a follower of Jesus, but he was wise enough to realize that if the message of Jesus was false, it would die like the message of the other false Messiahs. The Jewish terrorist, Saul, was equal to the Muslim, Bin Laden. He hated all the Jews who accepted Jesus as the Messiah. After the death of Stephen the believers in Jesus were scattered abroad. The believers left Israel traveling as far as Phenice, and Cyprus, and Antioch. Jerusalem was almost free from those who believed the message of the apostles.

Paul gives his own history in one of the later book of Acts. *"I am verily a man which am a Jew, born in Tarsus, a city in Cilicia, yet brought up in this city at the feet of Gamaliel, and taught according to the perfect manner of the law of the fathers, and was zealous toward God, as ye all are this day. And I persecuted this way* (followers of Jesus) *unto the death, binding and delivering into prisons both men and women. As also the high priest doth bear me witness, and all the estate of the elders: from whom also I received letters unto the brethren, and went to Damascus, to bring them which were there bound unto Jerusalem, for to be punished."* **Acts 22:3-5**

Writing to the Galatians he tells them about his past. *"For ye have heard of my conversation (association) in time past in the Jews' religion, how that beyond measure I persecuted the church of God, and wasted it: And profited in the Jews' religion above many my equals in mine own nation, being more exceedingly zealous of the traditions of my fathers. But when it pleased God, who* **separated me from my mother's womb,** *and called* *me by his grace, to reveal his Son in me, that I might preach him among the heathen; immediately I conferred not with flesh and blood: Neither went I up to Jerusalem to them which were apostles before me; but I went into Arabia, and returned again unto Damascus. Then after three years I went up to Jerusalem to see Peter, and abode with him fifteen days. But other of the apostles saw I none, save James the Lord's brother. Now the things which I write unto you, behold, before God, I lie not. Afterward I came into the regions of Syria and Cilicia; And was unknown by face unto the churches of Judaea which were in Christ: But they had heard only, That he which persecuted us in times past now preacheth the faith which once he destroyed. And they glorified God in me."* **Gal 1:13-24**

We have seen in our study that John the Baptist was called from his mother's womb, how Christ was conceived in the womb of Mary, and now we see also that Saul was also separated to be the apostle to the Gentiles from his mother's womb. For six years after Pentecost this man, Saul, persecuted the Jewish church of Jesus Christ. He had no idea what was in store for him.

He had rid Jerusalem of many of the believers in Jesus as their Messiah. In Jerusalem all the disciples of Jesus were sorely afraid on Saul. Even after his conversation when he went back to Jerusalem many of the disciples did not believe that he was now a disciple. Saul had heard about there being many believer in Jesus in the city of Damascus. *"And Saul, yet breathing out threatening and slaughter against the disciples of the Lord, went unto the high priest, And desired of him letters to Damascus to the synagogues, that if he found any of this way, whether they were men or women, he might bring them bound unto Jerusalem."* **Acts 9:1-2**

As Saul came close to he the Lord Jesus Christ and suddenly there shined a light from heaven around him. He fell to the ground. The voice of Jesus came to him. He was a changed man. He had met the Master and was now one of His.

nineteen

Saul becomes Paul

the Apostle to the Gentiles

And as he (Saul) journeyed, he came near Damascus: and suddenly there shined round about him a light from heaven: And he fell to the earth, and heard a voice saying unto him, *"Saul, Saul, why persecutest thou me?"* And he said, *"Who art thou, Lord?"* And the Lord said, *"I am Jesus whom thou persecutest: it is hard for thee to kick against the pricks."* And he trembling and astonished said, *"Lord, what wilt thou have me to do?"* And the Lord said unto him, *"Arise, and go into the city, and it shall be told thee what thou must do."* And the men which journeyed with him stood speechless, hearing a voice, but seeing no man.

And Saul arose from the earth; and when his eyes were opened, he saw no man: but they led him by the hand, and brought him into Damascus. And he was three days without sight, and neither did eat nor drink. And there was a certain disciple at Damascus, named Ananias; and to him said the Lord in a vision, "Ananias." And he said, "Behold, I am here, Lord." And the Lord said unto him, "Arise, and go into the street which is called Straight, and enquire in the house of Judas for one called Saul, of Tarsus: for, behold, he prayeth, And hath seen in a vision a man named Ananias coming in, and putting his hand on him, that he might receive his sight." Then Ananias answered, "Lord, I have heard by many of this man, how much evil he hath done to thy saints at Jerusalem: And here he hath authority from the chief priests to bind all that call on thy name." But the Lord said unto him, "Go your way: for he is chosen vessel unto me, to **bear my name before the Gentiles,** *and kings and the children of Israel. For I will shew him how great things he must suffer for my name's sake."*

And Ananias went his way, and entered into the house; and putting his hands on him said, Brother Saul, the Lord, even Jesus, that appeared unto thee in the way as thou camest, hath sent me, that thou mightest receive thy sight, and be filled with the Holy Ghost. And immediately there fell from his eyes as it had been scales: and he received sight forthwith, and arose, and was baptized. **Acts 9:3-18**

Paul gives the account of his conversion when he later in life returned to Jerusalem. *"And it came to pass, that, as I made my journey, and was come nigh unto Damascus about noon, suddenly there shone from heaven a great light round about me. And I fell unto the ground, and heard a voice saying unto me, "Saul, Saul, why persecutest thou me?" And I answered, Who art thou, Lord? And he said unto me, "I am Jesus of Nazareth, whom thou persecutest." And they that were with me saw indeed the light, and were afraid; but they heard not the voice of him that spake to me. And I said, "What shall I do, LORD?" And the Lord said unto me, "Arise, and go into Damascus; and there it shall be told thee of all things which are appointed for thee to do." And when I could not see for the glory of that light, being led by the hand of them that were with me, I came into Damascus. And one Ananias, a devout man according to the law, having a good report of all the Jews which dwelt there, Came unto me, and stood, and said unto me, "Brother Saul, receive thy sight." And the same hour I looked up upon him. And he said, "The God of our fathers hath chosen thee, that thou should know his will, and see that Just One, and should hear the voice of his mouth. For thou shalt be his witness unto all men of what thou hast seen and heard. And now why tarriest thou? arise, and be baptized, and wash away thy sins, calling on the name of the Lord. And it came to pass, that, when I was come again to Jerusalem, even while I prayed in the temple, I was in a trance; And saw him saying unto me, "Make haste, and get thee quickly out of Jerusalem: for they will not receive thy testimony concerning me." And I said, Lord, they know that I imprisoned and beat in every synagogue them that believed on thee: And when the blood of thy martyr Stephen was shed, I also was standing by, and consenting unto his death, and kept the raiment of them that slew him. And he said unto me, "Depart: for I will send thee far hence unto the Gentiles." And they gave him audience unto this word, and then lifted up their voices, and said, Away with such a fellow from the earth: for it is not fit that he should live.* **Acts 22:6-22**

Paul was called to be the chief (leader) of the apostles to the Gentiles. He was also called to suffer for the name of Christ. It is great to be called the leader of the message of salvation to the Gentiles. But it is another thing to be called to suffer greatly for the Lord. All his life after his conversion Paul walked a life close to death. His life would not be easy. He was called to be the apostle of the Gentile by those who were Jews who preached the Gospel of Kingdom which Peter preached at Pentecost. He was baptized for the washing away of his sins calling on the name of the Lord. He was converted by those who preached and knew the Gospel of the Kingdom.

After is conversion Saul *immediately preached Christ in the synagogues, that HE WAS THE SON OF GOD.* **Acts 9:20** Paul was sent by God to the Arabian wilderness. *"Neither went I up to Jerusalem to them which were apostles before me; but I **went into Arabia,** and returned again unto Damascus."* **Galatians 1:17** The Jews in the synagogues in Damascus did not believe him and Saul escaped. After the three years in the wilderness he went to Jerusalem. *"and when Saul came to Jerusalem, he assayed to join himself to the disciples: But they were all afraid of him, and believed not he was a disciple.* **Acts 9:26**

In the Arabian wilderness Jesus taught Saul, whose name God changed to Paul. (It is interesting that Jews today can change their first names to a Gentile name if they keep the first letter of their Jewish name. A Jewish friend of mine was named Ephraim at the time of his circumcision. He changed his name to Earl. But with Saul, God just changed the first letter of his name.) It is at this time in the Arabian wilderness that God taught him the mysteries of the Gospel of Grace to be mainly preached to the Gentiles but also to Jews. This gospel of Grace would be different than the message of the Gospel of the Kingdom as preached to the Jew. The Gospel of the Kingdom was for Jews only but the Gospel of Grace was for all who would believe it. John the Baptist's message was for Israel only. He never left Israel. The message taught by Jesus and proved by signs, wonders, and miracles. *"And Jesus departed from thence, and came nigh unto the sea of Galilee; and went up into a mountain, and sat down there. And great multitudes came unto him, having with them those that were lame, blind, dumb, maimed, and many others, and cast them down at Jesus' feet; and he healed them: Insomuch that the multitude wondered, when they saw the dumb to speak, the maimed to be whole, the lame to walk, and the blind to see: and they glorified the God of Israel."* **Matthew 15:29-31** Those who believed Jesus was the Son of God, their eyes were open, they walked in the ways of God, and spake the ways of the Lord. But Jesus message was limited (with two exceptions) to Israel. As he told his disciples, *"**Go not into the way of the Gentiles,** and into any city of the Samaritans enter ye not:"* **Matthew 10:5**

When the believing Jews were forced to leave Israel because of the persecutions against them, they went to the cities of the Gentiles. *"Now they which were scattered abroad upon the persecution that arose about Stephen traveled as far as Phenice, and Cyprus, and Antioch, **preaching the word to none but unto the Jews only.**"*

Acts 11:19 This message of the Kingdom was limited to Jews only. It was not a message to the Gentiles. God had a special message for the Gentiles nations "the Gospel of Grace."

It is important to know the difference of these two gospels. Without making a distinction it is like putting the two gospels in a blender and coming up with a third gospel, a gospel that makes confusion in the life of a child of God. Keep the two apart, and we understand the grace of God to a larger degree.

twenty

Gospel of the Kingdom

The book of Acts being a book of transition from the Gospel of the Kingdom as taught by John the Baptist, Jesus, Peter, Stephen and the other apostles, to the Gospel of Grace as taught by the apostle Paul. The gospel of the Kingdom has to be understood to have a grasp on the thirteen or fourteen books of Paul depending or not if Paul was the author of the book of Hebrews. To more understand what was preached by John the Baptist, Jesus, and the early church leaders, it is best to list the message of each of these.

John the Baptist came before Jesus preaching a message of repentance. When the angel Gabriel met with Zechariah in the temple, Gabriel said of John the Baptist, *"For he shall be great in the sight of the Lord, and shall drink neither wine nor strong drink; and he shall be filled with the Holy Ghost, even from his mother's womb. And* **many of the children of Israel shall he turn to the Lord their God.** *And he shall go before him in the spirit and power of Elijah,* **to turn the hearts of the fathers to the children, and the disobedient to the wisdom of the just; to make ready a people prepared for the Lord."** **Luke 1:15-17** John did baptize those who repented. He preached the baptism of repentance for the remission of sins **(See Mark 1:4)** When the Pharisees asked John what he was doing, John answered, *"I am the voice of one crying in the wilderness,* **Make straight the way of the Lord***, as said the prophet Isaiah."* **John 1:23**

The message of John the Baptist was:

1. To turn the hearts of the fathers to the children.
2. To turn many of the children of Israel to the Lord their God.
3. To turn the disobedient to the wisdom of the just.
4. To make ready the people of Israel for the Lord Jesus Christ.

5. To baptize those who repented and believed his message. (Repentance is to turn from their ungodly wicked ways to a life of righteousness before God, walking in all the commandments and ordinances of the Lord blamelessly.)

The message of Jesus to the children of Israel was:

1. To tell the people of Israel about the coming Kingdom of Heaven. (In the Lord's prayer Jesus said, *"Thy kingdom come thy will be done on earth as it is in heaven."*)

2. To show signs, wonders, and miracles to Israel that he was the Son of God. He made the blind see, the deaf hear, the lame walk, lepers clean, raise the dead, and preach the gospel to the poor. These signs, miracles, and wonders were done for one reason. The reason was to show to Israel that he was the Son of God.

3. To be tempted by Satan and in all things that man would be tempted of.

4. To appoint twelve men as apostles who would judge the twelve tribes of Israel when the Kingdom of Heaven came to earth.

5. To call Israel to repentance for the Kingdom of Heaven was at hand. (If all Israel would have repented and believed that He was the Son of God after his ascension he would soon return as the reigning Messiah.)

6. To teach the people of Israel by parables.

7. To fulfill the Law and the prophets.

8. To be be arrested by the Jews religious leader. To stand before these religious leaders of Israel calling him a blasphemer because he claimed to be the Son of God. To be beaten by these religious leaders of Israel then sent to Pilate for judgment. To be beaten, mocked and scorned by the Roman Soldiers.

9. To To be sentenced to the death on the cross, to die, and be raised from the dead.

10. To be the Lamb of God who would take away the sins of the world. Jesus, Son of man, Son of God, came to this world to be "**despised** *and* **rejected of men;** *he would be a* **man of sorrows,** *and* **acquainted with grief:** *and Israel hid as it were our faces from him; he was despised, and esteemed him not. He borne their griefs, and carried the sorrows of the world. Israel yet did esteem him stricken, smitten of God, and afflicted.* **But he was**

wounded for our transgressions, he was bruised for our iniqui-ties: the chastisement of our peace was upon him; and with his stripes we are healed. *All we like sheep have gone astray; we have turned every one to his own way; and the Lord has laid on him the iniquity of us all.* He was oppressed, and he was afflicted, by the religious leaders of Israel yet he opened not his mouth. He is brought as a lamb to the slaughter, and as a sheep before her shearers is dumb, so he opened not his mouth. He was taken from prison and from judgment: and who shall declare his genera-tion? for he was cut off out of the land of the living: for the transgression of my people was he stricken. He made his grave with the wicked, and with the rich in his death; because he had done no violence, neither was any deceit in his mouth. *Yet it pleased the Lord to bruise him; he hath put him to grief: when thou shalt make his soul an offering for sin, he shall see his seed, he shall prolong his days, and the pleasure of the Lord shall prosper in his hand.* The Lord He saw his travail of his soul, and shall be satisfied: by his knowledge shall my righteous servant justify many; for he shall bear their iniquities. Therefore will God divide him a portion with the great, and he shall divide the spoil with the strong; because he hath poured out his soul unto death: and he was numbered with the transgressors; and he bare the sin of many, and made intercession for the transgressors. "**Isaiah 53:3-12**.

The message of Peter at Pentecost was:

1. To let all of Israel know assuredly, that God had made Jesus, whom they crucified, both Lord and Christ (their Messiah).
2. To repent. (to turn from their wicked ways to a life of righteousness before God, walking in all the commandments and ordinances of the Lord blamelessly.)
3. To be baptized in the name of Jesus Christ for the remission of sins.
4. Then they would receive the promise of the Holy Spirit.
5. The promise was to Israel, even to the children of Israel afar off, as many as the their God would call.

This was the message at the time from John the Baptist to time of the early Jewish church. The early Jewish believers spread this message to **Jews only** throughout the then know world. It was not a message for Gentiles. It was the message that God had promised to Abraham, Isaac, and Jacob. It was a promise that the children of Israel would be a nation that went from the

River Euphrates to the river of Egypt. It was a message told Israel that some-day God would bring the Kingdom of Heaven down from heaven to earth and God would rule over them from Jerusalem. It was a message of hope of resurrection after death. Job said to be a great-grandson of Judah declared, *"For I know that my redeemer lives, and that* **he shall stand at the latter day upon the earth:"** Job 19:25

twenty one

Gospel of Grace

After the conversion of Paul, God called him to the Arabian wilderness to give him the Gospel of Grace which up to this time in history was unknown and a mystery. Even after the cross the twelve apostles did not understand what the meaning of the passion of Jesus was. They did not understand that Jesus's blood was being shed for the sins of the world. From the time of Christ's resurrection the animal sacrifices in the temple were meaningless. Jesus, the Lamb of God, had shed his blood for sin and to make animal sacrifices for the covering of sin ineffective. That is why just like with Moses writing the law which made personal sacrifices ineffective when the tabernacle and the priesthood began making sacrifices for sin. Just as there was forty years in the wilderness to put an end to family sacrifices and set up the priesthood of Aaron and his descendants as the only way for the children of Israel to have their sins covered. From the time of Christ's redemption, blood was shed for sin, and it would be forty years later that the temple would be destroyed, putting an end of the priesthood and their making atonement for the sins of Israel.

The apostle Paul mentions the mysteries seventeen times in his epistles. The mysteries have to do with the real meaning of the cross. It is the mystery of the Age of Grace. It is the mystery that God turned his attention to the Gentiles. The book of Romans was written by the apostle Paul to a mostly Jewish church in Rome founded by converts of Peter who returned to Rome. Paul had not been to Rome before he wrote the book of Roman in Corinth. The book of Romans is called the "Constitution of Christianity."

God's promise to Abraham was a promise to all mankind. *"And in thy seed shall all the nations of the earth be blessed; because thou hast obeyed my voice."* **Genesis 22:18** This was the foundation promise God gave Abraham that through his seed, the Lord Jesus Christ, all the nations of the world would be blessed with the grace of God. Grace is God's giving mankind undeserved favor instead of the deserved wrath of God.

Paul's introduction to the book of Romans affirms that Jesus was the Son of God and our Lord was of the seed of King David according to the flesh (Son of man), and declared to be the Son of God with the power by his resurrection from the dead, by whom we receive grace by faith among all nations. The gospel of Christ (grace) is the power of God unto salvation to every one that believes, to the Jew first and now also to the Gentiles. The cross is the righteousness of God revealed from faith to faith. The life of the believer is a life of faith. It was written in **Habakkuk 2:4** *"The just* (righteous) *shall live by faith."* The same was written by Paul, *"Without faith it is impossible to please God."* **Hebrews 11:6** All men were guilty of sin before God. Paul goes to address the sins of immoral Rome with all its perversion, tells that amoral man that he is also guilty of sin, and lastly of all the sin of the self-righteous religious Jews. He concludes with an absolute truth of the word of God. *"For all have sinned, and come short of the glory of God."* **Romans 3:23**

What does it mean to become short of the Glory of God? *"The sun shall be no more thy light by day; neither for brightness shall the moon give light unto thee: but the LORD shall be unto thee an everlasting light, and* **thy God thy glory.***"* **Isaiah 60:19** *"And the city had no need of the sun, neither of the moon, to shine in it:* **for the glory of God did lighten it,** *and the Lamb is the light thereof."* **Revelation 21:23** The brightness of God is his glory. In the holy city that comes down from heaven there will be no need for light, because His glory will fill the city with light. Three of Christ's apostles had a glimpse of the glory when Jesus appeared with Moses and Elijah. *"And it came to pass about an eight days after these sayings, he took Peter and John and James, and went up into a mountain to pray. And as he prayed, the fashion of his countenance was altered, and* **his raiment was white and glistering.** *And, behold, there talked with him two men, which were Moses and Elias: Who appeared in* **glory,** *and spake of his decease which he should accomplish at Jerusalem. But Peter and they that were with him were heavy with sleep: and when they were awake,* **they saw His glory,** *and the two men that stood with him.* **Luke 9:-32**

To fall short of the glory of God would mean that man would not see the light of the glory of God in the city of God. Man being with sin, and sin cannot be in the city of God. So, man has been left out. But that is the end of what Paul said. He continues with the end of the phrase, *"Being justified freely by his grace through the redemption that is in Christ Jesus."* **Romans 3:24**

Grace is what Peter, the other eleven apostles, and the Jewish believers did not understand. They believed like Peter that the Jews had - ***"Killed the Prince of life,*** *whom God hath raised from the dead."* **Acts 3:15** The early believers believed it was the Jews who had killed Jesus. They believed that Jesus was the Son of God, they had repented of their sins, were baptized for the remission of sins, and were filled with the Holy Spirit. This was their gospel. This was the Gospel of the Kingdom.

But the mystery of the reason for the death of Christ was not the work of the Jews and Roman government. They were all just pawns in the hands of God to bring forgiveness of sins to mankind, to redeem man from the power of Satan, and to give eternal life to all who put their faith in what God had done through his Son, the Lord Jesus Christ.

The mystery was planned before there was the planet called earth. *"And all that dwell upon the earth shall worship him, whose names are not written in the book of life of the* **Lamb slain from the foundation of the world."** **Revelation 13:8** It was not the plan of the Jews religious leaders but it was the plan of God before the foundation of the world they he would send God the Son into this world to be a perfect ransom for sinners, and put his wrath for sin upon the Son. He would be beaten by the Jews and Gentiles put on a cross, die, be buried, and would be raised again in three days by the power of the Holy Spirit. It was all God's plan to redeem a people both Jew and Gentile to call his own, and to live with God for eternity.

This plan voided all work my man to obtain salvation. It was all of God. Man could not add anything to the grace of God. All man had to do was to believe, trust, and put their faith in what Christ had done while on earth and add nothing to it. Faith plus Nothing.

With this message, the mystery of God, there would be no more need for baptizing for the remissions of sins, circumcision, keeping of the Law of Moses, keeping of the Jewish feast days, animal sacrifice, and anything man would add to what Christ had done. His work was a complete work. Christ blood was said, the final and all inclusive act of salvation. Faith plus Nothing.

There are three absolutes that goes from Genesis 1:1 to Revelation 22:21.

1. All have sinned and come short of the glory of God. **Roman 3:23**
2. Without the shedding of blood there is no remission of sin. **Hebrews 9:22**
3. Without faith it is impossible to please God. **Hebrews 11:6**

Paul took salvation from the work of man to the cross of Christ. It is the action of Christ, backed by faith alone, and sustained by our confidence in what Christ has done completely. Paul's message is the cross of Jesus Christ. So there it is. One sentence tells us that there is an all-powerful, all-loving, deity who sent His Son to earth as a **blood** offering, that whoever accepts that **blood** offering will live forever. The shedding of **blood** to cover the sins of mankind started in the Garden of Eden. Adam and Eve had eaten of the forbidden tree and realized they were naked. After they sinned, they imagined that they could get rid of sin with self-made garments of fig leaves. God came down and would not accept their self-made covering for their sins and announced a curse on mankind and his created earth.

God slew a lamb and took the skin of the **blood** shed animal and clothed Adam and Eve. The shedding of **blood** began there in the Garden of Eden for the covering for sin. It has never changed. God, the creator of this world and mankind, was the first to shed **blood** on this earth to cover the sin of mankind. The **blood is the only atonement for sin.** For the life of the flesh is in the **blood**: and I have given it to you upon the alter to make an atonement for your souls: for it is the **blood** that maketh an atonement for the soul. **(See Leviticus 71:11)**

In Israel there was the tabernacle and the temple. Every year there was the Day of Atonement (Yon Kipper). It was the only day the High Priest could enter the Holy of Holies. Before he could start the atonement for the sins of Israel he had to prepare himself to enter the Holy of Holies. He had to put on the altar a ram and a bullock first for the sins of him and his family. Then he had to wash in the laver to clean his body of any of this world's dirt and unrighteousness. Then he was to put on the altar a sacrifice for the people of Israel and take that **blood** into the Holy of Holies and sprinkle the **blood** on the floor and on the Mercy Seat. If all was done right without sin's presence the priest would leave the Holy of Holies and God came down and accepted the **blood** offering for the sin of the people of Israel. Then the priest would tell the people that God had accepted the sacrifice and an atonement was made for sins for that year. The people rejoiced that their sins were atoned for. Atonement means **"one with God."** Jesus, after he arose from the dead, took His own **blood** and applied it on the Mercy Seat that is in Heaven, once and for all and made atonement for the sins of man. He again made us **"one with God"** making us able to walk with God as Adam did in the Garden of Eden before the fall.

We, the believers, are also purchased by the **blood** of Jesus. Take heed therefore unto yourselves, and all the flock, over which the Holy Ghost hath made you overseers, to feed the church of God, which he hath purchased with his **blood: (See Act 20:28)** There was a ransom to be paid. Man had become the servant of Satan at the fall in the Garden of Eden. We were not God's any more, we were the property of Satan. To purchase us back from Satan took more than silver or gold. It took the **blood** of Jesus Christ, Son of God, Son of man, one with the Father, member of the Godhead. God the son left Heaven's glory dwelt in the tent of the body of man. He lived a sinless life, surrendered to man and was crucified on the cross giving His **blood** to purchase back man from the servitude of Satan.

The **blood** justified the believer with God. *"Much more then, being now justi-fied by his blood, we shall be saved from the wrath through Him."* **Rom 5:9** Upon that cross the wrath of God toward us was put on our Lord Jesus Christ. His **blood** justified us, made us in right standing with God the Father. Justified is a legal term making everything as it was before. Things were made right. But His **blood** did more than justify us. A better word if it was available in the English language would be "rightousified." To be "rightousified" is greater than just being justified. It is being made right with God. God sees us as righteous, and sinless, just as he see his Son, Jesus Christ.

The **blood** give us peace with God. *"And, having made **peace** through the **blood** of his cross, by him to reconcile all thing unto himself, by Him, I say, whether they be things on earth or things in Heaven."* **Col 1:20** Before the cross mankind was at odds with God. We had lost our relationship with the Father when Adam and Eve sinned in the Garden of Eden. But on the cross by the **blood** of Jesus Christ, the relationship was healed. We were again at peace with God. We could again walk and talk with our God. A reconciliation was made between man and God by the **blood** of Christ.

The **blood** sanctifies believers and makes them holy. For the bodies of those beasts, whose **blood** is brought into the sanctuary by the high priest for sin, are burned without the camp. Wherefore Jesus also, that He might **sanctify** the people with his own **blood,** suffered outside the gate. Sanctification is being made holy and set apart for God. His **blood sanctified** us, making us holy. Setting us apart from the world and put aside for God's use. **(See Heb 13:11-12)**

The **blood** cleanseth us from all sin. *"But if we walk in the light, as he is in the light, we have fellowship with one with another, and the **blood** of Jesus Christ his Son cleanseth us for all sin."* **I John 1:7** God is Light. To walk in this light, living free from the bondage of sin, is to make true fellowship and communion between believers possible. The **blood** of Jesus Christ cleanseth man from sins from the time Eve ate the forbidden fruit, to the time when the last sin is committed on this earth. It is a everlasting flood of His **blood** that continued to cleanseth man from sin. Praise God.

The **blood** has redeemed us to God. And they sung a new song, saying, Thou art worthy to take the book, and to open the seals thereof, for Thou was slain, and hast **redeemed** us to God by thy **blood** out of every kindred and tongue, and people, and nation: **(See Revelation 5:9)** "Redeemed by the **Blood** of the Lamb", is an old time favorite hymn. The **blood** of Jesus Christ paid the ransom for our sins, and we are again the Children of God. No longer are we a slave to Satan and his army, but we are now children of the Living God. Not just Israel, but Children of God from every race, language, people, and nation. It is an international salvation. We can look for a new heaven and a new world where only righteousness dwells.

Faith opens the door to God. For by grace are you saved though faith, and not that of yourselves: it is the gift of God, not of works, lest any man should boast **Eph 2:8-9** The shedding of the **Blood** of Jesus Christ is for the sins of this world. Christ was a perfect sacrifice without sin. Christ was the once and for all sacrifice. It needed to be done only once, not a yearly sacrifice as it was in old Israel. His **Blood** made an atonement for sin, his **Blood** purchased us back from the property of Satan and made us Children of God, his **Blood** made us justified before God, his **Blood** made us at peace with God, this **Blood** sanctified us for God's purpose, his **Blood** cleansed us for all sin, and his **Blood** redeemed us and we are no longer a slave of Satan. It is free to all those who put their faith in his **Blood.** Believe it and put your confidence in the shed **Blood** of the Lord Jesus Christ on Calvary's Cross.

Grace, Grace, God's Grace, His grace is greater than all our sins. *"For by* **grace** *are ye* **saved** *through* **faith;** *and that not of yourselves: it is the* **gift** *of God."* **Eph 2:8** We obtain God's grace only by placing our complete faith that we receive the gift of God, forgiveness of sin and eternal life.

IT IS FAITH PLUS NOTHING!!!!!

twenty two

Conflict between Gospels

The first conflict between the early church and the apostles church was in Antioch. The church in Antioch was the accepting of Greek speaking Jews receiving the message of the Kingdom of God. It upset the apostles and they sent Barnabas to Antioch to enquire about the matter. *"When he came, and had seen the grace of God, was glad, and exhorted them all, that with purpose of heart they would cleave unto the Lord. For he was a good man, and full of the Holy Ghost and of faith: and much people was added unto the Lord."* **Acts 11:23-24** The church at Antioch was a Jewish church. At Antioch is where the believers in Christ were first called Christians. It is strange that the term now means "Gentiles who have faith in Christ." The Jews today that believe Jesus as the Messiah are not called Christians but Messianic Jews.

Then Paul and Barnabas went out together to begin ministering to the Gentiles with the message of the Gospel of Grace. *"As they ministered to the Lord, and fasted, the Holy Ghost said, Separate me Barnabas and Saul for the work where-unto I have called them."* **Acts 13:2** It had been eleven years since the cross. Up to this time, the Gospel of the Kingdom as taught by Peter was the only gospel preached and that to the **Jews only.** Paul being called to be the apostle for the Gentiles began to preach in the cities of Asia to the Gentiles.

They sailed to the Island of Cyprus. It was the custom of Paul to always go to the synagogue first in all the cities he visited. Paul continued to preach in the cities of the Gentiles until his arrest in Jerusalem. In each city he would preach the message of the Gospel of Grace starting at the synagogue and then to the Gentiles in the city. After preaching, he would call the believers apart and teach them more deeply the things of God. It was not an easy road for Paul. The Jews who rejected the message of the cross would try to kill him or drive him out of the city. During his ministry he suffered much heartache. As the Gentile churches were established, the Jewish believers would go to the church and tell the Gentiles they had to be circumcised and follow the Law of Moses.

This conflict is brought forth in the book of Galatians. After his greeting to the church at Galatia Paul goes right after the issue at hand. The Jewish Christians came to the Galatia church and told them they had to follow the Gospel of the Kingdom as taught by Peter. The gospel that was preached to the Jews only at that time. Paul then got down to the point, *"I marvel that ye are so soon* **removed** *from him that* **called you into the grace of Christ unto another gospel:** *Which is not another; but there be some that trouble you, and would pervert the gospel of Christ. But though we, or an angel from heaven, preach any other gospel unto you than that which we have preached unto you,* **let him be accursed.** *As we said before, so say I now again, if any man preach any other gospel unto you than that ye have received,* **let him be accursed.** *For do I now persuade men, or God? or do I seek to please men? for if I yet pleased men, I should not be the servant of Christ."* **Galatians 1:6-10**

These are harsh words. Let those who came to the church at Galatia be **accursed or be damned**. He calls the Gospel of the Kingdom another gospel. It was another gospel. It was the gospel that Peter preached to the Jews. At that time the Gentiles were, *"That at that time ye* **were without Christ,** *being* **aliens** *from the commonwealth of Israel, and* **strangers** *from the covenants of promise,* **having no hope,** *and* **without God in the world."** **Ephesians 2:12** This was condition of all the Gentiles. After the call of Abraham and the promises made to Abraham, all other nations were without God, aliens, strangers, with no hope for salvation. That is the condition still to all who do not put their faith in Jesus Christ's atonement. Paul continues to write to the brethren in Galatia, *"But I* **certify** *you, brethren, that the gospel which was preached of me* **is not after man.** *For I neither received it of man, neither was I taught it, but* **by the revelation of Jesus Christ.** *For ye have heard of my conversation in time past in the Jews' religion, how that beyond measure I persecuted the church of God, and wasted it: And profited in the Jews' religion above many my equals in mine own nation, being more exceedingly zealous of the traditions of my fathers. But when* **it pleased God,** *who separated me from my mother's womb, and called me by his grace,* **to reveal his Son in me,** *that I might* **preach him among the heathen;** *immediately I conferred not with flesh and blood: Neither went I up to Jerusalem to them which were apostles before me; but I went into Arabia, and returned again unto Damascus. Then after three years I went up to Jerusalem to see Peter, and abode* *with him fifteen days. But other of the apostles saw I none, save James the Lord's brother. Now the things which I write unto you, behold, before God, I lie not."* **Galatians 1:11-20**

The Jewish believers were continually going into the Gentiles churches to take them out of Gospel of Grace and bring them to the Jewish Gospel of the Kingdom. The Kingdom was never promised to the Gentiles. It was a promise to the Jews only. But because Israel as a nation did not accept Jesus as their Messiah, God turned his back on Israel and went to the Gentiles with the Gospel of Grace. They were mixing the Gospel of the Kingdom with the Gospel of Grace. The mixture does not work. The Gospel of the Kingdom is the belief that Jesus was the Messiah, that man should repent (turn form his wicked selfish ways to a life of righteousness before God, walking in all the commandments and ordinances of the Lord blameless), to be baptized in the name of Jesus Christ for the remission of sins., and have hands laid on them to received the gift of the Holy Spirit.

The Gospel of Grace is best explained by Paul in his first letter to the Corinthians, *"Moreover, brethren, I declare unto you* **the gospel** *which I preached unto you, which also* **ye have received***, and wherein* **ye stand***; By which also* **ye are saved***, if ye keep in memory what I preached unto you, unless ye have believed in vain. For I delivered unto you first of all that which I also received, how that* **Christ died for our sins** *according to the scriptures; And that* **he was buried***, and that* **he rose again the third day** *according to the scriptures: And that he was seen of Cephas, then of the twelve: After that, he was seen of above five hundred brethren at once; of whom the greater part remain unto this present, but some are fallen asleep. After that, he was seen of James; then of all the apostles, and last of all he was seen of me also, as of one born out of due time."* **I Corinthians 15:1-8**

The Gospel of Grace which Paul preached was received by the Gentile Corinthians, which they were saved from everlasting punishment, and was where their faith stood, **that Christ died for sins, he was buried, and rose again on the third day.** It was all grace through faith plus nothing. No circumcision, no water baptism was required, no following the Law of Moses, just pure faith. When they put their faith in Christ, they received the Holy Spirit and then God sealed the Holy Spirit within their bodies.

It was fourteen years since Paul's conversion on the way to Damascus. It was eleven years since he started preaching the Gospel of Grace to the Gentiles. He had enough of the inference from the Jewish believers. Paul tells about this trip in his letter to the Galatians. *"Then fourteen years after I went up again to Jerusalem with Barnabas, and took Titus with me also. And I went up by revelation, and* **communicated unto them that gospel which I preach among the Gentiles,** *but privately to them which were of reputation, lest by any means I should run, or had run, in vain. But neither Titus, who was with me, being a Greek, was compelled to be circumcised: And that because of* **false brethren unawares brought in, who came in privily to spy out our liberty which we have in Christ Jesus, that they might bring us into bondage:** *To whom we gave place by subjection, no, not for an hour; that the truth of the gospel might continue with you. But of these who seemed to be somewhat, (whatsoever they were, it maketh no matter to me: God accepteth no man's person:) for they who seemed to be somewhat in conference added nothing to me: But contrariwise, when they saw that the gospel of the uncircumcision was committed unto me, as the gospel of the circumcision was unto Peter; (For he that wrought effectually in Peter to the apostleship of the circumcision, the same was mighty in me toward the Gentiles:) And when James, Cephas, and John, who seemed to be pillars, perceived the grace that was given unto me, they gave to me and Barnabas the right hands of fellowship; that we should go unto the heathen, and they unto the circumcision. Only they would that we should remember the poor; the same which I also was forward to do."* **Galatians 2:1-10**

In the book of Acts Paul meeting with the council at Jerusalem is also recorded. But in Acts we see Peter stepping in behalf of Paul. "And when there had been much disputing, Peter rose up, and said unto them, Men and brethren, ye know how that a good while ago God made choice among us, **that the Gentiles by my mouth should hear the word of the gospel, and believe.** And God, which knoweth the hearts, bare them witness, giving them the Holy Ghost, even as he did unto us; And put no difference between us and them, purifying their hearts by faith. Now therefore **why tempt ye God, to put a yoke upon the neck of the disciples, which neither our fathers nor we were able to bear?** But **we believe that through the grace of the LORD Jesus Christ we shall be saved,** even as they. Then all the multitude kept silence, and gave audience to Barnabas and Paul, declaring what miracles and wonders God had wrought among the Gentiles by them.

And after they had held their peace, James answered, saying, Men and brethren, hearken unto me: Simeon hath declared **how God at the first did visit the Gentiles, to take out of them a people for his name.** And to this agree the words of the prophets; as it is written, After this I will return, and will build again the tabernacle of David, which is fallen down; and I will build again the ruins thereof, and I will set it up: That the residue of men might seek after the Lord, and all **the Gentiles, upon whom my name is called,** saith the Lord, who does all these things. Known unto God are all his works from the beginning of the world. Wherefore my sentence is, that we trouble not them, which from among the Gentiles are turned to God: But that we write unto them, that they abstain from pollutions of idols, and from fornication, and from things strangled, and from blood. For Moses of old time hath in every city them that preach him, being read in the synagogues every sabbath day. Then pleased it the apostles and elders with the whole church, to send chosen men of their own company to Antioch with Paul and Barnabas; namely, Judas surname Barnabas and Silas, chief men among the brethren:

And they wrote letters by them after this manner; The apostles and elders and brethren send greeting unto the brethren which are of the Gentiles in Antioch and Syria and Cilicia. For as much as we have heard, that certain which went out from us have troubled you with words, subverting your souls, saying, Ye must be circumcised, and keep the law: to whom we gave no such commandment: It seemed good unto us, being assembled with one accord, to send chosen men unto you with our beloved Barnabas and Paul, Men that have hazarded their lives for the name of our Lord Jesus Christ. We have sent therefore Judas and Silas, who shall also tell you the same things by mouth. **For it seemed good to the Holy Ghost, and to us, to lay upon you no greater burden than these necessary things;** That ye abstain from meats offered to idols, and from blood, and from things strangled, and from fornication: from which if ye keep yourselves, ye shall do well. Fare ye well.

So when they were dismissed, they came to Antioch: and when they had gathered the multitude together, they delivered the epistle: Which when they had read, they rejoiced for the consolation. And Judas and Silas, being prophets also themselves, exhorted the brethren with many words, and confirmed them. And after they had tarried there a space, they were let go in peace from the brethren unto the apostles. Notwithstanding it pleased Silas to abide there still. Paul and Barnabas continued in Antioch, teaching and preaching the word of the Lord, with many others also. And some days after Paul said unto Barnabas, Let us go again and visit our brethren in every city where we have preached the word of the LORD, and see how they do. **(See Acts 15:7-36)**

The results of this meeting were very important to the Gentile church. James understood the importance of this meeting and the decision. He had the minutes of the meeting and addressed it to the Gentile churches in Antioch, Syria, and Cilicia. Not only did he write it, he sent two from Jerusalem, Judas and Silas with Paul to deliver the letter to the churches. This letter gave the approval of Paul and the other apostles that the Gospel of Grace was to be preached to the Gentiles and that the Jewish believers should not interfere with their ministry.

twenty three

Sufferings of Paul

During Paul's conversion he was told he would be the apostle to the Gentiles. He was also told he would have to suffer much for the sake of the Gospel of Grace. There was a time he was stoned and left for dead. Paul and Barnabas were in the city of Lystra. There a lame man was healed by the hands of Paul. The people of Lystra thought Paul and Barnabas were gods. Then certain Jews from Antioch and Iconium, turned the people of Lystra against Paul. The Jews stirred up the people that they stoned Paul, drew him out of the city, supposing he had been dead. Thinking he was dead some disciples stood around Paul and he rose up. The next day he departed to another city.

Paul wrote to the Corinthians about the false teachers that had been going to the churches established by Paul preaching another gospel, preaching another Jesus and accusing Paul of many things. Paul had to come to his own defense. He tells this to the saints at Corinth. These false teachers, like Paul were Jews, Hebrews, and sons of Abraham. But Paul remind them of the cost he has paid to be the chief apostle to the Gentiles.

"I am more; in labors more abundant, in stripes above measure, in prisons more frequent, in deaths often. Of the Jews five times received I forty stripes save one. Thrice was I beaten with rods, once was I stoned, thrice I suffered shipwreck, a night and a day I have been in the deep; In journeying often, in perils of waters, in perils of robbers, in perils by mine own countrymen, in perils by the heathen, in perils in the city, in perils in the wilderness, in perils in the sea, in perils among false brethren."

"In weariness and painfulness, in watching often, in hunger and thirst, in fastings often, in cold and nakedness. Beside those things that are without, that which cometh upon me daily, the care of all the churches. Who is weak, and I am not weak? who is offended, and I burn not? If I must needs glory, I will glory of the things which concern mine infirmities."

"The God and Father of our Lord Jesus Christ, which is blessed for evermore, knoweth that I lie not. In Damascus the governor under Aretas the king kept the city of the Damascenes with a garrison, desirous to apprehend me: And through a window in a basket was I let down by the wall, and escaped his hands." **II Corinthians 11:23 -33**

For nearly thirty years Paul gave his life for the preaching of Gospel of Grace. From Antioch he preached in the area what is now known as Asia minor, around to Europe starting in Greece and ended up in chains teaching the saints in Rome. He was an evangelist at times, and other times as a pastor teaching the new converts the deeper things in Christ.

The warning in the New Testament is the warning of false teachers. Jesus warned of false prophets that would come. *"Beware of false prophets, which come to you in sheep's clothing, but inwardly they are ravening wolves."* **Matthew 7:15** *"And many false prophets shall rise, and shall deceive many.* **Matthew 24:11** *For there shall arise false Christs, and false prophets, and shall shew great signs and wonders; insomuch that, if it were possible, they shall deceive the very elect."* **Matthew 24:24**. There is not one book in the New Testaments that does not warn against false prophets. Paul was not the only one who had to put up with false teachers, prophets, and false Christ.

Peter and John also warned against false prophets. Peter warned, *"But there were false prophets also among the people, even as there shall be false teachers among you, who privily shall bring in damnable heresies, even denying the Lord that bought them, and bring upon themselves swift destruction."* **II Peter 2:1** John also warned, *"Beloved, believe not every spirit, but try the spirits whether they are of God: because many false prophets are gone out into the world."* **I John 4:1**

All of the false prophets, and preachers have an element of truth with their false message. Today we have in the church world wide false teaching. One of the most damnable teachings in churches today is the acceptance of homosexuality in the pew and in the pulpit. Sin is sin and God does not change his definition of what sin is.

Paul was the chief of all the ministers of the Gospel of Grace. He willing paid a great price for his journeys into the Gentile world with the message of salvation through faith in the atoning work of Christ. His word to Timothy as he approached the end of his ministry and life was, *"Henceforth there is laid up for me a* **crown of righteousness**, *which the Lord, the righteous judge, shall give me at*

that day: and not to me only, **but unto all them also that love his appearing."**
II Timothy 4:8

Summing up the perils of Paul during his thirty year journey of giving the message of the Gospel of Grace is a long list:

- A Hebrew (Jew). He was a Israelite. A seed of Abraham. A minister of Jesus Christ.
- Labored abundantly for Jesus Christ. Beat with strips above all others.
- Imprisoned for preaching Christ. Left for death because of his preaching for Christ.
- Received 39 stripes five times for Christ. (That is 195 stripes.) Was stoned once for Christ.
- Three times beaten with rods for Christ. Travels often from city to city for Christ.
- Three times was in ship wrecked during his travels for Christ. Had perils of the water for Christ.
- Had perils of being robbed for Christ. Suffered perils of the Gentile heathens for Christ.
- Suffered perils of the Jewish people because of his message to the Gentile for Christ.
- Suffered in the cities for Christ and in the perils of the wilderness for Christ.
- Suffered from perils of false brethren for Christ. Got weary in the preaching of Christ.
- Had suffered painfulness for Christ. Had times of hunger in serving Christ.
- Had to be on watch all the time during his ministry for Christ.
- Had times of thirst in serving Christ. He fasted often for Christ.
- Suffered the cold for Christ. Suffered nakedness for Christ.

The man who for his first thirty years was a Jew's Jew. He was taught under Gamaliel and was a member of the religious leaders of Israel. He was present when many followers of Christ were put to death. But, he met the Lord Jesus Christ on the road to Damascus. He could sing, "For all things were changed when I met the Master. When He found me a new day broke out all around me. For, then, I met the Master now, I belong to Him."

We also can met the Master of life. He was the Lamb of God who took away the sins of the world while suffering for us on the cross, paying our sin debt, giving us his righteousness, and eternal life. It is all by faith not anything of ourselves. We can ask Jesus into our hearts, give our lives to Jesus, be baptized in the name of the Father, Son, and Holy Ghost, or any other that we put our faith in for salvation, but God only recognizes is the blood of his Son. Faith in our works by mouth or water does not take the place of faith in the atoning work of Christ.

For my grace are we saved through faith not of works and having something to brag about doing. We have to take the "I" out of salvation and place it all in Christ. Without faith in the atoning blood of Jesus, we cannot find salvation. We have to realize to believe, trust, and have faith in Christ alone. Faith plus nothing.

twenty four

Doctrine of Grace

Paul after evangelizing a city would separate the believers from the world around them and teach them doctrine. Many of today's Christians do not like to think of doctrine. Paul said to the saints in Rome, "But God be thanked, that **you were the servants of sin,** but ye have obeyed from the heart that form of **doctrine which was delivered you." Romans 6:17** Knowing the doctrine of Paul to the Gentile is a foundation for faith and Christian living. The doctrines of Paul are outlined as follows:

Doctrine of All men are unrighteous before God:

When Adam sinned he brought sin to all men. The Bible in the book of Romans tell the believer, "That all have sinned and come short of God's glory. Man is born with a sin nature. We don't have to teach man to lie, steal, or covet. It is the Adamic nature within us that a child does not have to be taught to lie. The Adamic sin nature comes from male the and not from the female. *"For as in **Adam all die**, even so in Christ shall all be made alive."* **I Corinthians 15.22** Mary was conceived by the Holy Spirit. The Adamic sin nature was not in Jesus because he was conceived of the Holy Spirit not of the seed of man. *"As it is written, There is none righteous, no, not one:"* **Romans 3:10.** Man being unrighteous cannot communicate with God. The remedy is the grace of God.

Doctrine of Salvation:

The doctrine of salvation is all a work of God. God planned it before the foundation of the world. God knew that man would fall into sin. God determined that the Son of God would take on the image of man, come to earth, live a sinless life, then let man crucify him on a cross, die on the that cross, be buried and on the third day rise again from the grave by the power of the Holy Spirit. He would satisfy everything demanded by God for man to have communion again with Him. The response of man would only be to believe, trust, and have faith in the fact that the Son of God, the Lord Jesus Christ, did all that was required by God to pay sin's debt, redeem man from Satan, give man the righteousness of the Lord Jesus Christ, and have eternal life with God.

Doctrine of the Blood:

Without the shedding of blood there is not remission of sin. **Hebrews 9:22.** It started with the sin of Adam and Eve. They tried to cover their sin by their own work of making a covering of their nakedness with fig leaves. God would not accept their own work. He took an animal(s), shed the blood of the animal and make a covering for them with the skin of the animal. The shedding of blood was required for a covering for sin until Christ once and for all shed his blood for the sin of all mankind. Before the cross the blood of animals only covered man's sin till Christ came from heaven and shed his blood for the sin of man. The blood of Jesus was not spilled. It was shed. To spill is an accidental occurrence. **The blood of Jesus was a planned occurrence, not an accident.**

Doctrine of Grace:

Grace is the undeserved favor or merit instead of deserved wrath or punishment. It is an unmerited divine gift given by God. Grace was planned before the creation of the universe and before their was such a creature as man. Grace started in heaven. "And I beheld, and I heard the voice of many angels round about the throne and the beasts and the elders: and the number of them was ten thousand times ten thousand, and thousands of thousands; Saying with a loud voice, Worthy is the Lamb that was slain to receive power, and riches, and wisdom, and strength, and honor, and glory, and blessing.

And all that dwell upon the earth shall worship him, whose names are not written in the book of life of **the Lamb slain from the foundation of the world." Revelation 5:11-12 & Revelation 13:8** God had ordained before the foundation of the earth that the Son of God to be the visible image of the invisible God. Not only that by his grace he, *"According as he hath **chosen us in him before the foundation of the world,** that we should be holy and without blame before him in love: Having **predestinated us** unto the adoption of children by Jesus Christ to himself, according to the good pleasure of his will, to the praise of the **glory of his grace,** wherein he hath made us accepted in the beloved."* **Ephesians 1:4-6.** Grace started before the foundation.

Salvation begins and finishes by God and by him alone, as with Lydia, a Jewish women, whose heart was made ready by the Holy Spirit. "And a certain woman named Lydia, a seller of purple, of the city of Thyatira, which worshiped God, heard us: **whose heart the Lord opened,** that she attended unto the things which were spoken of Paul." **Acts 16:14**

Understanding God's grace takes the "I" out of salvation. He is alpha and omega of our salvation. My own experience with salvation started with "I." Every year the young people of the church would go to a summer camp. In the first year I was there, most of the young people had "asked Jesus into their hearts." Two or three of us had not "asked Jesus into our hearts." I did want to be an odd ball so I too went forward in the morning chapel and "asked Jesus into my heart." I put the date in my Bible. So, when asked from then on about my salvation I could answer, "Yes, I asked Jesus into my heart on such and such date." When I got older I wanted to join the church. I went before the elders and pastor. They asked me about my faith. I told them that "I have asked Jesus to come into my heart at camp on such and such a date." That is all it took and I became a member. I was working in a business and met many people of the reformation churches. They were very honest, good, and godly folks. The Holy Spirit started working on my heart. I had asked "Jesus in my heart" they did not, yet they were very godly people. But not having asked Jesus into their hearts they were unsaved. At the same time we had a distributor who called on the business and took me to lunch. He always had his Bible with him and we would discuss the Bible. I was being convicted of sin in my life just like those honest good folks who did not ask Jesus into their hearts. The Holy Spirit gently made me seek for an answer to my confusion. Then one night while meditating on my salvation, I realized that my work of "asking Jesus into my heart" was not Biblical at all. It was part of works salvation. I then realized I was a sinner and that Christ died and paid the penalty for all of my sins. It was not what I did, but what God had done for me on the cross.

A few weeks later I got into a serious auto accident and was very close to death. I was on a hospital gurney with a white sheet over me. I saw that sheet as snow. I realized that God looked down on me and all he could see was the righteousness, that Jesus gave to me in exchange for my sin. As I laid there I had a vision of Jesus holding me. I had such peace knowing that God hand done everything for me to give me eternal life. "Grace, Grace, God's Grace, Grace that is greater that all my sin."

Doctrine of Faith: (Saving Faith)

The word faith is used in many ways. There are several religions in the world today that are called faiths. There is the Islamic faith, a Jewish faith, Hindu faith, Buddhist faith, the Christian faith and many many other religions also called faiths. Today the faith of Christendom numbers more that a billion people. Among the many people in Christendom there is the true church of God. A blood bought faith that brings salvation comes only by the grace of God. *"A faith that is the substance of things hoped for, the evidence of things not seen."* **Hebrews 11:1** *"A faith that comes by hearing, and hearing by the word of God."* **Romans 10:17**

Paul asked the brethren at Corinth about their faith, *"This only would I learn of you,* **Received ye the Spirit** *by the works of the law, or by the* **hearing of faith?** *Are ye so foolish? having begun in the Spirit, are ye now made perfect by the flesh? Have ye suffered so many things in vain? if it be yet in vain. He therefore that ministers to you the Spirit, and worketh miracles among you, does he it by the works of the law, or by the hearing of faith?"* **Galatians 3:2-5** The brethren at Galatia started with "Faith plus nothing" but then false teachers came in and were trying to put the new believers under law. When believers starting adding works to faith alone, they are telling God his grace was insufficient. We must stand always on **God' gift.** *"For by* **grace** *are ye* **saved** *through* **faith;** *and that not of yourselves: it is the* **gift** *of God:* **Ephesians 2:8** . There is nothing to be added.

The Doctrine of the Baptism of the Holy Spirit:

The baptism of the Holy Spirit is what was promised by God and preached by John the Baptist. *"And I knew him not: but he that sent me to baptize with water, the same said unto me, Upon whom thou shalt see the **Spirit** descending, and remaining on him, the same is he which **baptizes with the Holy Spirit.**"* **John 1:33** This first time the baptized believers with God the Holy Spirit was at Pentecost when the one hundred twenty believers were in the upper room. It was followed by the apostles laying hands on the Jewish believers. Again, when Peter went to Cornelius the Holy Spirit fell on them at the same time they believed. It never has stopped. When a believer put his or her faith in the atonement of our Lord Jesus Christ, the Holy Spirit comes and dwells in the new believer till death. *"When they heard the of the atonement of Jesus and His giving his life for the sin of man, his death and resurrection, they believed and the Holy Spirit indwelt them. The Holy Spirit was sealed by God himself. "In whom ye also trusted, after that ye heard the word of truth, the gospel of your salvation: in whom also after that ye believed,* **ye were sealed with that holy Spirit of promise."** **Ephesians 1:13**. Today the church puts little emphasis on the Holy Spirit dwelling in the believer. This was also true of the early church. Paul writes to the Corinthians about the Holy Spirit, *"What? know ye not that your body is the temple of the Holy Ghost which is in you, which ye have of God, and ye are not your own?"* **I Corinthians 6:19**

Doctrine of Hope:

We say, "Well, I hope so." Hope is to desire with expectation of obtainment. Hope is to expect with confidence. Job was a man of hope. Through all his trials he always had hope that God would bring him through. Fifteen times in the book of Job, Job refers to his hope. The prophet Jeremiah in the Old Testament tell about a blessed man. *"Blessed is the **man that trusts** (Has Faith) in the Lord, and whose hope the Lord is."* **Jeremiah 17:7** In Paul's Epistle to Titus he gives this advice and comfort to Titus, *"Looking for that blessed hope, and the glorious appearing of the **great God and our Savior** Jesus Christ."* **Titus 2:13** Oh, what a wonderful hope that we can claim today in a world that is in total confusion. Therefore, we can look for that **glorious appearing** of our God and Savior, the Lord Jesus Christ. In this verse it refers to our Lord Jesus Christ not only as God but also our Savior. Amen.

Doctrine of Love:

Oh, the love of God is greater far than tongue, pen, or computer words could ever tell. The verse in the Bible almost every believer knows tells us, *"For God so **loved** the world, that he gave his only begotten Son, that whosoever believeth in him should not perish, but have everlasting life."* **John 3:16** God's love for this world and his people cost him the death of the Son of God on the cross. But praise God, that after three days with the power of the Holy Spirit he was raised from the dead. *"And hope maketh not ashamed; because the **love of God** is shed abroad in our hearts by the Holy Ghost which is given unto us."* **Romans 5:5.** When we put our faith in the blood of Jesus, the Holy Spirit come into our bodies to dwell there the rest of our lives, and the Holy Spirit brings with him the Love of God. God seals the Holy Spirit in our bodies and nothing can take the Holy Spirit or the Love of God from us. Paul tells us, *"Nor height, nor depth, nor any other creature, shall be able to **separate us from the love of G**od, which is in Christ Jesus our Lord."* **Romans 8:39**

For many years I saw God with a baseball bat on his shoulder ready to bop me every time I sinned. Realizing that the baseball bat was already used by God at Calvary upon His Son, God had taken his wrath against me on Jesus. I did not any longer have to fear him. Then I saw God as my friend. I could talk to him about problems in my life including the problems with the sin in my life. Then I learned to love him because he loved me so much. Now, I can tell my God I love him when I am in prayer. I can lift up my hands and praise Him for this great love. The heavens as a scroll and every writing instrument on earth could not be enough pen and paper to write the love of God.

Doctrine of Propitiation:

This is a uncommon word which most of us do not know the meaning of. In the tabernacle in the wilderness and the temple, everything in the walls of these structures pointed to the future slaying of the Lord Jesus Christ on the cross, and God's complete way to the salvation of man. Christ did everything that was required by God for the redemption of man. That satisfaction of the God's holy nature and law of man's sin were paid for by the blood of Christ. This is known in scripture as **propitiation.**

Doctrine of Reconciliation:

Reconciliation is the removal, by the death of Christ for man's obstacles of righteousness which man's sin had set up between God and man. Man through Christ can have a relationship with God.

Doctrine of Justification:

Justification is an English legal term which mean "Just as though you never sinned." It was the best word the could use to explain the plan of the actual conferring of the gift of righteousness upon all who by faith believe, without any distinction. It is a change of a sinner's standing before God from one of condemnation to one of righteousness. In other words it is being righteousified.

Doctrine of Redemption:

Redemption is the buying back of the soul of man through the blood of Jesus Christ from sin. *"To* **redeem** *them that were under the law, that we might receive the adoption of sons."* **Galatians 4:5** *"Who gave himself for us, that he might* **redeem** *us from all iniquity, and purify unto himself a peculiar people, zealous of good works."* **Titus 2:14** Man was made out of the dust of the earth with dominion over all the earth. After Adam and Eve's sin, God lost us to Satan, prince of the world, but on the cross Jesus paid the redemption price to bring us back to himself.

Forgiveness of Sin:

Jesus took on the wrath of God upon the sin of man on the cross, paying the penalty for sin for all on mankind. Man has forgiveness of sin forever. No more would man be responsible for his sin. Man would still be responsible for his unbelief in refusing to accept God's gift of Salvation. *"As far as the east is from the west, so far hath he removed our transgressions from us."* **Psalms 103:12** Start walking east and you can walk for eternity and you will never find the west. God has promised to never to remember our sins. *"For I will be merciful to their unrighteousness, and their sins and their iniquities will I remember no more."* **Hebrews 8:12** Our sins are buried in the sea of God's forgiveness.

Doctrine of Remission of Sins:

God has Removed the transgression from the sinner, so that for all time and eternity his sin shall not be upon him.

Doctrine of Incorporation:

We were united with Christ on the cross by God's sovereign act. We are crucified with Christ, buried with him, and will arise with him. "Therefore, having been **justified by faith,** we have **peace with God through our Lord Jesus Christ,** through whom also we have access by faith into this grace in which we stand, and rejoice in hope of the glory of God." **Romans 5:1-2.**

Doctrine of In Habitation:

The fact that the Body of Christ and each member individually is inhabited or indwelt by the Holy Spirit. Many times we forget we are indwelt by God the Holy Spirit. He is always there whether we close to Him or far away. God personally sealed the Holy Spirit within us. The seal of God cannot be broken.

To write all that God has done for us would take a life time. Each day we see more and more what Christ is doing in our lives. He is the one who hears our prayers, he is our attorney when Satan accuses us before God. As the hymn tells us, "The **love of God is** greater far than tongue or pen can ever tell. It goes beyond the high star, and reaches to the lowest hell. The guilty pair, bow down with care, **God gave his Son to win, his erring child He reconciled and pardon from his sin. Oh, love of God how rich, how pure, how measureless and strong, it shall for ever move endure,** the saint's God great song." Praise God.

Doctrine of Mercy:

Mercy is withheld justice. The Law of Moses called for the death of David by for his adultery with Bathsheba and killing her husband. This was the Law given by God to Moses. David knew that was his fate. He would have to be stoned to death. David appealed to God to blot out the sin from God's record.

God did what he asked. David received mercy. David cried to God, *"Have mercy upon me, O God, according to thy loving kindness: according unto the* **multitude of thy tender mercies** *blot out my transgressions. Wash me thoroughly from mine iniquity, and cleanse me from my sin. For I acknowledge my transgressions: and my sin is ever before me. Against thee, thee only, have I sinned, and done this evil in thy sight: that thou mightest be justified when thou spoke, and be clear when thou judges."* **Psalm 51:1-4**

In other Psalms David pleads for God's mercy. Return, O LORD, deliver my soul: oh save me for thy **mercies'** sake. Remember, O LORD, thy tender **mercies** and thy loving kindnesses; for they have been ever of old. Make thy face to shine upon thy servant: save me for thy **mercies'** sake. Make thy face to shine upon thy servant: save me for thy **mercies'** sake. Praise God for Mercy.

twenty five

Paul and His Love for the Jews

Paul the apostle to the Gentiles could not forget his love for his own people Israel. He would give up his own salvation to everlasting punishment for the salvation of Israel. This would be impossible, but that was a desire of the Apostle Paul. In writing his epistle to the Romans he had to stop in the middle of writing to tell about his beloved Israel. Romans nine, ten, and eleven are his expressed love for Israel. He opens chapter nine with his sorrowful heart toward his native people Israel. "I say the truth in Christ, I lie not, my conscience also bearing me witness in the Holy Ghost, That I have **great heaviness** and **continual sorrow** in my heart. **For I could wish that myself were accursed from Christ for my brethren, my kinsmen according to the flesh:** Who are Israelites; to whom pertains the adoption, and the glory, and the covenants, and the giving of the law, and the service of God, and the promises; Whose are the fathers, and of whom as concerning the flesh Christ came, who is over all, God blessed for ever. Amen." **Romans 9:1-6**

Not all of the children of Abraham were given the promises that God gave Abraham. Only in Isaac did the covenant of God to Abraham continue. Ishmael and the the sons of Keturah were given a gift from Abraham and sent to the east wilderness of Arabia. Isaac had twin boy. The covenant of God to Abraham was passed down to Isaac and Esau, but the eldest of the twins was to be the heir of the covenant. But it was written, Jacob have I loved, but Esau have I hated. Was God unrighteous for choosing Jacob over Esau. But God had said to Moses, "I will have mercy on whom I will have mercy, and I will have compassion on whom I will have compassion." From Jacob came the twelve patriots. From these three came all the descendant of Jacob who would receive the covenant promises God gave to Abraham, Isaac, and Jacob. From outside the covenant all men were without God. "That at that time ye were **without Christ**, being **aliens** from the commonwealth of Israel, and strangers from the covenants of promise, **having no hope, and without God in the world**." **Ephesians 2:12**

Paul in Romans nine refers to the prophet Hosea. *"And I will sow her unto me in the earth; and I will have mercy upon her that had not obtained mercy; and I will say to them which were not my people,* (the Gentiles who accept the message of salvation) *Thou art my people; and they shall say, Thou art my God."* **Hosea 2:23** But God has not turned his back on Israel forever. Paul quotes from the book of Isaiah giving hope to Israel. *"Isaiah also cried concerning Israel, Though the number of the children of Israel be as the sand of the sea, a remnant shall be saved: For he will finish the work, and cut it short in righteousness: because a short work will the Lord make upon the earth. And as Isaiah said before, Except the Lord of Sabbath had left us a seed, we had been as Sodom, and been made like unto Gomorrah."* **Romans 9:27-29** Since Abraham was called by God, God had always had his remnant that kept faith in God. When Elijah was alone depressed believing he was the only one left that served God. God answered him saying, *"Yet I have left me seven thousand in Israel, all the knees which have not bowed unto Baal, and every mouth which hath not kissed him."* **1 Kings 19:18**

Paul's prayer and heart's desire is that all Israel to be saved. The religious leaders of Israel had a zeal for God, but not according to the knowledge of the Old Testament's promises. They did not know God's righteousness and went about to establish their own righteousness. God told Israel in the Torah of Moses, "But the word is very nigh unto thee, in thy mouth, and in thy heart, that thou may do it." **Deuteronomy 10:30** It was the word of faith which they stumbled over and establishing their own righteousness. *"**That if thou shalt confess with thy mouth the Lord Jesus, and shalt believe in thine heart that God hath raised him from the dead, thou shalt be saved.** For with the heart man believeth unto righteousness; and with the mouth confession is made unto salvation. For the scripture saith, Whosoever believeth on him shall not be ashamed. For there is no difference between the Jew and the Greek (Gentiles): for the same Lord over all is rich unto all that call upon him."* **Romans 10:9-12.** Salvation was always available to the Jews. Even though Paul was the Apostle to the Gentiles he was also called to preach to the Jews. When going into a city, Paul always went to the synagogues first before going to the Gentiles.

Paul closes these three chapters in Romans giving a prophesy as to the future of Israel. God has always loved the apple of his eye. *"For thus saith the Lord of hosts; After the glory hath he sent me unto the nations which spoiled you: for he that touches you touches the apple of his eye"* **Zechariah 2:8.**

His love for Israel is everlasting. As God had said to Elijah, *"I have reserved to myself seven thousand men, who have not bowed the knee to the image of Baal.* **Even so then at this present time also there is a remnant according to the election of grace."** **Romans 11:4-5.** There has always been a remnant of Israel who know God. Paul then tell makes the redeeming statement about God's mercy on Israel. *"And* **so all Israel shall be saved:** *as it is written,* **There shall come out of Zion the Deliverer, and shall turn away ungodliness from Jacob:** *For this is my covenant unto them, when* **I shall take away their sins.** *As concerning the gospel, they are enemies for your sakes: but as touching the election, they are beloved for the father's sakes.* **For the gifts and calling of God are without repentance.** *For as ye in times past have not believed God, yet have now* **obtained mercy** *through their unbelief: Even so have these also now not believed, that through your mercy they also may obtain mercy. For God hath concluded them all in unbelief, that he might have mercy upon all."* **Romans 11:25-32**

Two years after the death of Paul in 70AD, Jerusalem was destroyed by The Roman army, led by the future Emperor Titus, with Tiberius Alexander as his second-in-command, besieged and conquered the city of Jerusalem which had been occupied by it's Jewish defenders in 66 AD. The siege ended with the sacking of the city and the destruction of its famous Second Temple. The destruction of both the first and second temples are still mourned annually as the Jewish feast of Tisha B'Av. The Arch of Titus celebrating the Roman sack of Jerusalem and the Temple, still stands in Rome.

The people of Jerusalem were almost all massacred and the ones who survived were taken captured by the Romans and were scattered throughout the Roman Empire. The temple was so destroyed that the Romans filled the temple site with dirt and planted vegetation over the site. The cities of Israel were destroyed and the promised land that flowed with milk and honey became desolate for the next 1900 years. Earthquakes shook the land frequently, the early and later rains stopped, and what little rain that came ended in swamps filled with mosquitoes that carried many diseases. Mark Twain on his trip to Europe and Africa in 1867 traveled through the land and called it the most desolate land in the world. He said of the land of Israel, "A desolate country whose soil is rich enough, but is given over wholly to weeds… a silent mournful expanse…. a desolation…. we never saw a human being on the whole route…. hardly a tree or shrub anywhere. Even the olive tree and the cactus, those fast friends of a worthless soil, had almost deserted the country." "A fast walker could go outside the walls of Jerusalem and walk entirely around the city in an hour. I do not know how else to make one understand how small it is." "The mighty Mosque of Omar, and the paved court around it, occupy a fourth part of Jerusalem. They are upon Mount Moriah, where King Solomon's Temple stood. This Mosque is the holiest place the Mohammedan knows, outside of Mecca. Up to within a year or two past, no christian could gain admission to it or its court for love or money. But the prohibition has been removed, and we entered freely for baksheesh."

Jesus had told his disciples that the Temple would be destroyed. *"And Jesus went out, and departed from the temple; and his disciples came to him for to shew him the buildings of the temple. And Jesus said unto them, See ye not all these things? verily I say unto you, There shall not be left here* **one stone upon another, that shall not be thrown down."** Matthew 24:1-2.

God had warned Israel if they did not follow in his ways he would scatter the people throughout the world. With that warning also came the promise he would gather them back into their own land. *"And I will bring you out from the people, and will* **gather** *you out of the countries wherein ye are* **scattered***, with a mighty hand, and with a stretched out arm, and with fury poured out."* **Ezekiel 20:34.** *"I will accept you with your sweet savor, when I bring you out from the people, and* **gather** *you out of the countries wherein ye have been* **scattered***; and I will be sanctified in you before the heathen."* **Ezekiel 20:41.** "Thus saith the Lord GOD; When I shall have **gathered** the house of Israel from the people among whom they are **scattered**, and shall be sanctified in them in the sight of the heathen, then shall they dwell in their land that I have given to my servant Jacob." **Ezekiel 28:25.**

twenty six

Did The Church Replace Israel

The interest in the movement for a homeland for the Jews in Palestine was supported by the Evangelical Churches. The Roman Catholic and the Reformation Churches did not support the movement. Their theology taught that God had replaced Israel with the church. That meant that all the promises of Abraham, Isaac, and Jacob became the promises to the church. It all started with Origen Adamantius.

Origen Adamantius was an early theologian who lived from 184 AD to 254AD. He was from Alexandria, Egypt and was a very respectable theologian. He brought into the church theology the concept of infant baptism and replacement theology. It was accepted by the Roman Catholic church and Martin Luther brought these doctrines into the Reformation. The concept of replacement has to do with the future of Israel. Replacement Theology - reduced to its simplest form - teaches that the Church has replaced Israel in God's plan. The term "Replacement Theology" is relatively new and unfamiliar to many people **(in some cases, even those who believe in it).** The Church "supersedes" Israel. Its proponents teach that God has set aside Israel and made the Church "new Israel," the new and improved people of God.

Replacement Theology is closely associated with Reformed (or Covenant) Theology, the brand of theology historically linked to John Calvin (1509-1564) and the Protestant Reformation. Reformed/Covenant Theology, in turn, is closely associated with amillennialism, an eschatological view with a spiritualized (rather than literal-historical) interpretation of the prophetic Scriptures. The natural affinity these views (that is, Replacement Theology and amillennialism) seem to have for each other is understandable because Replacement

Theology relies so heavily on a non-literal and allegorical interpretation of the biblical promises to Israel.

Although many of the early Reformers and Puritans - including even Calvin himself - wrote about the nation of Israel one day being restored by the grace of God and experiencing a national regeneration, that is an increasingly marginalized, **minority view in Reformed Christianity today** (which is ironic, since we have seen the amazing rebirth of the nation of Israel, just as the Word of God predicted!). And even among those who allow for an end-time work of the Spirit of God among the Jewish people, there is still a reluctance to acknowledge that God is not finished with His people Israel as a nation, or to acknowledge the prospect of a future Kingdom on the Earth.

This view stands in contrast to the teachings of Dispensational Premillennialism, which affirms the **continuing role that Israel plays** (in tandem with the Church) **in the outworking of God's plan of redemption.** These views are held by most evangelical Churches. D. L. Moody and William E. Blackstone were leaders in America supporting the Zionist Movement and calling for the a homeland for the Jews. The American evangelicals have always been in the forefront in support of Israel after the nation was founded in 1948.

The incredible irony here is that only a few centuries earlier, the Church had been almost exclusively Jewish! The Messiah was Jewish; the writers of the Bible were Jewish; the apostles were Jewish; the earliest Christians were Jewish; the first congregation was Jewish (located in Jerusalem); and the first missionaries were Jewish! Another incredible fact is that the first church where believers in Christ were first called Christians, was the Jewish church in Antioch.

In fact, a council of Church leaders - including Paul, Barnabas, Peter and James - was convened at Jerusalem (Acts 15) so the leaders of the new and growing Messianic Movement (known first as "the sect of the Nazarenes," Acts 24:5) could decide upon what conditions non-Jews would be admitted into the fellowship with the saints! But here, within just a few generations, the shoe was already on the other foot! Gentile believers were in control of the Church now. Jewish doctrines (the earthly Kingdom in particular) were considered erroneous and even seditious. And non-Jewish, Gentile, Church leaders were laying down the terms for Jewish believers in Jesus Christ who wished to be baptized.

Israel will be saved in the same way believers from all ages and generations have been saved; that is, they will be saved by grace, through faith

(See Ephesians 2:8-10). The problem with saying that God rejected His people Israel is that the term "rejection" implies permanence and finality. Paul's forceful statements in **Romans 11:1,** *"I say then, Hath God cast away his people? God forbid."* probably indicate that people were claiming, even in his day, that God had "cast away" His people Israel. They were saying that Israel had "stumbled' and "fallen" from her former position **(See Romans 11:11-12)**. Paul rejected any such notion ("**God Forbid**" in verses 1 and 11). Then he goes on to say that even if we insist on saying that they were rejected, then we are forced to the conclusion that the rejection is only temporary. Even if we insist on saying that they did stumble and fall, then it must also be said that their fall brought salvation to the rest of the world (Gentiles) - and Israel's fall, too, is only temporary because they are destined to be restored one day to a position of "fullness" **(See Romans 11:12)**.

The **"fullness of the Gentiles"** (Romans 11:25) refers to the time when the full number of Gentile believers has been added to the Church and the last person has come to salvation. Likewise, the "fullness" of the Jewish people **(Romans 11:12)** refers to the time when "**all Israel shall be saved**" **(Romans 11:26)**. As we saw earlier, that means the Jewish people in whole will recognize and receive their Messiah, Jesus of Nazareth.

The truth is that God is no more finished with Israel than He is finished with the Gentiles. Neither one has been replaced by the other; and God's plan for both remains intact, in spite of their failures. This is really the crux of the issue. Replacement Theology says that Israel was rejected by God and that the rejection was permanent and irrevocable; however, we say that God's calling on Israel was permanent and irrevocable, in spite of her many sins and shortcomings **(See Romans 11:29.)**

Is Replacement Theology really worth arguing about? Or is this discussion much ado about nothing? **One reason it's important is to call attention to questionable theology,** no matter how deeply entrenched it may be in traditional Christianity is that sooner or later, bad theology always leads to bad practice - and in this case, it already has! Replacement Theology has provided the basis for all sorts of mischief, persecution, and atrocities against the Jewish people throughout Christian history.

For example, Martin Luther, the father of the Protestant Reformation, accepted the Replacement Theology that started in the Roman Catholic Church which that was started by Origen. Near the end of his life, he said that synagogues and Jewish schools should be burned to the ground, Jewish people run out of their homes, their prayer books and Talmudic writings burned, and the rabbis forbidden to preach or teach on penalty of death. Luther also declared that Jewish people in Germany should be confined to their own homes and neighborhoods. This plan the Nazis implemented literally when they quarantined Jewish families in ghettos in Poland and other places before shipping them to the death camps for extermination. One historian writes: It is difficult to understand the behavior of most German Protestants in the first Nazi years unless one is aware of two things: their history and the influence of Martin Luther. The great founder of Protestantism was both a passionate anti-Semite and a ferocious believer in absolute obedience to political authority. He wanted Germany rid of the Jews. Luther's advice was literally followed four centuries later by Hitler, Goering, and Himmler (William L. Shirer, *The Rise and Fall of the Third Reich* [New York: Simon & Shuster, 1960], p. 236).

No one is suggesting that anyone who believes in Replacement Theology is an anti-Semite or would agree with Luther's statements. But it is an incontestable fact that ideas similar to those of Replacement Theology have inspired some horrible atrocities against the Jewish people.

The trend in America away from the Replacement Theology was in 1820's under the preaching of Charles Finney and shook the church in America. This was follow by in the end of the nineteenth century with the preaching of D. L. Moody and William E. Blackstone with hundreds of other lessor known preachers focusing on the second coming of Christ, the rapture of the church, the seven year tribulation and the rebirth of the nation of Israel. This teaching of Moody and Blackstone and many other preachers were known as premillennialism. The belief was based on the fact that God would restore Israel as a nation before the second coming of Christ.

At the same time Europe was blaming all the wrongs of Europe on the Jews. In 1727 Queen Catherine of Russia banned all Jews from Russia. In Poland the Jews were partitioned in one area of Warsaw know as the ghetto. The Russian Jews then were sent to the cold western part of Russia known as Siberia. Starting in 1881 at the time of Moody and Blackstone, supported a homeland for the Jews in Palestine, the Russian pogroms (an organized massacre) often officially encouraged massacre or persecution of a minority group, especially one conducted against Jews. This pogroms in Russia started a migration of Jews from Russia to come to America. The Zionist organization had bought much of the desolate land in Palestine, and the Russia Jews left Russia for Palestine living on the land bought by the Zionist Movement.

In the early twentieth century there was a growth in the evangelism and a more aggressive preaching about the belief of the second coming of Christ, the rapture of the church, the seven year tribulation and the rebirth of the nation of Israel. Also, the Evangelicals became more aggressive in sharing and promoting the good news. In this sense, an evangelical Christian is a believer who holds to the inspiration, inerrancy, and authority of Scripture, the Trinity, the deity of Christ, and salvation by grace through faith alone.

The evangelicals encouraged the government to allow the Jews to come to America. Today in America there are as many Jews as there are Jews in Israel. America has welcomed the Jews and have treated them the same as any other ethnic group. They have been able to prosper in American and been a great asset to our nation.

The Orthodox Church in America and the Roman Catholic church have not changed their stand on Replacement Theology. The replacement theology is believed by seventy to eighty percent of the American church. The thirty percent that are evangelicals have lead the nation in recognizing the nation of Israel as a fulfillment of prophesy in the Bible. Their influence in the political field has kept the government in support of Israel as a nation.

Some say the returning people to Israel are not really the children of Abraham, Isaac, and Jacob. They say they are Gentiles that said they were Jews to further their political, religious, and economic position. If this were true, why would these false Jews suffer the pogrom, life in the Polish ghetto, and the holocaust? Why would they practice circumcision to show they were Jews when they could say, "We are not Jews at all but have used the name of Jews for our own advantage." These Jews who are returning to Israel are the same people who suffered the pogroms, ghettos, and the furnaces of Hitler. And why would they be hated so much by the Arabs if they were not real Jews. It does not make sense.

Today there is a nation of Israel. It will be there when Christ returns to **Zion.** There and them all Israel will know that the Jesus of Nazareth was truly the Messiah.

twenty seven

Israel A New Beginning

In the 1740's the Great Awaking sparked by the preaching of Jonathan Edwards, spread through our nation. A Second Awaking began in 1820 under the leadership of Charles Finney. It was a shock to the churches of America. Under Finney's leadership the church started to focus on the second coming of Jesus Christ. Along with the interest in the second coming of Christ came an interest in the rebirth of the Nation of Israel. Powerful evangelist like D. L. Moody and William E. Blackstone were proclaiming this message. Russian Jews were pouring into America touching the hearts of many Americans Christians. They provided the new Jews from Russia with food, clothing, and medical attention. Blackstone started a movement throughout America promoting a Jewish homeland in Palestine. Also supporting Blackstone for a homeland for the Jews were D. L. Moody and T. DeWitt Talmage. Many other political and business leaders followed including the Mayors of Chicago, Baltimore, New York, and Boston. Many senators, representatives, and government leaders followed including B. F Jacobs of the Security and Stock Exchange and Cyrus McCormick of McCormick Harvester Company.

America has been a haven for the Jewish people. The first Jewish people came to America in 1654. They were welcomed to America and fought in the Revolutionary War on the side of America. In 1881 Czar Alexander II of Russia was assassinated. The Russian Government blamed the Jews for his death. The terrible pogrom in 1881 resulted in the murder of hundred of Jews with thousands injured, and their homes and property destroyed. The Jews wanted to leave Russia and knew of the haven that America provided for them. In 1877, there were two hundred and fifty thousand Jews in America. Thirty years later, the population grew to three million. Today there are nearly seven million Jews in America and nearly seven million in Israel. It is estimated there are another seven million still scattered throughout the rest of the world.

Since the beginning of the Twentieth Century the world has seen the regathering of Israel. There were Jew leaders who called for the return of the Jews to Palestine for decades before Theodor Herzl (1860-1904) wrote his influential pamphlet, "The Jewish State." But Herzl's work pushed the formation of a political movement to establish a Jewish homeland in Palestine. The first Zionist Congress, convened by Herzl, was held in Basel, Switzerland, in 1897.

The American Jewish community became part of the Zionist Congress in 1897. The Zionists starting buying the desolate land which was once called Israel from the government of Turkey. Slowly some of the Jews from Russia went back to the promised land. It was rough going with many dying of sickness caused by the mosquitoes in the swamps. They made water reservoirs out of the swamps and used the water in the reservoirs to irrigate the land. As more Jews came back to what was once the land of Israel the early and later rains once again watered the barren land. With more Jews coming each year the population became larger and larger. After World War II the Jewish refugees in Europe went there too.

On November 2, 1917, during World War I, Lord Arthur Balfour, the British Foreign Secretary declared the "The Balfour Declaration," it was a 67-word declaration contained within a brief letter recognizing the establishment of a Jewish homeland in Palestine. The declaration statement read as follows:

"His Majesty's Government view with favor the establishment in Palestine of a national home for the Jewish people, and will use their best endeavors to facilitate the achievement of this object, it being clearly understood that nothing shall be done which may prejudice the civil and religious rights of existing non-Jewish communities in Palestine, or the rights and political status enjoyed by Jews in any other country."

Before World War I there was just a trickle of Jews returning to Israel. The freedom that America was giving to the Jews and the opportunity for the Jews in America was too tempting to migrate to America rather than the desolate land of Palestine. The Zionists were buying what ever land they could in Palestine from the Turks.

In 1914 World War I started. In 1917 it was apparent that the Allied Nations were winning the war. The British defeated the Turks and ended the Ottoman Empire. In the middle of the fifteenth century, the Ottoman Empire was established as a world empire. It went up to the southern border of the Holy Roman Empire, most of the Mideast Islamic nations and northern Africa. On December 9, 1917 British General Edmund Allenby captured Jerusalem. The Turks left without firing a shot. After almost six hundred years Palestine was free from Islamic rule.

After World War I, the League of Nations placed the British government in charge of Palestine. The Arab nations tried to restrict Jewish emigration. There were riots in many of the cities of Palestine against the immigration of the Jews. The Arabs massacred many of the Jews in Palestine. In Hebron alone they killed every Jew living there. The pressure of the Arab people forced the British to reduce the land designated by the League of Nations to just the land West of the Jordan River and create the new nation of Trans-Jordan which in now the nation of Jordan.

As mentioned before, few Jews came to Palestine between World War I and World War II. Jews from Russia went back to the promised land. It was rough going with many dying of sickness caused by the mosquitoes in the swamps. They made water reservoirs out of the swamps and used the water in the reservoirs to irrigate the land. As more Jews came back to what was once the land of Israel the early and later rain once again watered the barren land.

World War II was the main factor that would send the Jews back to Palestine and provide the rebirth of the nation of Israel. The Holocaust drove many of the Jewish survivors out of Europe and into Palestine. By 1948, there were six hundred thousand Jews living in Palestine. World War II had prepared the hearts of the European Jews the desire to migrate to Palestine and established a new nation there. With the killing of six million Jews by Hitler and his henchmen, the Nazis were not able stop the rebirth of Israel.

In 1948 one of the first things (but one of the few things the UN did right) the United Nations did was to accept Israel as a nation. Russia soon recognized Israel as a nation. President Harry Truman's advisers were all against the recognition Israel as a nation. President Truman did not know which way to go with most in his cabinet and his advisers as they were not in favor of new nation Israel. One night President Truman remembered this mother telling him that someday he would do something great. Being a God fearing family, his mother's statement came to his mind. Knowing the scriptures regarding Israel, President Truman went against his cabinet and advisers and recognized Israel as a nation. On May, 14, 1948 Israel became a nation with a government and borders.

When President Truman received the document for the recognition at that time, it did not have a name for the new nation. The provisional government of Israel could not decide what that name of the new nation should be. There was a debate over the name for the new nation. They had to choose between the nation of Judah or the nation of Israel. "Israel" was the name they chose for the new nation. On the document Truman received called it the "new Jewish state." Truman crossed out the word "the new Jewish state" and wrote in long hand "State of Israel."

The document then read as follows: "This government has been informed that a Jewish state has been proclaimed in Palestine, and recognition has been requested by the provisional (the word provisional was written in long hand by Truman) government thereof. The United State recognizes the provisional government as the de facto authority of the new nation of Israel. It was signed by Harry Truman and dated by his hand writing. "Approved May 14, 1948."

With the announcement of the new Israeli state, the Arab nations sur-rounding Israel pledged to destroy the new Jewish state. They were ready to drive this new nation into the Mediterranean Sea. The1948 Arab–Israeli War was fought between the the nation of Israel and a military coalition of Arab states consisting of Egypt, Syria, Iraq, Saudi Arabia and the Arab forces inside Israel.

The war was preceded by a period of civil war in the territory between Jewish forces and Palestinian Arab forces in response to the United Nation Partition Plan. An alliance of Arab states intervened on the Palestinian side, turning the civil war into a war between sovereign states. The fighting took place mostly on the former territory of the British Mandate and for a short time also in the Sinai Peninsula and southern Lebanon.

As a result of the war, the nation of Israel kept nearly all the area that had been recommended by the the United Nation Resolution 181 and took control of almost sixty percent of the area allocated to the proposed Arab state, includ-ing the Jaffa, Lydda, and Ramle area; Galilee part of the Negev Desert, and some territories in the West Bank. Trans-Jordan took control of the remainder of the West Bank and East-Jerusalem, putting it under military rule and the Egyptians took control of the Gaza Strip. No Arab Palestinian state was created in the Armistice agreement that was signed between all belligerents except Iraqis and Palestinians.

Important demographic changes occurred in the country. Between six hundred thousand and seven hundred sixty thousand Palestinian Arabs fled or were expelled from the area that became Israel and became Palestinian refugees. On the other hand, around ten thousand Jews were forced to leave their homes in Palestine. The war and the creation of Israel also triggered the Jewish exodus from Arab lands. In the three years following the war, about seven hundred thousand Jews immigrated to Israel.

As the new nation was formed, there was a need for a state language. Jews from all the countries they were scattered, spoke a different language or dialect. To correct this problem they called on Eliezer Ben-Yehuda. The Old Testament prophesied about this problem. *"For then will I turn to the people a* **pure language,** *that they may all call upon the name of the* LORD, *to serve him with one consent."* **Zephaniah 3:9.** Hebrew is an ancient Semitic language. The earliest Hebrew texts date from the second millennium B.C. and evidence suggests that the Israelite tribes who invaded Canaan spoke Hebrew. The language was likely a commonly spoken dialect until the fall of Jerusalem in 587 B.C.

The Jews were in Babylonian captivity for seventy years. After the captivity, most of the Jews were settled in Babylon and were speaking the language of the Babylonians. When Nehemiah lead the return to Israel only forty-two thousand of the Jews went with him. The vast majority stayed in Babylon. Once Jews were exiled, Hebrew began to disappear as a spoken language, though it was still preserved as a written language for Jewish prayers and holy texts. After their return to Israel, Hebrew was most likely used only for liturgical purposes. The priests and religious leaders still knew the Hebrew language. But they found the people did not understand it. When a priest would read the Torah, another priest would interpret what was said in Arabic. Up until a century ago Hebrew was not a spoken language. Jewish communities generally spoke Yiddish, a combination of both Hebrew and German. The Spanish Jews spoke Ladino and a combination of Hebrew and Spanish. Of course, Jewish communities also spoke the native language of whatever countries they were living in. Jews still used Hebrew (and Aramaic) during prayer services, although Hebrew was not used in everyday conversation.

That all changed when Eliezer Ben-Yehuda made it his personal mission to revive Hebrew as a spoken language. He believed it was important for the Jewish people to have their own language if they were to have their own land. In 1880 he said: "in order to have our own land and political life... we must have a Hebrew language in which we can conduct the business of life."

Ben-Yehuda had studied Hebrew while a Yeshiva student and was naturally talented with languages. When his family moved to Palestine, they decided that only Hebrew would be spoken in their home. It was a difficult task, since Hebrew was an ancient language that lacked words for modern things like "coffee" or "newspaper." Ben-Yehuda set about creating hundreds of new words using the roots of biblical Hebrew words as a starting point. Eventually he published a modern dictionary of the Hebrew language that became the basis of the Hebrew language today. Ben-Yehuda is often referred to as the father of modern Hebrew. Today Hebrew is the official spoken language of the State of Israel. It is also common for Jews living outside Israel (in the Diaspora) to study Hebrew as part of their religious upbringing. Yiddish (meaning "Jewish") is a Jewish hybrid language that has been spoken by Jews from eastern and central Europe since the Middle Ages. Today Yiddish is spoken by about four million Jews, located primarily in Argentina, Canada, France, Israel, Mexico, Romania, and the United States. In the late 20th century, a Russian-Yiddish dictionary and a few novels in Yiddish were published by Russian Jews. In Israel, Yiddish is a second language to Hebrew and is cultivated mostly by older Israelis who have an eastern European background.

Ben-Yehuda set up schools to teach the Hebrew language. Every new immigrant that came to Israel had to go to Hebrew school to learn the Hebrew language. Because of this one man's vision the prophesy of **Zephaniah was fulfilled,** *"For then will I turn to the people a* **pure language,** *that they may all call upon the name of the* LORD, *to serve him with one consent ."*

twenty eight

Israel Arab Wars

After the 1948 war with its Arab neighbors no major war between the Jews and Arabs until 1967. The 1967 War would be known as the Six Day War. Egypt and Syria mobilized their troops and planned an attack on Israel from the north and from the south. Saudi Arabia kept out of this war. The Egyptian army went north across the Sinai heading for Israel's south border. There were United Nation's peacekeepers in the Sinai and Egypt demanded that they leave. Egypt closed Israel's port on the Gulf of Aqaba which cut off Israel's trade to the orient.

On June 5, the Israel army did an air attack on both Egypt and Syria crushing both invading armies. In five days the armies of Egypt and Syria were defeated. The war began on June 5 with Israel launching surprise bombing raids against Egyptian air-fields after a period of high tension that included an Israeli raid into the Jordanian-controlled West Bank. Israel initiated aerial clashes over Syrian territory. Syrian artillery then attacks against Israeli settlements in the vicinity of the border followed by Israeli response against Syrian positions in the Golan Heights and encroachments of increasing intensity and frequency (initiated by Israel) into the demilitarized zones along the Syrian border. The war culminating in the Egyptian imposition of a naval blockade on Eilat and ordering of the evacuation from the Sinai Peninsula of the U.N. buffer force. On the last day of the war Jordan got into the war. The next day Jordan lost Jerusalem and the West Bank.

Within six days, Israel had won a decisive land war. Israeli forces had taken control of the Gaza Strip and the Sinai Peninsula from Egypt, the West Bank, the Golan Height and East Jerusalem from Syria and Jordan. Today these territories are still in dispute and the cause of much of the tension in the Middle

East. When the war ended, Israel gave back to Egypt part of the Sinai and gave some land back to Syria but not the Golan Heights. Jordan was able to take control of the Dome of the Rock site on the mount of Zion. But Israel had gained the Golan Heights which gave Israel safety. Israel moved into the West Bank. After many years Israel gave the Gaza Strip control to the "so called" Palestine State.

Dispute over these territories between Israel and the Arab nation did not stop. In 1973, Egypt and Syria attacked Israel during the Jewish Holiday of Yom Kippur.. Israel was not ready for the attack. **Yom Kippur,** also known as **Day of Atonement**, is the holiest day of the year for the Jewish people. Its central themes are atonement and repentance. Jewish people traditionally observe this holy day with a period of fasting and intensive prayer, often spending most of the day in synagogue services. Yom Kippur completes the annual period known in Judaism as the High Holy Days or the Days of Awe.

The attack, known as the Yom Kippur War, was a complete surprise to Israel. Israel was nearly defeated. But Israel began a powerful counterattack. Egyptian and Syrian forces crossed ceasefire lines to enter the Israeli-held Sinai Peninsula and the Golan Heights respectively, which had been captured and occupied since the 1967 Six Day War. Both the United States and the Soviet Union initiated massive resupply efforts to their respective allies during the war, and this led to a near-confrontation between the two nuclear superpowers.

The war began with a massive and successful Egyptian crossing of the Suez Canal. After crossing the cease-fire lines, Egyptian forces advanced virtually unopposed into the Sinai Peninsula. After three days, Israel had mobilized most of its forces and managed to halt the Egyptian offensive, settling into a stalemate. The Syrians coordinated their attack on the Golan Heights to coincide with the Egyptian offensive and initially made threatening gains into Israeli-held territory. Within three days, however, Israeli forces had managed to push the Syrians back to the pre-war ceasefire lines. They then launched a four-day counter-offensive deep into Syria. Within a week, Israeli artillery began to shell the outskirts of Damascus. As Sadat began to worry about the integrity of his major ally, he believed that capturing two strategic passes located deep in the Sinai would make his position stronger during the negotiations. He therefore ordered the Egyptians to go back on the offensive, but the attack was quickly repulsed. The Israelis then counterattacked at the seam between the two Egyptian armies, crossed the Suez Canal into Egypt, and began slowly advancing southward and westward during a week of heavy fighting which inflicted heavy casualties on both sides.

By October 24, the Israelis had improved their positions considerably and completed their encirclement of Egypt's Third Army and the city of Suez. The Camp David Accords that followed led to the return of the Sinai to Egypt and normalized relations—the first peaceful recognition of Israel by an Arab country. This new peace treaty lasted for thirty years. The Arab nations with a population of nearly one hundred sixty million came against Israel with a population about five million. The odds were overwhelmingly against Israel. But in six days they had the Arab nations on their knees.

Israel is there to stay. God was the one who scattered them throughout the nation and He is the one who is gathering them from all the nations back to the promised land. Since the Yom Kippur War, the nations of the world along with the United Nations have been concerned about the land taken by Israel during these wars. The United Nations has been against Israel's right to the Golan Height, the West Bank and East Jerusalem. Just as the prophet Zechariah wrote, *"And in that day will I make **Jerusalem** a **burdensome stone for all people:** all that burden themselves with it shall be cut in pieces, though all the people of the earth be gathered together against it."* **Zechariah 12:3**

The nations of the world have a continued need for oil for their energy. The Mideast Nations have control of one third of the world's oil supply. The nations of the world do not want this supply cut off. So, the nations of the world to please the Arab oil nations have been pushing Israel to go back to the borders prior to the Six Day War. Since the beginning of the Nation of Israel in 1948, Jerusalem has been a burdensome stone on the nations of the world as told by the scriptures.

twenty nine

The Burdensome Stone

The gathering the descendants of Abraham, Isaac, and Jacob started in 1880 with the creation of the Zionist Movement. It is not finished as it continues on today. It started with the Russian Jews trickling back to the desolate land of Palestine. They drained the swamps and made water reservoirs to provide water to grow crops in formerly fertile land that laid desolate for nearly nineteen hundred years. It was hard for the early settlers. The lack of water and disease carried by the mosquitoes took the lives of many at that time. But as they worked, the early and later rains started to return to the land.

Then came World War I and the Lord Balfour Declaration to make a homeland for the Jewish people. World War I prepared the land for the return of the descendents of Israel. After World War I more Jews came to Palestine. The period between World War I and World War II brought tension between the returning Jews and the Arabs. As the Jews became successful in the tilling of the land many poor Arabs came to work for the Jewish farmers.

World War II made a big difference in God fulfilling his covenant with the children of Israel. The Nazi Holocaust set the events for a massive return of the Jews to their homeland. Six million Jews were killed during Nazi Holocaust. After the war, the Arab land which was controlled by the Ottoman Empire was divided by the British. The Jewish people were to get all of the land that is now Jordan to the Mediterranean Sea. The Arab people protested leaving the land West of the Jordan River to Israel except the West Bank. The land given to Israel had to be shared with the Arabs living there.

The nation of Israel after the 1967 Six Day War made Jerusalem its capital. This act made Jerusalem a burdensome stone for the Nations of the world. Most religions of the world including most of Christendom do not recognize

God's everlasting covenant to Israel. In Christendom, most believe that the covenant was given to Christendom because of the failure of the Jews to recognize Jesus as their Messiah.

God is using the return of the children of Israel to the promised land to show His word is literal and true. The rebirth of Israel confronts the false teaching of Origen on the Replacement Theology. Israel is the burdensome stone breaking the teaching of Replacement Theology.

Islam does not recognize the covenant God gave to Abraham, Isaac, and Jacob. They believe that the covenant did not go to Isaac but went to Ishmael, Abraham's first son. *"And God said, Sarah thy wife shall bear thee a son indeed; and thou shalt call his name Isaac: and I* **will establish my covenant with him for an everlasting covenant,** *and with his seed after him. And as for Ishmael, I have heard thee: Behold, I have blessed him, and will make him fruitful, and will multiply him exceedingly; twelve princes shall he beget, and I will make him a great nation.* **But my covenant will I establish with Isaac,** *which Sarah shall bear unto thee at this set time in the next year."* **Genesis 17:19-21.**

God choosing Isaac over Ishmael has been the foundation of the Arab-Israel conflict which will continue until the Messiah returns to Zion. The United Nations has made more resolutions against Israel than all the other nations put together. The United States has been Israel's support since it was made a nation in 1948. But the support of Israel started to change in 1991.

This was the first phase in God's plan in restoring His people, Israel, to the land God promised their fathers. The second phase is the judging of the nations for their unbelief in not recognizing God's covenant with Abraham, Isaac, and Jacob. The third will usher in the second Coming of the Son of God to Israel to reign from Zion over Israel and the nations of the world. Today we are in the second phase of God's plan. The nations of the world want to divide Israel and Jerusalem. The nations of the world have to appease the Arab nation because of their need for oil. The goal of the Arab nations is to drive all Israel into the sea, so there will be not one square inch of Palestine owned by the Jews. The United States under George H. W. Bush made the first move as an American President for the dividing of the land of Israel. After President Bush led America to a victory over Iraq in Operation Desert Storm, he took it upon himself to create a peace plan for Israeli-Palestine dispute.

In October of 1991 he convened the Madrid Peace Process. President Bush was to use the United State's power to pressure Israel into a peace process with the Palestinian, Syrians, and Egyptians. The process was to have Israel surrender land for peace. The prophet Joel warned the nations of the world not to part His land. *"For, behold, in those days, and in that time, when I shall bring again the captivity of Judah and Jerusalem, I will also gather all nations, and will bring them down into the valley of Jehoshaphat, and will plead with them there for my people and for my heritage Israel,* **whom they have scattered among the nations, and parted (Divided) my land."** Joel 3:1-2.

In 1993 the Madrid Peace Plan evolved into the Oslo Accords, which set a time table for Israel to withdraw from the parts of the land gained during the 1967 and 1973 wars. The Oslo Accord focused on the city of Jerusalem. By 1998, seven years since the Madrid Peace Plan, the dividing of the city of Jerusalem has failed. The United States was the leader in the land for peace process. After George H. W. Bush was defeated by Bill Clinton, Clinton continued with the plan to divide land for peace. President Clinton pressured Israel to give up large sections of land to the Palestinians. He condemned Israel for building apartments in East Jerusalem.

But it was President George W. Bush who committed the United States to support the Palestinian state. In a speech before the United Nations, he was the first President to use the term "Palestinian State." His speech before the United Nations made it clear. He said, "The American government is committed to a just peace in the Middle East. We are working toward a day when two states, Israel and Palestine live peacefully together within secure and recognized borders." His "Road Map to Peace" included a two state solution with Arab and Israel living side by side. President Bush continued by stating that Israeli occupation of the Palestinian land since 1967 had to end. The United Nations followed with Resolutions 242 and 338 requiring Israel to withdraw from large sections of land including East Jerusalem.

Since 1991, America's policy is no longer in tune with God's agenda for Israel. Starting with President George H. W. Bush's administration, the Clinton administration, and followed by the George W. Bush administration our government has supported a "Road Map to Peace" plan. Since the George W. Bush administration, the United States has been plagued by many disasters starting with the September 11, 2001 attack on America by Islam terrorists. We have seen the destruction of Hurricane Andrew, Hurricane Katrina, and recently Hurricane Sandy. We have been stuck in a win less war in Afghanistan. We have seen a stock market fall disaster followed with a housing balloon crash where many American lost their homes or found themselves upside down in their mortgages. The real unemployment of the American workers is close to twenty percent. Our national debt is out of control. All of these disasters started with America's desire to divide or part the promise land.

Israel will stand as a nation with or without the support of America. The God of Abraham, Isaac, and Jacob is still on the throne. He has not forgotten his covenant with Israel. He will continue to gather his people from all the nations of the earth to return to Israel. Israel was and always will be the **"Apple of His Eye."**

thirty

Israel Today

Israel today is in the midst of the Arab Spring revolution with the Islam nations of the mid-east. There is trouble in Egypt, Syria, Lebanon, Jordan, Libya, and Tunisia. The nations of the world including America are for the creation of a Palestinian State within the borders of Israel. They want it now. In resent United Nation vote on Palestine the United States, Israel and seven other nations voted on the side of Israel. All the other member countries of the United Nations voted in favor of the Palestinian.

Iran is working diligently on the making of an atomic bomb. President Ahmadinejad openly declares that Iran will use the bomb against Israel largest city, Tel Aviv. If Iran hits first, most of Israel's population will be wiped out. So, as the world watches, there is no other answer for Israel is to strike first. **Israel is near the prophesy of Psalm 83.**

*"Keep not thou silence, O God: hold not thy peace, and be not still, O God. For, lo, thine enemies make a tumult: and **they that hate thee** have lifted up the head. They have taken crafty counsel against thy people, and consulted against thy hidden ones. **They have said, Come, and let us cut them off from being a nation; that the name of Israel may be no more in remembrance.***" (verses 1-4) These words are now being spoken by the Islamic nations that surround Israel. They want to drive Israel into the Mediterranean Sea. Many say that if it was not for the United States, Israel would have been destroyed years ago. But that is not the case. If it were not for the **God of Israel** and his promises to Israel, they would have been destroyed years ago. He is their true defender.

*"For they have **consulted together with one consent:** they are confederate against thee:"* (Verse 5) The Psalmist lists all the nations surrounding Israel as they were called during the writing of the Psalm. They are the sons of Ishmael,

Esau, and the children of Abraham by his wife (after Sarah died) Keturah. These nations say, *"Let us take to ourselves the houses of God in possession."* (Verse 12)

*"**O my God**, make them like a wheel; as the stubble before the wind. As the fire burns wood, and as the flame sets the mountains on fire; So persecute them with thy tempest, and make them afraid with thy storm. Fill their faces with shame; that they may seek thy name, O LORD. Let them be confounded and troubled for ever; yea, let them be put to shame, and perish: That men may know that thou, whose name alone is **JEHOVAH**, art the most high over all the earth."* (Verse 13-18)

The desolate land is now a land filled with milk and honey. The fields are green with rich grains and vegetables. The orchards blossom with the best of citrus fruits. Today little Israel supplies Europe with ninety percent of its citrus fruit.

The technology development by Israel is the best of any nation. With a small army they have defeated the Arab nations in three wars. The wars of 1948, 1967, and 1973 have increased the borders of Israel. They have an army that is ready to move within minutes. The Jews are less than three tens of one percent of the world's population, yet the Jews have taken close to twenty percent of the world's highest achievement awards. These awards include the Nobel Peace Prize, the Pulitzer Prize, and all of the major motion picture film making awards.

The religious Jews are making preparations for a new temple. They are making the holy items that will be used in the third temple that will be built. They are setting up a priesthood using DNA testing to find the Aaron descendants to serve as priests. They are searching under the temple site. They have found some of the foundational stones of the destroyed temple and many other rooms that were used under the site for the storage of water and other things used in the old temple.

A group of four has set the beginning of 2014 for a peace agreement between Israel and the Palestinians. The group of four consist of representatives from the United Nations, Europe, United States, and Russia. By the end of the year 2012 they want Israel and the Palestinians to have defined borders for the two states. With uprising in Syria, Egypt and possibly Jordan makes this goal almost impossible. These uprisings got to be known as the Arab Spring. It started in December 18, 2010 with a rebellion in Tunisia lead by the Muslim

Brotherhood followed by a rebellion in Libya, Egypt and Syria. As the year 2013 ended the rebellion continues in Syria and Egypt.

The years 2012 and 2013 was a year of turmoil in the Mid East. Israel and the Palestinians in Gaza were about to come to an all out war. The United Nations worked out a truce between the two forces. Israel had their army along the Gaza border ready to move in with tanks and soldiers. After the truce nearly seventy percent of the people of both sides wanted the conflict to continue and fight it out to the end.

The Mid East is ready to explode, with Iran's desire to complete their atomic bomb capability as soon as possible. Egypt is ready to break the Camp David Accords and move troops into the Sinai toward the southern border of Israel. Will the group of four be able to bring a peace agreement which all the nations of the Mid East will agree to? Will this agreement be the covenant that Daniel prophesied about over two thousand years ago? Will it signal the beginning of the seven year of tribulation or the time of Jacob's trouble?

In any case the world is close to tribulation and the second coming of our Lord Jesus Christ, the Messiah of Israel.

thirty one

Rapture of the Church

The rapture of the church is a tenant of the evangelical churches. The Reformation churches and the Roman Catholic churches do not accept the church being raptured. Most of the churches that do not accept the rapture of the church believe that the church of Jesus Christ will make the world better and prepare the world for the coming of Christ.

The argument of the Reformed churches conclude that the world rapture is not in the Bible. That is true of the King James Version and the new translations of the Bible. The pilgrims were in America before their was a King James Version of the Bible. It was not until the sixteen century that King James of England ordered the churches to come up with a Bible they all could agree on.

The first English translations of the Bible came from the Latin Vulgate Bible. The Latin Vulgate Bible was completed in the forth century. It was largely the work of St. Jerome who was commissioned by Pope Damasus I in 382. The Vulgate Bible used the word "rapture" in referring to the taking out of the church before the time of Jacob's trouble or the tribulation. By the thirteenth century this revision had come to be called the versio vulgata that is, the "commonly used translation", and ultimately it became the definitive and officially promulgated Latin version of the Bible in the Roman Catholic Church. Its widespread adoption led to the eclipse of earlier Latin translations, which are collectively referred to as the Vetus Latina.

With the first translations of the English Bible, they did not have a world for "rapture" so they used the term "gather together unto him." The first two verses in Thessalonians is where we find this. *"Now we beseech you, brethren,* **by the coming of our Lord Jesus Christ, and by our gathering together unto** *him, That ye be not soon shaken in mind, or be troubled, neither by spirit, nor by word, nor by letter as from us, as that the day of Christ is at hand."* **II Thessalonians 2:1-2.**

The doctrine of the rapture of the church and the future of the people of Israel is what sets the main difference between the Evangelical Churches and the Reformation Churches. The message of salvation is held the same in both churches, that is, Jesus Christ paid the sin debt of the world by his atoning blood, his death on the cross, and his being raised from the dead after three days. The doctrine of the rapture and the belief that God is not through with his dealing with the nation of Israel make a difference how one looks at the world today and what is happening in the Mid East. It makes a difference how we look at the work of the United Nations and a one world government.

I was talking to a Reformed man about the world today. I mentioned that we have to be looking at the nation of Israel and what is happening in Israel. His reply was, "What does Israel have to do with what is happening in the world today?" To the Evangelical it means everything. We have seen the Holocaust with its six million unmercifully killed. We have seen the nation of Israel come into being again after two thousand five hundred years on May 14, 1948. We have seen that one hundred sixty million Arabs could not defeat five million Jews. We have seen the United Nations concern about the nation of Israel and the many resolutions made against Israel. We see the world's concern over Israel without caring about the million African Christians being killed by the Muslim Africans.

Paul was the apostle to the Gentile world. He wrote in his letter to the Christians in Corinth in the fifteenth chapter of his first epistle about the resurrection of the dead. The Christians at Corinth were very carnal in their life as Christians. They were easily shaken in their faith. Paul begins with what he preached to them and what they believed. *"Moreover, brethren, **I declare unto you the gospel** which I preached unto you, which also **ye have received**, and wherein **ye stand**; By which also ye are **saved**, if ye keep in memory what I preached unto you, unless ye have believed in vain. For I delivered unto you first of all that which I also received, **how that Christ died for our sins according to the scriptures; And that he was buried, and that he rose again the third day according to the scriptures:** And that he was seen of Cephas, then of the twelve: After that, he was seen of above five hundred brethren at once; of whom the greater part remain unto this present, but some are fallen asleep. After that, he was seen of James; then of all the apostles. And last of all he* *was seen of me also, as of one born out of due time."* **I Corinthians 15:1-8** These eight verses gives the summary of the message that Paul preached to us Gentiles. It is the gospel of salvation. The saints at Corinth **received** the gospel and **stood in faith** in this gospel Paul declared. It was the gospel which they believed and were **saved** from eternal damnation.

The gospel of what was declared to them was, *"**How that Christ died for our sins according to the scriptures; And that he was buried, and that he rose again the third day according to the scriptures:**" It was good news to the Gentiles that the Lord had given Paul during his three years in the Arab wilderness. This gospel has not changed one iota. It is the same gospel that will save people today if they believe (put complete faith in) and have forgiveness of sins and eternal life.*

The saints at Corinth had a question about the resurrection. Paul answers the question saying, "Now if Christ be preached that he rose from the dead, how say some among you that there is no resurrection of the dead? But if there be no resurrection of the dead, then is Christ not risen: **And if Christ be not risen, then is our preaching vain, and your faith is also vain.** *Yea, and we are found false witnesses of God; because we have testified of God that he raised up Christ: whom he raised not up, if so be that the dead rise not. For if the dead rise not, then is not Christ raised: And if* **Christ be not raised, your faith is vain; ye are yet in your sins.** *Then they also which are fallen asleep in Christ are perished. If in this life only we have hope in Christ, we are of all men most miserable.* **But now is Christ risen from the dead, and become the first fruits of them that slept.** *For since by man came death, by man came also the resurrection of the dead.* **For as in Adam all die, even so in Christ shall all be made alive.** *But every man in his own order: Christ the first fruits; afterward they that are Christ's at his coming."* **I Corinthians 15:12-23.** It is utmost important for our salvation that we believe that Christ arose from the dead. One can be a good person believing that Jesus was born and lived, but without the belief that Christ after his crucifixion was raised from death to life, their belief is in vain for salvation.

If Christ was not raised from the dead how can we expect to be raised from the dead? The foundation of our salvation and our being resurrected or raptured is in vain. Paul said we should then eat, drink and be merry because there is no hope for the future after death. Christ was the first to have risen from the dead. The saints of Christ will follow after him.

There will be a time when all the saints of God shall be called to be with him, *"Behold, I show you a* **mystery;** *We shall not all sleep, but we shall all be changed,*

In a moment, in the twinkling of an eye, at the last trump: for the trumpet shall sound, and the dead shall be raised incorruptible, and we shall be changed. For this corruptible must put on incorruption, and this mortal must put on immortality. So when this corruptible shall have put on incorruption, and this mortal shall have put on immortality, then shall be brought to pass the saying that is written, Death is swallowed up in victory. O death, where is thy sting? O grave, where is thy victory? The sting of death is sin; and the strength of sin is the law. But thanks be to God, which giveth us the victory through our Lord Jesus Christ. Therefore, my beloved brethren, be ye steadfast, unmovable, always abounding in the work of the Lord, for as much as ye know that your labor is not in vain in the Lord." **I Corinthians 15:51-58.**

These final verses in I Corinthians fifteen is full of promise to the believer in the atonement of Christ. Up to this point in history the Gentiles were aliens from God without hope in this world. But now there is hope for all who put complete faith in Christ's atonement.

The people of Israel had hope for resurrection. Job a descendant of Abraham said, *"For I know that my* **redeemer lives,** *and that* **he shall stand at the latter day upon the earth."** **Job 19:25.** Job like all the children of Israel were looking forward to the God's earthly kingdom. They did not look for a heavenly home but the Kingdom of Heaven to come to earth and God would be their King. The hope of the children of Israel will be fulfilled in the end time known as the millennium. The Kingdom of Heaven will come to earth and God will be King and rule from Mount Zion. But this is not the hope of those Jews and Gentile who are under the Gospel of Grace. The Lord's prayer tells the event clearly. **"Thy Kingdom come thy will be done on earth as it is in heaven."**

The forty years between the death of Christ and the Roman destruction of the temple and cities of Israel God called and choose the apostle Paul to go to the Gentile world with the Gospel of Grace. Under the Gospel of the Kingdom preached for the first eight years after the crucifixion to the Jews, only the message was as Peter called "**Repent,** and be **baptized** every one of you **in the name of Jesus Chris**t for the **remission of sins,** and ye shall receive the gift of the Holy Ghost." **Acts 2:38** Paul's message of the Gospel of Grace as told to the saints at Corinth, *"How that* **Christ died for our sins** *according to the scriptures; And that* **he was buried,** *and that* **he rose again the third day** *according to the scriptures:"* **I Corinthians 15:1-8.** The Gospel of the Kingdom and the Gospel of Grace were both the gospel of Salvation, one for the Jews and one for the Gentiles. The Gospel of the Kingdom required the Jews to keep the Law of Moses. That included daily prayers and working of the temple. Does that mean that all those who believed in the Gospel of the Kingdom were doomed to hell after the destruction of the temple? God forbid. Thousands of thousands of Jews were killed by Titus when the temple and cities of Israel were destroyed and those who escaped death were scattered throughout the Roman Empire. The promise land of Israel would become desolate for the next 1900 years. But after the temple was destroyed by the Romans, it ended the Gospel of the Kingdom until after the rapture of the church. Then God will send the one hundred forty-four Jewish evangelist to preach to the end time Jews the Gospel of the Kingdom

After the destruction of the temple and the land of Israel, the number of Gentile believers under the Gospel of Grace became much greater than the Jewish believers. The Jewish believers under the Gospel of the Kingdom became part of the Gentile believers under the Gospel of Grace. *"And a certain Jew named Apollos, born at Alexandria, an eloquent man, and mighty in the scriptures, came to Ephesus. This man was instructed in the way of the Lord; and being fervent in the spirit, he spake and taught diligently the things of the Lord, **knowing only the baptism of John.** And he began to speak boldly in the synagogue: whom when Aquila and Priscilla had heard, **they took him unto them, and expounded unto him the way of God more perfectly.** And when he was disposed to pass into Achaia, the brethren wrote, exhorting the disciples to receive him: who, when he was come, helped them much which had believed through grace: For he mightily convinced the Jews, and that publicly, showing by the scriptures that Jesus was Christ."* **Acts 18:24-28.** God knew the early Jewish Christians, no one was going to take them out of his hand. His mighty hand would make known to them the Gospel of Grace.

Peter in his epistles has a different message than his message after Pentecost. *"Peter, an apostle of Jesus Christ, to the strangers scattered throughout Pontus, Galatia, Cappadocia, Asia, and Bithynia, Elect according to the foreknowledge of God the Father, **through sanctification of the Spirit,** unto obedience and sprinkling of **the blood of Jesus Christ:** Grace unto you, and peace, be multiplied."* **I Peter 1:1-2.** In Peter's second epistle he closes with calling Paul the beloved apostle. *"And account that the long suffering of our Lord is salvation; **even as our beloved brother Paul also according to the wisdom given unto him** hath written unto you; As also **in all his epistles,** speaking in them of these things; in which are some things hard* *to be understood, which they that are unlearned and unstable wrest, as they do also the other scriptures, unto their own destruction."* **II Peter 3:15-16.** Peter and the Jewish believers came to understand more fully the message of grace.

Paul's with his first epistle to the Thessalonians did not want the people to live without the knowledge of what happen after death. *"But I would not have you to be ignorant (not having knowledge of), brethren, concerning them which are asleep* (dead), **that ye sorrow not, even as others which have no hope. For if we believe that Jesus died and rose again,** *even so them also which sleep in Jesus* **will God bring with him.** *For this we say unto you by the word of the Lord, that we which are alive and remain unto the coming of the Lord shall not prevent them which are asleep.* **For the Lord himself shall descend from heaven with a shout, with the voice of the archangel, and with the trump of God: and the dead in Christ shall rise first: Then we which are alive and remain shall be caught up together with them in the clouds, to meet the Lord in the air: and so shall we ever be with the Lord.** *Wherefore comfort one another with these words."* I **Thessalonians 4:13.** It is not hard to understand these words and get comfort from them. What a promise that is given to all those who believe that there will be a day when the Lord shall descend from heaven with a great shout and the voice of the archangels with trumpet of God, the dead saint shall arise from where they were buried, and the saints which are alive will follow those saints who have died will meet the Lord in the air and ever be with the Lord. We are so close today for that trumpet to sound and for all the saints of God from Adam to the time he calls us to himself. As Paul said in his epistle to Titus said, *"Looking for that* **blessed hope***, and the glorious appearing of the great God and our Savior Jesus Christ."* **Titus 2:13.**

In Paul's epistles to Timothy and Titus he gives the mantle of his apostleship to each of them. It was time for his departing of this world and to be present with his Lord. In these three epistles, he gives warning of events and things that would happen to the church of Jesus Christ before the blessed hope, the rapture of the church. *"This know also, that in the last days perilous times shall come. For men shall be lovers of their own selves, covetous, boasters, proud, blasphemers, disobedient to parents, unthankful, unholy, Without natural affection, truce breakers, false accusers, incontinent, fierce, despisers of those that are good, Traitors, heady, highminded, lovers of pleasures more than lovers of God; Having a form of godliness, but denying the power thereof: from such turn away."* **II Timothy 3:1-5.** Is this happening in Christendom today. Is Christendom having a form godliness, but denying the power given to the church?

Paul concludes his epistle to Titus with hope. *"For the grace of God that brings salvation hath appeared to all men, Teaching us that, denying ungodliness and worldly lusts, we should live soberly, righteously, and godly, in this present world;* **Looking for that blessed hope, and the glorious appearing of the great God and our Savior Jesus Christ; Who gave himself for us, that he might redeem us from all iniquity, and purify unto himself a peculiar people, zealous of good works***.* "Titus 2:11-14.

Jesus gave the same hope, *"And he shall send his angels with a great sound of a trumpet, and they shall gather together his elect from the four winds, from one end of heaven to the other. Now learn a parable of the fig tree; When his branch is yet tender, and puts forth leaves, ye know that summer is nigh: So likewise ye, when ye shall see all these things, know that it is near, even at the doors.* **Verily I say unto you, This generation shall not pass, till all these things be fulfilled.***"* Matthew 24:31-34.

The fig tree, Israel, God is gathering to the promised land. There is now over seven million Jews back in the promised land. Jerusalem has become a millstone around the necks of the nations. We are close to the shout of the angel and the trumpet of God to sound and the appearing of our Lord Jesus Christ in the air to met the saints of God.

The rapture or resurrection of the saints is the blessed hope of the believer in the present world. There is no other hope than the appearing of the great God and our Savior the Lord Jesus Christ. We shall behold Him our Savior and Lord. Amen.

thirty two

Time of Tribulation

After the saints of the Lord have been removed from the earth, the world will be without the salt that has kept man from evil. The tribulation could happen soon after the rapture or a short time later. The tribulation starts with the confirming of a covenant with the nation of Israel by the Antichrist. This confirming of a covenant could be a confirming of one of the many peace agreement which have been made with Israel in the pass years, or could it be that the Antichrist will confirm the Abrahamic Covenant? *"And he shall **confirm the covenant** with many for one week: and in the midst of the week he shall cause the sacrifice and the oblation to cease, and for the overspreading of abominations he shall make it desolate, even until the consummation, and that determined shall be poured upon the desolate."* **Daniel 9:27.** The confirmation will be for seven years. For the first three and a half years, Israel will build up the third temple and will be making animal sacrifices in the new temple. But at the beginning of the second three and a half years, the Antichrist will break the covenant and will sit in the temple declaring himself to be God.

During this seven years of tribulation, God will raise up one hundred forty-four thousand Jewish witnesses to go to the nations of the world preaching the Gospel of the Kingdom to come. There will be a message of salvation during these bitter seven years. In Jerusalem there will be two of the Old Testament prophets who would speak with great fire power coming out of their mouths against the Antichrist. They will have power to shut the heavens so it would not rain upon the earth. The world will want to kill them but will not be able. They will speak against the Antichrist until the last few day before the return to Christ. At that time, the two prophets will be killed and will lay out in public for three day for all the world to see that they are dead. There will be rejoicing around the world because of the death of the two prophets. It will be as a big celebration party with the giving of gifts because of the joy over their deaths. But suddenly after the three days the prophets will stand up. The party is over, great fear will be upon all the nations and peoples of the earth. The earth shall quake. *"And they heard a great voice from heaven saying unto them,* **Come up hither.** *And they ascended up to heaven in a cloud; and their enemies beheld them. And the same hour was there a great earthquake, and the tenth part of the city fell, and in the earthquake were slain of men seven thousand: and the remnant were frightened, and gave glory to the God of heaven."* **Revelation 11:12-13.**

There are many people, nations, and animals mentioned in both of the books of Daniel and Revelation. There will be the Antichrist, the false prophet, and the two witnesses. Many of the scholars of eschatology have several scenarios as to the identity of character of the players in the tribulation. If God wanted the church to know who all these players, were he would have told so in His book. The Book of Revelation is about what will be happening to the nations of the world and their anger against the nation of Israel. Israel is the focus point of the tribulation. It is the time of Jacob's trouble, and a time of God's wrath against the nations of the world.

The Antichrist is also called the Son of Perdition, the man of sin, or the little horn. The Apostle Paul calls him the Son of Perdition, *"Let no man deceive you by any means: for that day shall not come, except there come a falling away first, and that* **man of sin** *be revealed, the* **son of perdition;** *Who opposes and exalts himself above all that is called God, or that is worshiped; so that he as God sitteth in the temple of God, showing himself that he is God."* **II Thessalonians 2:3-4.** This Antichrist will oppose God and exalts him to be higher than God. Not only the God of Abraham he will exalt himself above but also shall exalts himself being greater than the gods of the heathens, thereby attempting to be a god to all nations and religions. Most eschatology scholars agree that in the middle of the seven years he will go to the temple on Mount Zion and declare himself to be God.

What nation shall the Antichrist come from? This has been debated by eschatology Bible scholars for the past century. Some say that the Antichrist will come from Europe and some say that he will come from the Mid East. Having read many of the books on eschatology, it is still a mystery of where and who will make up the ten nations confederacy. Who will be the Antichrist and the False Prophet is still a mystery. But where ever he will come from, he will confirm a covenant with Israel and will be declared God at the middle of the tribulation. Does it really matter if the Antichrist comes from Europe, the Mid East or even South America? Who ever the Antichrist is, what he will do is the important issue. But this I know, he will be present in the seven years of the tribulation and will lead the nations of the world to Armageddon.

The **Antichrist** will be assisted by the **False Prophet**. The identity of who the false prophet will be is uncertain by the eschatology scholars. Saint Malachy, a twelfth century sainted priest of the Roman Catholic Church, predicted that the one hundred thirteenth pope will be the false prophet. The present Pope Benedict VI is the one hundred twelfth pope. According to Saint Malachy Pope Benedict will die or retire in the year 2012 or early 2013. The prediction of the session of the Popes is highly respected by the Vatican. He predicted that the pope following Pope Benedict will take the name of Peter or Leo. There are other scholars who put the false prophet coming from other than the Roman Catholic church. It is ironic that Saint Malachy is of the Roman Catholic Church and he is the one who predicted that the false prophet will come from the Roman Catholic Church.

There will be an **alliance of ten nations.** Some say these nations will be the rebirth of the Roman Empire in Europe. When Greece became the tenth nation of the European Union some were sure that was it. But the European Union now has a membership of twenty-seven nations. Others say it will be alliance of ten Mid-East nations. Among these ten nations will rise up a small nations or the little horn nation. This small nation will become strong and take over three of the end time ten nation alliance. The leader of the small nation will become the Antichrist. In Europe no one really knows who this small nation is. Some believe that the three nations that the Antichrist takes over are the Netherlands, Belgium, and Luxemburg. Those who feel that the ten nations in the Mid-East fell that the Kurds in northern Iraq will rise up and take over three of the lower Muslim nations that were part of the Soviet Union.

In Daniel chapter seven and Revelation chapter thirteen there are **four beasts** mentioned. The four beast will be a lion, bear, leopard and a dreadful, terrible, exceedingly strong beast. The beast will have great iron teeth and will have ten horns. The scholars of eschatology differ much as to who or what these four beast represent.

The books of Daniel and Revelation are books of prophecy of the final seven years before the coming of the Lord Jesus Christ to rule and reign over Israel and the world. The Kingdom of Heaven will come down from heaven and Christ shall rule from Mount Zion in the city of Jerusalem. The devil, the Antichrist, and the False Prophet will be cast into the lake of fire.

The scene opens in the fourth chapter of the book of the Revelation. The scene opens in heaven at the throne of God. Around the throne are twenty-four elders sitting before the throne. The scene is filled with praise to the Lord God Almighty. The twenty-four elders cast their crown of gold before the throne. They say, *"Thou art worthy, O Lord, to received glory, honor, and power for you have created all things, that were created."* Revelation 4:11.

Chapter five of Revelation opens with Lord holding in his right hand a book (scroll) with seven seals that sealed the scroll. The question is asked, *"Who is worthy to open the scroll, and to loose the seals."* No man could be found to open the seals. In the midst of the elders, stood **the Lamb of God**. The same Lamb of God which John the Baptist had introduced to Israel many years before by saying, "Behold **the Lamb of God** which taken away the sins of the world." The elders and those around the throne began to sing, "Thou art worthy to take the scroll and open the seals thereof; **for thou has redeemed us to God by thy blood of every kindred, tongue, people, and nations:** And have made us unto our God kings and priest and we shall reign on the earth." And the host of angels joined in saying with load voices, **"Worthy is the Lamb** that was slain to receive power, riches, wisdom, strength, honor, glory, and blessing for ever and ever."

Chapter six opens with the removing of the seals. The first seal was removed and a white horse appeared with a man sitting on the horse with a bow, a crown was given him and he went forth to conquer. The second seal was removed and a red horse appeared with a man sitting on the horse with a great sword. Power was given him to take peace from the earth and man would kill one another. The third seal was removed and a black horse appeared with a man sitting on the horse holding a pair of balances in his hand saying, "A measure of wheat or four measures of barley for a days wages but do not hurt the oil and wine." The forth seal was removed and a pale (green) horse appeared with a man sitting on the horse whose name was Death and Hell. Power was given him over one forth of the earth to kill with sword, hunger, and with death.

What are the **four horses of the Apocalypse?** This is also been debated by the end time eschatology Bible scholars for the past century. The first horse is a white horse, the second a red horse, the third a black horse, and the forth horse a pale or green horse. Some say the white horse represents the coming of the Antichrist, the red horse the coming a great war, the black horse is a great famine that follows the war, and the pale horse is pestilences. Others say that the white horse is the Holy Roman Empire reborn, the red horse being the world under communism, the black horse the world under capitalism, and the green or pale horse is the world under the rule of Islam. Again, having read many of the books it makes one wonder if any of the books are right.

Babylon the Great *is the great prostitute that sits upon many waters. "The kings the earth have committed fornication and the inhabitants of the earth have been made drunk of the wine of her fornication."* **Revelation 17:2.** This great prostitute has committed fornication with all the world. She has worldwide power over the leaders and inhabitants of the world. Judah turned from following the law of Moses and the temple atonement to wickedness of the nations surrounded it. They went from dwelling in safety of the city of Jerusalem to the captivity of Babylon. Christendom has fallen from the precepts of the Word of God to captivity into the precepts of Babylon. Babylon the city has been destroyed. The world's commerce that started in Babylon is influencing the world's commerce, economics, education, the arts, government and religion, taking it from righteousness to a system of dishonesty and deceit. This Babylonian system will bring the armies of the world against Jerusalem and the Lamb of God. Scholars differ about what or who is Babylon the Great. Some say the city of Babylon will be rebuilt. Some think that it is the city of Dubai in the United Arab Emirates. Other scholars say it is a wicked economic and commerce system that has influenced the leaders and people of this world. What ever it is, it will be destroyed in the tribulation years.

The prophet Jeremiah summarized the future of Israel and Judah and the tribulation being the time of **Jacob's trouble.** The word that came to Jeremiah from the LORD, saying, *"Thus speaks the LORD God of Israel, saying, Write thee all the words that I have spoken unto thee in a book. For, lo, the days come, saith the LORD, that **I will bring again the captivity of my people Israel and Judah,** saith the LORD: and **I will cause them to return to the land that I gave to their fathers, and they shall possess it.** And these are the words that the LORD spake concerning Israel* *and concerning Judah. For thus saith the* LORD; *"We have heard a voice of trembling, of fear, and not of peace. Ask ye now, and see whether a man doth travail with child? wherefore do I see every man with his hands on his loins, as a woman in travail, and all faces are turned into paleness? Alas!* **for that day is great, so** *that none is like it: it* **is even the time of Jacob's trouble,** *but he shall be saved out of it. For it shall come to pass in that day, saith the* LORD *of hosts, that I* **will break his yoke from off thy neck,** *and will* **burst thy bonds, and strangers shall no more serve themselves of him: But they shall serve the** LORD **their God,** *and David their king, whom I will raise up unto them. Therefore fear thou not, O my servant Jacob, saith the* LORD; *neither be dismayed, O Israel: for, lo, I* **will save thee from afar, and thy seed from the land of their captivity; and Jacob** (children of Israel) **shall return, and shall be in rest, and be quiet, and none shall make him afraid."** Jeremiah 30.

Most of Christendom believes that God has forsaken Israel and replaced it with the Church. This was a false doctrine started by Origen of Alexandria, Egypt at the beginning of the fifth century. It has stayed with Christendom since. Most of Christendom looks at Israel today without any knowledge of the promises of God to Abraham, Isaac, Jacob, and their descendants. They cannot see that God is the one who is bringing back his people from his scattering them throughout the world some nineteen hundred years ago.. During this time of Jacob's trouble all nations will turn against Israel. Even our beloved United States of America will some day force the American Jews to leave our country and return to Israel. When the Jews were being killed by the millions in Russia during pogroms or when the six million Jews were sent to the gas chambers and ovens of Germany the world did not have any doubt they were the descendants of Abraham, Isaac and Jacob. But when they started to return to Palestine and become a nation then the world doubted they were Jews. When Jerusalem today is like a millstone around the necks of the nations, then was it not God gathering the "apple of his eye," Israel back into the promised land?

The fifth seal was removed and under the altar were the souls of those who slain for the testimony of the word of God. They cried, *"**How long, O Lord, holy and true,** do you not **judge and avenge** our blood on those that dwell on earth?" The time of tribulation on earth is to judge and avenge those who died for the sake of the Lord Jesus Christ. White robes were given the martyrs under the altar and told to rest for a little while until their fellow servants* (the hundred and forth Jewish evangelists) *should be killed. The sixth seal was opened and there was a great earthquake and the sun* *became black and the moon to turn red. The stars in heaven would fall on the earth like fruit from a tree. The heaven departed and all kings, great men, chief captains, mighty men, bondmen, and free men hid themselves in the dens, caves, and rocks of the mountains. They would call, "Rocks fall on us and hide us from the face of him on the throne and from the* **wrath of the Lamb.** *For the great day of his wrath is come, and who shall be able to stand?"* **Revelation 6:17.**

After the wrath of God poured out on earth after the sixth seal, the **one hundred and forty thousand Jewish evangelist** are sealed. They will consist of twelve thousand from twelve tribes of Israel. Then the four angels stood on the four corners of the earth holding back the winds. When the rains of the earth are dependent on the winds to blow across the oceans. Without wind there is little or no rain. But even in the tribulation **God's grace** is made known. *"After this there appeared a great multitude so great than no man could number them. They were clothed in white robes with palms in their hands and cried with a loud voice,* ***"SALVATION TO OUR GOD WHICH SITS UPON THE THRONE, AND UNTO THE LAMB."*** *Then all the elders and angels around the throne worshiped God saying, "Amen: blessing, glory, wisdom, thanksgiving, honor, power, and might be to our God for ever and ever, Amen." Who were the multitude? They are those who came out of the great tribulation and have* **washed their robes in the blood of the Lamb.** *The* **Lamb** *will then feed them and lead them to living waters, and God shall wipe away all the tears from their eyes."* **See Revelation 7.**

The last of the seven seals is removed from the scroll. There was silence in heaven for the space of thirty minutes. Then came seven angels with seven trumpets and stood before God. One of the angels took a censer (a vessel that holds incense) filled with fire and cast it to the earth and there were voices, thunderings, lightnings, and an earthquake. The seven angels which had the trumpets prepared themselves to sound.

The first angel sounded. There followed hail and fire mixed with blood which was cast on the earth. Then a third part of the trees and grass on the earth were burnt up. The second angel sounded and a great burning fiery mountain was cast into the sea and a **third part of the sea became blood. A third of the sea creatures died and a third part of the ships of the sea were destroyed.** The third angel sounded. A great burning star from the heavens fell upon a third part of the rivers and springs of the earth. The name of the star was Wormwood. When the Wormwood star fell on earth a third of the waters of the earth became contaminated. Many men will die from the contaminated water. (It is interesting to know that the Russian word for Wormwood is chernobyl. The nuclear reactor in the city of Chernobyl went out of control resulting in a city of fifty thousand people becoming a ghost town. It happen some twenty-six years ago and the city sits vacant today. Russia estimated the the disaster caused the death of nearly nine hundred and eighty thousand people.)

The forth angel sounded. **A third part of the sun, moon, stars were smitten and darkened and a third part of the daytime was like night.** Another angel said with a loud voice, "Woe, woe, woe, to the inhibitors of the earth for the last three trumpets are about to sound." The fifth angel sounded and a star fell from heaven to the earth with the key to the bottomless pit. The bottomless pit was opened and smoke came from the pit and the sun and air were darkened and **out of the pit came locusts upon the earth with a sting like a scorpion.** They were commanded not to hurt the green trees and grass but sting man for a period of five months. **The sting would cause men to seek death but unable to find it.** This was the first of the three woes.

The sixth angel sounded its trumpet and the four angels which are bound in the Euphrates River were loosen. The four angels in a year, a month, a day, and hour **would slay a third part of mankind.** The two thirds that were not slain by the four angels did not repent of their sin of murders, sorceries, thefts or fornication . **They continued to worship idols made by their own hands, devils, and idols of gold, silver, brass and wood.**

Between the sixth and seventh trumpet is the mid point of the tribulation. A measuring rod was given to John. He was to measure the temple of God, the altar, and them that worship there. John was not to measure the part that was given to the Gentiles. The holy city will be tread under foot for the next three and a half years. The two witnesses are given power for the final half of the tribulation also called the great tribulation. If any man on earth would try to hurt them fire shall come out of the mouths of the two prophets and devour them. The prophets will have power to shut off the rain from heaven, to turn water into blood, and smite the earth with plagues. **At this time Israel will flee into the wilderness to a place to hide prepared by God** and will be hid there until the return of Christ. Satan and his legion of fallen angels are cast out of heaven. *"And I heard a loud voice saying in heaven,* **Now is come salvation,** *and strength, and the kingdom of our God, and the power of his Christ: for the accuser of our brethren is cast down, which accused them before our God day and night.* **And they overcame him by the blood of the Lamb**, *and by the word of their testimony; and they loved not their lives unto the death. Therefore rejoice, ye heavens, and ye that dwell in them. Woe to the inhabiters of the earth and of the sea! for the devil is come down unto you, having great wrath, because he knoweth that he hath but a short time."* **Revelation 12:10-12.**

The first beast (the Antichrist) rises out of the sea having seven heads and ten horns. Scholars have different views as to what nations the seven heads and seven horns represent. Out of these nations will rise a little horn who will overtake three of the first ten horns. This little horn will be the Antichrist and the world will worship him. Then a second beast will come out of the earth. He will have the same power as the Antichrist and cause the world to worship the Antichrist. **He will cause all men to receive a mark on their right hand or their foreheads. No one will be able to buy or sell without his mark. His number will be six hundred sixty-six.** All those who have the mark will have the wrath of God poured out on them.

"And the seventh angel sounded; and there were great voices in heaven, saying, The kingdoms of this world are become the kingdoms of our Lord, and of his Christ; **and he shall reign for ever and ever."** **Revelation 11:15.** The seventh angel sounds and introduces the seven angels with vials or bowls **filled with the wrath of God.**

The first angel's vial is poured upon the earth. **Grievous sores came upon all those who received the mark of the beast.** The second angel's vial is poured upon the sea and **the sea becomes as the blood of dead men.** The third angel's vial is poured upon **the rivers and springs that they too will become blood.** The fourth angel's vial is poured upon the sun and power was given him to **scorch men with fire.** Man then blasphemes the name of God and they repented not or to give God glory. The fifth angel's vial is then poured on the seat of the beast and his **kingdom. It became dark the people of his kingdom gnawed their tongue in pain and blasphemed God** and repented not of their deeds. The sixth angel's vial is poured upon the Euphrates River. The water of the Euphrates dried up to make way for the kings of the east. God then gathers all the armies of the earth to the valley of Armageddon. The seventh angel's vial is poured out into the air. And a great voice came out of the temple of heaven and from the throne saying, *"It is done!"* Then **there**

were thunders, lightnings, and a mighty earthquake such as was never was before. The city of Jerusalem was departed into three parts. *"And there fell upon men a* **great hail out of the heavens** *weighting about one hundred pounds, and man blasphemed God because of the plague of hail for the plague was exceedingly great."* This is followed by the fall of Babylon. Some scholars say that Babylon will be rebuilt but other say it is the fall of the world's system of economics, education, government, and finance.

Jesus prophesied the about this time of **Jacob's trouble,** *"And Jesus went out, and departed from the temple: and his disciples came to him for to show him the buildings of the temple. And Jesus said unto them, "See ye not all these things?" verily I say unto you, "There shall not be left here one stone upon another, that shall not be thrown down."* Here Jesus was prophesying about the destruction of the temple that happened in 70 BC. When the temple was destroyed there was much gold between the stones in the temple. The Roman soldiers moved every stone to find the gold. Afterward they completely destroyed the temple area and filled it with dirt and planted vegetation where the temple site was. Then Jesus was on the mount of Olives with his disciples and they came to him again with a question.

"And as he sat upon the mount of Olives, the disciples came unto him privately, saying, "Tell us, when shall these things be? and what shall be the **sign of thy coming, and of the end of the world?"** This is the question of the ages. What are the signs of the Second coming of Jesus? What are the signs of the end of the world? In Matthew 24 the chapter is Christ's answer to their question.

"And Jesus answered and said unto them, "Take heed that no man deceive you. **For many shall come in my name, saying, I am Christ; and shall deceive many."** (Verse 4-5) There are many today saying they are the Christ. Islam claims that the Twelfth Imam or the Mahdi is the Messiah. Iran's former president, Ahmadinejad, said that his mission is to cause crisis in the world today to bring the hidden Mahdi from his cave and arise and be the savior of the world. *"And ye shall hear of wars and rumors of wars: see that ye be not troubled: for all these things must come to pass, but the end is not yet. For nation shall rise against nation, and kingdom against kingdom: and there shall be famines, and pestilences, and earthquakes, in divers places. All these are the beginning of sorrows."* (Verse 6-8) Do we hear about wars and rumors today. Today the United States is at war for eleven years. We have troop going to Turkey to calm the uprising in Syria. The world is trying to get a truce agreement between Israel and the Palestinians. We see uprising in

Egypt. We see North Korea building weapons of mass destruction. There has been rebellions in Tunisia, Libya, Egypt, Syria, and rumors of a rebellion coming to Jordan. The Arab world is boiling over with its hate for Israel. They do not want peace with Israel. They want to completely destroy Israel and drive the Israelis into the sea. The world is crying, "Peace, Peace but there is no Peace."

Today many of the eschatological teachers and scholars agree there are three wars to come. First will be the **war of Psalms 83**. *"Keep not thou silence, O God: hold not thy peace, and be not still, O God. For, lo,* **thine enemies make a tumult***: and they that* **hate thee have lifted up the head.** *They have* **taken crafty counsel against thy people,** *and consulted against thy hidden ones. They have said,* **Come, and let us cut them off from being a nation; that the name of Israel may be no more in remembrance.** *For they have consulted together with one consent: they are confederate against thee:"* **Psalms 83:1-5.** There has been bitterness of the nations and cities just east of the Jordan River since Israel became a nation in 1948. They tried to cut off Israel in the 1948 attack against Israel, then the 1967 attack, and then the 1973 Yon Kipper attack. But there is going to be one more attack against Israel and by the sons of Abraham through Ishmael and the sons of Abraham from his wife after Sarah died, Keturah. The Psalmist ends the chapter with a call to God, "O *my God, make them like a wheel; as the stubble before the wind. As the fire burns a wood, and as the flame sets the mountains on fire; So persecute them with thy tempest, and make them afraid with thy storm. Fill their faces with shame; that they may seek thy name, O LORD. Let them be confounded and troubled for ever; yea, let them be put to shame, and perish:* **That men may know that thou, whose name alone is JEHOVAH, art the most high over all the earth."** **Psalms 83:13-18.** The purpose of this war is to show the world that the God of Israel is the true God and the most high over all the earth. The term "most high" has always been the term for God for the Gentile world. The war of Psalm 83 will be a quick war and Israel will be the conqueror and will possess their land to the East of the Jordan River.

The second of these three wars will be the **war of Ezekiel 38**. The nations of Iran (Persia), a nation to the far north of Israel, (some believe this is the nation of Turkey some believe it will be Russia) , the Islamic nations in the Mid-East and Northern African Islamic nations. At the end of the war God will cause great delusions on those who have come against Israel as it was at the time of Gideon so that they will kill one another. *"And I will call for a sword against* *him throughout all my mountains, saith the Lord GOD:* **every man's sword shall be against his brother.** *And I will plead against him with pestilence and with blood; and I will rain upon him, and upon his bands, and upon the many people that are with him, an overflowing rain, and great hailstones, fire, and brimstone. Thus will I magnify myself, and sanctify myself; and I will be known in the eyes of many nations, and they shall know that I am the LORD."* **Ezekiel 38:21-23.** The war will cause much death. Only one sixth of those who come against Israel in this war will survive. "Therefore, thou son of man, prophesy against Gog, and say, Thus saith the Lord GOD; Behold, I am against thee, O Gog, the chief prince of Meshech and Tubal: And I will turn thee back, and leave but the sixth part of thee, and will cause thee to come up from the north parts, and will bring thee upon the mountains of Israel: And I will smite thy bow out of thy left hand, and will cause thine arrows to fall out of thy right hand. **Ezekiel 39:1-3** If the nation from the far north is Turkey, it's arm forces number over a million. If five sixth are killed in the Ezekiel War, that will mean that nearly nine hundred thousand of their armed forces will be destroyed.

The third and final war will be **Armageddon** when all the nations of the world turn against Israel and Christ returns and will personally destroy all the armies of the nations coming against her. The blood will flow to the depth of a horse's bridle. This will be the war to end all wars. At this time the Kingdom of Heaven will come with Christ and Mount Zion will be the throne of God. All the wars against Israel in the twentieth century have ended up with Israel being the winner. Many claim that God has interred in miraculous ways to give Israel victory over its Arab enemies.

Going back to Matthew 24 and the answer Jesus gave the disciples about the end of the age. *Jesus said 'Then shall they deliver you* (Israel) *up to be afflicted, and shall kill you*(Israel) *: and ye* (Israel) *shall be hated of all nations for my name's sake. And then shall many be offended, and shall betray one another, and shall hate one another. And many false prophets shall rise, and shall deceive many. And because iniquity shall abound, the love of many shall wax cold. But he that shall endure unto the end, the same shall be saved."* Israel is the nation that shall be afflicted, killed and be hated by all nations of the world. Jerusalem, the city of God, is the city that all the nations of the world want to be the holy city of God for all religions of the world. The religious leaders of the world will deceive the nations of the world about Jerusalem. Sin will abound during this time of tribulation, many of the Jewish people will lack any type of love, but those who endure will be saved when Christ returns, and they will see the nail prints and will know he was the Jesus who was slain on Mount Calvary. *"And I will pour upon the* **house of David**, *and upon the* **inhabitants of Jerusalem**, *the spirit of grace and of supplications: and* **they shall look upon me whom they have pierced,** *and they shall mourn for him, as one mourns for his only son, and shall be in bitterness for him, as one that is in bitterness for his firstborn."* **Zechariah 12:10.**

Jesus continues to answer the question of the disciples as to the End of the Age, *"And this gospel of the kingdom shall be preached in all the world for a witness unto all nations;* (This will be the work of the one hundred forty four thousand Jews. They will not be preaching the Gospel of Grace but the Jewish Gospel of the Kingdom) *and then shall the end come. When ye therefore shall see the abomination of desolation,* (The Antichrist going into the Jewish temple and declaring himself as God.) *spoken of by Daniel the prophet, stand in the holy place, (whoso reads, let him understand:) Then let them which be in Judaea flee into the mountains: Let him which is on the housetop not come down to take any thing out of his house: Neither let him which is in the field return back to take his clothes. And woe unto them that are with child, and to them that give suck in those days! But pray ye that your flight be not in the winter, neither on the sabbath day: For then shall be great tribulation, such as was not since the beginning of the world to this time, no, nor ever shall be. And except those days should be shortened, there should no flesh be saved: but for the elect's sake those days shall be shortened."* This will occur in the center of the seven year tribulation. The Antichrist declares himself as God, Christ then warns the Jews in Jerusalem and the cities of Judah to flee to the mountains. God has a place in the mountains prepared for the ones who flee. Some scholars say it will be the present area called Petra. When this happens it will be the beginning of the last three and a half years of the tribulation called the Great Tribulation.

The tribulation time will be a time that will distress all the earth. It will be far worse that the two world wars put together. It will be a time worse than the pogrom and the holocaust put together for the people of Israel. But in the midst of all the tribulations to mankind, there is also the **grace, mercy, and love of God.** God will personally hide his remnant of Israel and there will salvation of such a number of Gentiles that no man can number. These will be the ones who have put faith in our Lord Jesus Christ will not take the mark of the beast. They will be killed as martyrs for Christ.

Jesus continues to answer the question of the disciples, *"Then if any man shall say unto you, Lo, here is Christ, or there; believe it not. For there shall arise false Christs, and false prophets, and shall show great signs and wonders; insomuch that, if it were possible, they shall deceive the very elect. Behold, I have told you before. Wherefore if they shall say unto you, Behold, he is in the desert; go not forth: behold, he is in the secret chambers; believe it not."* There will be the False Prophet and he will have many other who will go out to the world declaring the Antichrist is God. The False Prophet will show many sign and wonders to deceive the world that the Antichrist is God.

Jesus continues to answer the question of the disciples, *"For as the lightning cometh out of the east, and shines even unto the west; so shall also the coming of the Son of man be."* The Eastern Gate of Jerusalem has for many years been filled in. The Eastern Gate will then be opened for Jesus's second coming, to be King of kings and LORD of lords to take the throne of David and rule the world from Mount Zion.

Jesus continues in chapter 24 of Matthew to answer the question of the disciples, ***"For wheresoever the carcase is, there will the eagles be gathered together. Immediately after the tribulation of those days shall the sun be darkened, and the moon shall not give her light, and the stars shall fall from heaven, and the powers of the heavens shall be shaken: And then shall appear the sign of the Son of man in heaven: and then shall all the tribes of the earth mourn, and they shall see the Son of man coming in the clouds of heaven with power and great glory. And he shall send his angels with a great sound of a trumpet, and they shall gather together his elect from the four winds, from one end of heaven to the other."*** When all the nations armies are destroyed by the Words of Christ spoken with a tongue of a two edged sword. The birds will be eating the flesh of those who have died. Jesus will reign over Israel and the world from the Mount of Olives. The TV camera will be there so all the world can see Christ's return. They will hear the voice of angels and the trumpet sound. The angels shall gather the Jews from where God has hid them. *"And I will pour upon the **house of David**, and upon the **inhabitants of Jerusalem,** the spirit of **grace and of supplications:** and **they shall look upon me whom they have pierced, and they shall mourn for him,** a*s one mourns for his only son, and shall be in bitterness for him, as one that is in bitterness for his firstborn."* **Zechariah 12:10** . *"And one shall say unto him, What are these wounds in thine hands? Then he shall answer, "Those with which I was wounded in the house of my friends."* **Zachariah 13:6.**

Jesus continues to answer the question of the disciples, *"Now learn a parable of the fig tree; When his branch is yet tender, and puts forth leaves, ye know that summer is nigh: So likewise ye, when ye shall see all these things, know that it is near, even at the doors. Verily I say unto you, This generation shall not pass, till all these things be fulfilled. Heaven and earth shall pass away, but my words shall not pass away."* This is a warning to all to be watchful. Israel is the fig tree. The fig tree was planted in 1948. It has been over sixty years since the planting of the fig tree. The generation that planted the fig tree in 1948, shall not die until we see the return of Christ. Many in Christendom today are not being watchful. They have seen the rebirth of Israel in Palestine, they hear the news about the trouble in Israel and Jerusalem, but yet they do not heed the warning.

Jesus continues to answer the question of the disciples, *"But of that day and hour knoweth no man, no, not the angels of heaven, but my Father only. But as the days of Noah were, so shall also the coming of the Son of man be. For as in the days that were before the flood they were eating and drinking, marrying and giving in marriage, until the day that Noe entered into the ark, And knew not until the flood came, and took them all away; so shall also the coming of the Son of man be. Then shall two be in the field; the one shall be taken, and the other left. Two women shall be grinding at the mill; the one shall be taken, and the other left.* **Watch therefore:** *for ye know not what hour your Lord doth come. But know this, that if the good man of the house had known in what watch the thief would come, he would have watched, and would not have suffered his house to be broken up.* **Therefore be ye also ready:** *for in such an hour as ye think not the Son of man cometh. Who then is a faithful and wise servant, whom his lord hath made ruler over his household, to give them meat in due season?* **Blessed is that servant, whom his lord when he cometh shall find so doing.** *Verily I say unto you, That he shall make him ruler over all his goods. But and if that evil servant shall say in his heart,* **My lord delays his coming; And shall begin to smite his fellow servants, and to eat and drink with the drunken; The lord of that servant shall come in a day when he looks not for him, and in an hour that he is not aware of, And shall cut him asunder, and appoint him his portion with the hypocrites: there shall be weeping and gnashing of teeth.** Matthew 24

Jesus ends his answer with a warning that the world should be watching after Israel became a nation. Today at the end of 2013 the Group of Four (United Nations, America, European Union, and Russia) has given the Palestinians and

192 | David Visser

Israel a limited time to reach an agreement that would end the conflict between the two parties. The Mid-East at this time is in turmoil, Syria is having a rebellion, Egypt in in rebellion once again, and Jordan is in fear of a uprising in their nation. The United States of America is in a no win war in Afghanistan. Iran is building a nuclear bomb and when the work is completed they say they will use it to destroy Israel. Israel is in a position that they have to act first to have their nation from nuclear destruction.

The world runs on oil. Without oil this world will crumble. We need oil for our automobiles, for heat in the winter, for fertilizer for our crops and for the movement of the armies, navies, and air forces of the world. The Mid-East Islamic nations hold most of the available oil in the world today. They hate Israel and use the demand for oil to make the nations of the world hate Israel too. The hatred will continue until Christ returns. A world without Mid-East oil is a world in trouble. Food production for the world today is dependent on oil to feed the whole world. The world is held hostage to oil.

The United States supplied the world with oil during World War II. America's oil reserves are getting lessor every year. We are not using available oil in the waters off our coast. We are more dependent on foreign oil everyday. The cost of oil has made America a debtor nation. At the end of World War II we were the worlds largest creditor nation where today we are the world largest debtor nation. America did a total flip-flop.

Near the end of the tribulation, God will cause the fall of Babylon the Great. (either a real city or a system of commerce). The leaders of the nation and the merchants who have accumulated great wealth from the Babylonian system shall see their abundances and delicacies fall into ashes. The sin of Babylon has reached into heaven and God remembers their iniquities. God in heaven is going to give those who are part of Babylon double the trouble that she has given other nations of the earth. In one day shall plagues, death, mourning, and famine destroy her.

After her destruction merchants of gold, silver, precious stone, pearls, fine linen, silk, and fine vessels of ivory, wood, brass, iron and marble shall weep. The ship masters, the company of ships, sailors, and all who trade across the seas see the destruction from afar and cry, *"Alas, alas, that great city, (Babylon) wherein were made rich and all had ships in the sea by reason of her costliness! For in one hour she is made desolate."* **Revelation 18:19.** The very wealthy of the world who bought these luxuries will be destroyed in one hour. All the things that the wealthy took so much pride in are gone. It took only one hour.

The question that scholars are asking, "Will the city of Babylon be rebuilt or is the present city of Dubai, which is center of Arab oil riches, be modern Babylon?" Other scholars say the city is New York City is the new Babylon or the whole nation of America. Others say it is the present world of commerce and economics owned by the very rich and powerful of the this world which is the Babylon that will be destroyed.

The time is at hand. Jesus answers to the End of Age is at hand. His coming in the clouds of the air to gather his bride. His bride will those in Christendom who truly have their faith in the blood atonement of the Lord Jesus Christ on Mount Calvary. There is only one way. Without the shedding of blood there is no forgiveness for sin. Without faith it is impossible to please God. He is the rewarder of all those who seek him. Therefore, be ready, **He is coming SOON!**

Many books have been written on the tribulation. Most of the writers speculate on what nations will be the ten nation confederacy. They speculate on where the Antichrist shall come from. They speculate of where the Antichrist and False Prophet will be from. There are several scenarios as to who is who. Some say they will come from Europe, others from the Mid-East Islamic countries. The Bible does not tell us. **But it does tell us about the wrath of God.** One cannot express the vastness of the tribulation. The scriptures are true, there is going to be a time of Jacob's trouble which all the nations of the earth will have to come to grips with. It is a dire situation to fall into the arms of an angry God. *"The same shall drink of the wine of the* **wrath of God***, which is poured out without mixture into the cup of his indignation; and he shall be tormented with fire and brimstone in the presence of the holy angels, and in the presence of the Lamb."* **Revelation 14:10.**

Heaven is not quiet while the earth is in tribulation. As the return of Christ to earth is about to happen there will be a wedding in heaven. *"And I heard as it were the voice of a great multitude, and as the voice of many waters, and as the voice of mighty thunderings, saying, "Alleluia: for the Lord God omnipotent reigns. Let us be glad and rejoice, and give honor to him: for the marriage of the Lamb is come, and his wife hath made herself ready."* **Revelation 19:6-7.** To the bride (the true church of God) was arrayed in fine linen, clean white, for the fine linen is the righteousness (which was given to the saints in exchange of their sins) of saints. *"Write, Blessed are they which are called unto the marriage supper of the Lamb. And he saith unto me, These are the true sayings of God."* **Revelation 19:9.**

When the marriage supper is complete, it is time for the bridegroom (the lord Jesus Christ) to return with his bride to earth to put an end to wickedness of man. *"And I saw heaven opened, and behold a* **white horse;** *and he that sat upon him was called* **Faithful and True,** *and in righteousness he doth judge and make war. His eyes were as a flame of fire, and on his head were many crowns; and he had a name written, that no man knew, but he himself. And he was clothed with a vesture dipped in blood:* **and his name is called The Word of God.** *And the armies which were in heaven followed him upon white horses, clothed in fine linen, white and clean. (the saints who are now the bride of Christ.) And out of his mouth goes a sharp sword, that with it he should smite the nations: and he shall rule them with a rod of iron: and he treads the wine press of the fierceness and* **wrath of Almighty God.** *And he hath on his vesture and on his thigh a name written,* **KING OF KING AND LORD OF LORDS** *And I saw an angel standing in the sun; and he cried with a loud voice, saying to all the fowls that fly in the midst of heaven, "Come and gather yourselves together unto the supper of the great God; That ye may eat the flesh of kings, and the flesh of captains, and the flesh of mighty men, and the flesh of horses, and of them that sit on them, and the flesh of all men, both free and bond, both small and great." And I saw the* **beast** *(the Antichrist), and the kings of the earth, and their armies, gathered together to make war against him that sat on the horse, and against his army. And the* **beast** *(the Antichrist) was taken, and with him the* **false prophet** *that wrought miracles before him, with which he deceived them that had received the mark of the beast, and them that worshiped his image. These both were cast alive into a lake of fire burning with brimstone. And the remnant were slain with the sword of him that sat upon the horse, which sword proceeded out of his mouth: and all the fowls were filled with their flesh."* **Revelation 19:11-21.**

"And I saw an angel come down from heaven, having the key of the bottomless pit and a great chain in his hand. **And he laid hold on the dragon, that old serpent, which is the Devil, and Satan, and bound him a thousand years,** *And cast him into the bottomless pit, and shut him up, and set a seal upon him, that* **he should deceive the nations no more, till the thousand years should be fulfilled:**

and after that he must be loosed a little season. And I saw thrones, and they sat upon them, and judgment was given unto them: (the twelve Apostles) and I saw the souls of them that were beheaded for the witness of Jesus, and for the word of God, and which had not worshiped the beast, neither his image, neither had received his mark upon their foreheads, or in their hands; and **they lived and reigned with Christ a thousand years."** **Revelation 20:1-4.**

thirty three

Kingdom of Heaven on Earth

"For unto us a child is born, unto us a son is given: and the **government shall be upon his shoulder:** *and his name shall be called* **Wonderful, Counselor, The mighty God, The everlasting Father, The Prince of Peace**. *Of the increase of his government and peace there shall be no end, upon the throne of David, and upon his kingdom, to order it, and to establish it with judgment and with justice from henceforth even for ever.* **The zeal of the Lord of hosts will perform this."** Isaiah 9:6-7.

When Jesus was in the synagogue in Nazareth he stood up and read from Isaiah. *"The Spirit of the Lord GOD is upon me; because the LORD hath anointed me to* **preach good tidings** *unto the meek; he hath sent me to* **bind up the broken-hearted,** *to* **proclaim liberty to the captive**s, *and the* **opening of the prison** *to them that are bound; To* **proclaim the acceptable year of the LORD,"** Isaiah **61:1-2** Jesus stopped in the middle of verse two. Up to that point in the verse was a description of his first coming. After that point it pertained to his second coming. At Christ returns to reign the thousand year reign he finishes the rest of the prophesy, "and the day of vengeance of our God (the time of tribulation or Jacob's trouble); (then the millennium) to comfort all that mourn; To appoint unto them that mourn in Zion, to **give unto them beauty for ashes,** the **oil of joy for mourning,** the **garment of praise for the spirit of heaviness;** that they might be called trees of righteousness, the planting of the LORD, that he might be glorified.

And they shall build the old wastes, they shall raise up the former desolations, and they shall repair the waste cities, the desolations of many generations. And s**trangers shall stand and feed your flocks,** and the sons of the **alien shall be your plowmen and your vine dressers.**

But ye shall be named the **Priests of the LORD:** men shall call you the **Ministers of our God:** you shall eat the riches of the Gentiles, and in their glory shall ye boast yourselves. For your shame ye shall have double; and for confusion they shall rejoice in their portion: therefore in their land they shall possess the double: **everlasting joy shall be unto them.**

For I the LORD love judgment, I hate robbery for burnt offering; and I will direct their work in truth, and **I will make an everlasting covenant with them.** And their seed shall be known among the Gentiles, and their offspring among the people: all that see them shall acknowledge them, that they are the seed which the LORD hath blessed.

I will greatly rejoice in the LORD, my soul shall be joyful in my God; for he hath **clothed me with the garments of salvation,** he hath **covered me with the robe of righteousness,** as a bridegroom decks himself with ornaments, and as a bride adorns herself with her jewels. For as the earth brings forth her bud, and as the garden causes the things that are sown in it to spring forth; so the Lord GOD will cause righteousness and praise to spring forth before all the nations." **Isaiah 61:2-11**

"Blessed and holy is **he that has part in the first resurrection**: on such the second death shall be powerless, but they **shall be priests of God and of Christ,** and **shall reign with him a thousand years." Revelation 20:6** The scene has changed. God shall dwell with his people on earth. They shall be priests and rulers during this millennium (thousand years) reign with Christ. When Christ returns he will bring with him the **Kingdom of Heaven.** The earth for a thousand years will be free of war and tribulation. The tribulation did not destroy all of mankind or beast. The world's population when the tribulation started was about seven billion people. When Christ return the earth's population has shrunk to about two billion. The nation of Israel will be firmly planted in the land that their God promised Abraham, Isaac and Jacob. It is the land from the Euphrates River to the Nile River. The Lord Jesus Christ will be on the throne of David on Mount Zion in Jerusalem. It is the beginning of the Millennium Age. The marriage of the Lamb had happened. The bride of Christ will be with the bridegroom (the Lord Jesus Christ) on earth to rule and reign with him. They will not be part of Israel but they will be ruling and reigning with him over the two billion Gentile people still alive on the earth. There will be plenty of work to do to reclaim the earth from the damage of the tribulation.

Jesus spoke much about the Kingdom of Heaven and what it was going to be like. **The Kingdom of Heaven is totally Jewish. It is part of the Abrahamic Covenant.** The gospel of Matthew is where the Kingdom of Heaven is most expressed in the scripture. *"From that time Jesus began to preach, and to say, "Repent: for the **kingdom of heaven** is at hand."* King Jesus the Son of David, the Son of God was in their midst. If they would have believed Jesus, the kingdom of heaven would have been theirs then. But they did not accept him as their king, but instead put him to death.

The kingdom of heaven was for the poor in spirit, for those who were persecuted for righteousness sake, for those who teach men the commandments, and for those who righteousness exceeded the righteousness of the scribes and Pharisees. But, that is all. Man must be as righteousness as God in Heaven is righteous. It is impossible. That is why Christ gave his life on the cross make all who believe, to cleanse them of **all** unrighteous.

Jesus prophesied, *"That many shall come from the east and west, and shall sit down with Abraham, and Isaac, and Jacob, in the **kingdom of heaven**. Verily I say unto you, Among them that are born of women there hath not risen a greater than John the Baptist: notwithstanding he that is least in the kingdom **of heaven** is greater than he. He answered and said unto them, Because it is given unto you to know the mysteries **of the kingdom of heaven**, but to them it is not given."* Here we see that all the Old Testament men of faith will be there when the kingdom of heaven come down from heaven to earth at the second coming of Christ. The Kingdom of Heaven when on earth will be for his people Israel. The kingdom will start at the Euphrates River and end at the river of Egypt which in the Nile River. What is in store for Gentiles believers, Paul knew, but could not tell of its greatness.

Another parable spake he unto them; *"The **kingdom of heaven** is like unto leaven, which a woman took, and hid in three measures of meal, till the whole was leavened."* All these things spake Jesus unto the multitude in parables; and without a parable spake he not unto them: That it might be fulfilled which was spoken by the prophet, saying, *"I will open my mouth in parables; I will utter things which have been kept secret from the foundation of the world."* Then Jesus sent the multitude away, and went into the house: and his disciples came unto him, saying, *"Declare unto us the parable of the tares of the field."* He answered and said unto them, "He that Sows to the good seed is the Son of man; The field is the world; the **good seed are the children of the kingdom;** but the **tares are the children** *of the wicked one; The enemy that sowed them is the devil; the harvest is the end of the world; and the reapers are the angels. As therefore the tares are gathered and burned in the fire; so shall it be in the end of this world. The Son of man shall send forth his angels, and they shall gather out of his kingdom all things that offend, and them which do iniquity; And shall cast them into a furnace of fire: there shall be wailing and gnashing of teeth. Then shall the righteous shine forth as the sun in the kingdom of their Father. Who hath ears to hear, let him hear."* Matthew 13:33-43.

Again Jesus said unto them, "The kingdom of heaven is like unto treasure hid in a field; the which when a man hath found, he hides, and for joy thereof goes and sells all that he hath, and buys that field. Again, the kingdom of heaven is like unto a merchant man, seeking goodly pearls: Who, when he had found one pearl of great price, went and sold all that he had, and bought it. Again, the kingdom of heaven is like unto a net, that was cast into the sea, and gathered of every kind: Which, when it was full, they drew to shore, and sat down, and gathered the good into vessels, but cast the bad away. So shall it be at the end of the world: the angels shall come forth, and sever the wicked from among the just, And shall cast them into the furnace of fire: there shall be wailing and gnashing of teeth." Jesus saith unto them, "Have ye understood all these things?" They say unto him, "Yea, Lord." Then said he unto them, *"Therefore every scribe which is instructed unto the kingdom of heaven is like unto a man that is an householder, which brings forth out of his treasure things new and old."* Matthew 13:44-52. At the same time came the disciples to Jesus, saying, *"Who is the greatest in the kingdom of heaven?"* And Jesus called a little child unto him, and set him in the midst of them, And said, *"Verily I say unto you, Except ye be converted, and become as little children, ye shall not enter into the kingdom of heaven. Whosoever therefore shall humble himself as this little child, the same is greatest in the kingdom of heaven."* Matthew 18:1-4. But Jesus said, *"Suffer little children, and forbid them not, to come unto me: for of such is the kingdom of heaven."* Matthew 19:14.

And Jesus said unto them, "The kingdom of heaven is like unto a man that is an householder, which went out early in the morning to hire laborers into his vineyard. And when he had agreed with the laborers for a penny a day, he sent them into his vineyard. And he went out about the third hour, and saw others standing idle in the marketplace, And said unto them; Go ye also into the vineyard, and whatsoever is right I will give you. And they went their way. Again he went out about the sixth and ninth hour, and did likewise. And about the eleventh hour he went out, and found others standing idle, and saith unto them, Why stand ye here all the day idle? They say unto him, Because no man hath hired us. He saith unto them, Go ye also into the vineyard; and whatsoever is right, that shall ye receive. So when even was come, the lord of the vineyard saith unto his steward, Call the laborers, and give them their hire, beginning from the last unto the first. And when they came that were hired about the eleventh hour, they received every man a penny. But when the first came, they supposed that they should have received more; and they likewise received every man a penny. And when they had received it, they murmured against the good man of the house, Saying, "These last have wrought but one hour, and thou hast made them equal unto us, which have borne the burden and heat of the day." But he answered one of them, and said, "Friend, I do thee no wrong: didst not thou agree with me for a penny? Take that thine is, and go thy way: I will give unto this last, even as unto thee. Is it not lawful for me to do what I will with mine own? Is thine eye evil, because I am good?" **"So the last shall be first, and the first last: for many be called, but few chosen."** This is a lengthy parable to show that is not the time of service that matters. It is service that counts. The thief on the cross realized that Jesus was the Messiah and turned and asked for mercy. His life as child of God was less than a day. But after nineteenth hundred years he had set an example of the love of God.

And Jesus going up to Jerusalem took the twelve disciples apart in the way, and said unto them, *"Behold, we go up to Jerusalem; and the Son of man shall be betrayed unto the chief priests and unto the scribes, and they shall condemn him to death, shall deliver him to the Gentiles to mock, and to scourge, and to crucify him: and the third day he shall rise again."* (Here Jesus told the twelve that he would be betrayed unto the religious leaders, be condemned to death, delivered to the Gentiles who would mock, scourge and crucify him, and on the third day arise from the death. This went over their heads, they never heard or understood what Jesus had just told them. Their interest was in a ruling and reign Christ with the twelve as his assistants.) *Then came to him the mother of Zebedees children with her sons, worshiping him, and desiring a certain thing of him. And he said unto her, "What will thou" She saith unto him, "Grant that these my two sons may sit, the one on thy right hand, and the other on the left,* **in thy kingdom.**" *But Jesus answered and said, "Ye know not what ye ask. Are ye able to drink of the cup that I shall drink of, and to be baptized with the baptism that I am baptized with?" They say unto him, "We are able." And he saith unto them, "Ye shall drink indeed of my cup, and be baptized with the baptism that I am baptized with: but to sit on my right hand, and on my left, is not mine to give, but it shall be given to them for whom it is prepared of my Father."* **Matthew 20:1-24.**

Jesus said unto the scribes and Pharisees, "But woe unto you, scribes and Pharisees, hypocrites! for ye shut up the **kingdom of heaven** *against men: for ye neither go in yourselves, neither suffer ye them that are entering to go in. Woe unto you, scribes and Pharisees, hypocrites! for ye devour widows' houses, and for a pretense make long prayer: therefore ye shall receive the greater damnation. Woe unto you, scribes and Pharisees, hypocrites! for ye compass sea and land to make one proselyte, and when he is made, ye make him twofold more the child of hell than yourselves."* **Matthew 23:13-15.**

"The **kingdoms** *of this world are* **becoming the kingdoms of our Lord, and of his Christ;** *and he shall* **reign for ever and ever."** **Revelation 11:15.** *"And I heard a loud voice saying in heaven, Now is come* **salvation, and strength,** *and the* **kingdom of our God,** *and the* **power of his Christ:** *for the accuser of our brethren is cast down, which accused them before our God day and night."* **Revelation 12:10.**

During the thousand years reign of Christ the land of Israel shall flower like a rose. As God promised them many years before, *"But I have said unto you, Ye shall inherit their land, and I will give it unto you to possess it, a land that flows with* **milk and honey:** *I am the LORD your God, which have separated you from other people."* **Leviticus 22:24.** The spring and later rains shall come each year with just the amount of water needed for the best of crops. The flowers and grains of the fields and orchards will bloom in abundances. The bees will have millions blossoms to suck the nectar from. Their hives will be flowing with honey. The green grass and fields of grain will be abundant to feed the cattle who will produce an abundance of milk. The land will be so rich that the reapers cannot keep up with the sowers. *Behold, the days come, saith the LORD, that the plowman shall overtake the reaper, and the treader of grapes him that sows seed; and the mountains shall drop sweet wine, and all the hills shall melt. And I will bring again the captivity of my people of Israel, and they shall build the waste cities, and inhabit them; and they shall plant vineyards, and drink the wine thereof; they shall also make gardens, and eat the fruit of them. And I will plant them upon their land, and they shall no more be pulled up out of their land which I have given them, saith the LORD thy God.* **Amos 9:13-15.** This will be for every year of the millennium. The vineyards will be filled with large clusters of grapes so large that one man cannot carry them. Every promise that God gave Abraham, Isaac, and Jacob will be fulfilled.

And there shall come forth a rod out of the stem of Jesse, and a Branch shall grow out of his roots: And the spirit of the Lord shall rest upon him, the spirit of wisdom and understanding, the spirit of counsel and might, the spirit of knowledge and of the fear of the Lord; And shall make him of quick understanding in the fear of the Lord: and he shall not judge after the sight of his eyes, neither reprove after the hearing of his ears: But with righteousness shall he judge the poor, and reprove with equity for the meek of the earth: and he shall smite the earth: with the rod of his mouth, and with the breath of his lips shall he slay the wicked. And righteousness shall be the girdle of his loins, and faithfulness the girdle of his reins. The wolf also shall dwell with the lamb, and the leopard shall lie down with the kid; and the calf and the young lion and the fatling together; and a little child shall lead them. And the cow and the bear shall feed; their young ones shall lie down together: and the lion shall eat straw like the ox. And the sucking child shall play on the hole of the asp, and the weaned child shall put his hand on the cockatrice' den. They shall not hurt nor destroy in all my holy mountain: for the earth shall be full of the knowledge of the Lord, as the waters cover the sea. And in that day there shall be a root of Jesse, which shall stand for an ensign of the people; to it shall the Gentiles seek: and his rest shall be glorious. **Isaiah 11:1-10.**

"Then the eyes of the blind shall be opened, and the ears of the deaf shall be unstopped. Then shall the lame man leap as an hart, and the tongue of the dumb sing: for in the wilderness shall waters break out, and streams in the desert. And the parched ground shall become a pool, and the thirsty land springs of water: in the habitation of dragons, where each lay, shall be grass with reeds and rushes. And an highway shall be there, and a way, and it shall be called The way of holiness; the unclean shall not pass over it; but it shall be for those: the wayfaring men, though fools, shall not err therein. No lion shall be there, nor any ravenous beast shall go up thereon, it shall not be found there; but the redeemed shall walk there: And the ransomed of the LORD *shall return, and come to Zion with songs and everlasting joy upon their heads: they shall obtain joy and gladness, and sorrow and sighing shall flee away."* **Isaiah 35:5-10.**

The remaining Gentiles on earth at the end of the tribulation will be in their own nation being ruled by the bride of Christ. They will be able to have children and multiply greatly. At the end of the millennium the earth again will be filled with people. During this time there will be not more wars. *"And* **he shall judge among the nations,** *and shall rebuke many people: and they shall beat their swords into plowshares, and their spears into pruning hooks: nation shall not lift up sword against nation, neither shall they learn war any more.* **Isaiah 2:4.**

thirty four

After the Millennium

The Millennium will come to an end after one thousand years. There is still more that God has to do to bring redemption and judgment to this world. When Jesus was on earth at his first coming he told of future resurrections. The first shall be those who put their faith in the atoning blood of Christ and a second resurrection of judgment for all who died in unbelief in his blood atonement. *"Verily, verily, I say unto you, The hour is coming, and now is, when **the dead shall hear the voice of the Son of God: and they that hear shall live**. For as the Father hath life in himself; so hath he given to the Son to have life in himself; And hath **given him** (The Lord Jesus Christ) **authority to execute judgment also**, because he is the Son of man. Marvel not at this: for the hour is coming, in the which all that are in the graves shall hear his voice, And shall come forth; they that have done good, unto the resurrection of life; and they that have done evil, unto the resurrection of damnation."* **John 5:25-29.**

Again, in the final book in the Bible, the book of Revelation, the second resurrection is brought forth. *"But the rest of the dead lived not again until the thousand years were finished. This is the first resurrection. Blessed and holy is he that hath part in the first resurrection: on such the second death hath no power, but they* (Israel) *shall be priests of God and of Christ, and shall reign with him a thousand years."* **Revelation 20:5-6.**

The end of the millennium is not the end of the world. But at the end of the millennium there will be, as previously mentioned, billions of people on this earth. The millennium did not stop reproduction of man or beast. The Gentile people on earth after the millennium have never been tempted by Satan. Satan had been bound during the thousand years. The millennium people, like us today, have to be tempted by Satan to see if they will believe in the righteousness of God or will fall for Satan's lies.

"And when the thousand years are expired, Satan shall be loosed out of his prison, And shall go out to deceive the nations which are in the four quarters of the earth, Gog, and Magog, to gather them together to battle: the **number of whom is as the sand of the sea.** *And they went up on the breadth of the earth, and* **compassed the camp of the saints about, and the beloved city***: and fire came down from God out of heaven, and devoured them.* **And the devil that deceived them was cast into the lake of fire and brimstone, where the beast and the false prophet are, and shall be tormented day and night for ever and ever.** *And I saw a great white throne, and him that sat on it, from whose face the earth and the heaven fled away; and there was found no place for them."* **Revelation 20:7-11.**

The Gentile people during the millennium lived in peace and prosperity. *"And he shall judge among the nations, and shall rebuke many people: and they shall beat their swords into plowshares, and their spears into pruning hooks: nation shall not lift up sword against nation, neither shall they learn war any more."* **Isaiah 2:4.** But like Adam and Eve, they will soon fall for Satan's lies and deceptions. They will melt their plows and pruning hooks into weapons. Who will be their enemy? **Israel.** Just like it is in our generation, the ones the world says the evil enemy is – Israel. As man did during the war of Armageddon, they will bring their armies against the Mount of Zion in Jerusalem. Why does Satan hate Israel, the people of God, so much? It is where God will dwell.

"Great is the LORD, *and greatly to be praised in the city of our God, in the mountain of his holiness.* **Beautiful for situation, the joy of the whole earth, is mount Zion** *(in Jerusalem of Judah)* **,** *on the sides of the north, the* **city of the great King.** *God is known in her palaces for a refuge.* **For, lo, the kings were assembled, they passed by together.** *They saw it, and so they marveled; they were troubled, and hasted away. Fear took hold upon them there, and pain, as of a woman in travail. Thou breaks the ships of Tarshish with an east wind. As we have heard, so have we seen in the* **city of the** LORD **of hosts, in the city of our God: God will establish it for ever.** *We have thought of thy loving kindness, O God,* **in the midst of thy temple.** *According to thy name, O God, so is thy praise unto the ends of the earth: thy right hand is full of righteousness. Let* **mount Zion** *(in Jerusalem of Judah) rejoice, let the daughters of Judah be glad, because of thy judgments.* **Walk about Zion,** *and go round about her: tell the towers thereof. Mark ye well her bulwarks, consider her palaces; that ye may tell it to the generation following.* **For this God is our God for ever and ever: he will be our guide even unto death."** Psalm 48.

After the final war of Gog and Magog as they are about to attack Israel, fire will come down from heaven and devour the army. ***"And the devil that deceived them was cast into the lake of fire and brimstone, where the beast and the false prophet are, and shall be tormented day and night for ever and ever.*** *And I saw a great white throne, and him that sat on it, from whose face the earth and the heaven fled away; and there was found no place for them.* **And I saw the dead, small and great, stand before God; and the books were opened:** *and another book was opened, which is the book of life: and the dead were judged out of those things which were written in the books, according to their works. And the sea gave up the dead which were in it; and death and hell delivered up the dead which were in them: and* **they were judged every man according to their works.** *And death and hell were cast into the lake of fire. This is the second death. And whosoever was not found written in the book of life was cast into the lake of fire."* **Revelation 20:10-15.**

The judgment will not be for sin. The judgment for sin was done at Calvary when the wrath of God was poured out of our Lord Jesus Christ for the sins of the world. Everyone shall be judged according to their works. Their works will be filthy rags because they refused to believe God. They were in total unbelief. Self righteousness will never cut it. *"But we are all as an unclean thing, and all our righteousness is as* **filthy rags;** *and we all do fade as a leaf; and our iniquities, like the wind, have taken us away."* **Isaiah 64:6.**

The judgment will be over soon. All those who name was not in the book of Life will be cast into the lake of fire. **(See Revelation 20:15.)** But the end is not over. Redemption of the earth and universe has to be done. Sin has put its stain on the earth and all the heavens.

thirty five

The New Heavens and New Earth

The sin and deceit of Satan has stained the whole creation. The creation itself will have to be redeemed back to God. Peter in his second epistle makes reference to this. *"Look for and hasting unto the coming of the day of God, wherein the* **heavens being on fire shall dissolved,** *and the elements shall* **melt with fervent heat.***"* **2 Peter 3:12**

The Twenty-second chapter of Revelation in the Bible tells what is going to happen. *"And I saw a new heaven and a new earth: for the first heaven and the first earth were passed away; and there was no more sea. And I John saw the holy city, new Jerusalem, coming down from God out of heaven, prepared as a bride adorned for her husband. And I heard a great voice out of heaven saying,* **"Behold, the tabernacle of God is with men, and he will dwell with them, and they shall be his people, and God himself shall be with them, and be their God."**

And **God shall wipe away all tears** *from their eyes; and there shall be* **no more death,** *neither* **sorrow, nor crying, neither shall there be any more pain:** *for the former things are passed away. And he that sat upon the throne said, Behold, I make all things new. And he said unto me, Write: for these words are true and faithful. And he said unto me, "It is done. I am Alpha and Omega, the beginning and the end. I* **will give unto him that is thirsty of the fountain of the water of life freely."**

He that overcomes shall inherit all things; and **I will be his God, and he shall be my son.** *But the fearful, and unbelieving, and the abominable, and murderers, and whore mongers, and sorcerers, and idolaters, and all liars, shall have their part in the lake which burns with fire and brimstone: which is the second death.*

An angel talked with me, saying, "Come hither, I will show thee the bride, the Lamb's wife. And he carried me away in the spirit to a great and high mountain, and shewed me that great city, the holy Jerusalem, descending out of heaven from God, Having the glory of God:

and her light was like unto a stone most precious, even like a jasper stone, clear as crystal; And had a wall great and high, and had twelve gates, and at the gates twelve angels, and names written thereon, which are the names of the twelve tribes of the children of Israel."

"The wall of the city had twelve foundations, and in them the names of the twelve apostles of the Lamb. And he that talked with me had a golden reed to measure the city, and the gates thereof, and the wall thereof. And the city is foursquare. The city was pure gold, like unto clear glass. The city had twelve gates were twelve pearls: every several gate was of one pearl: and the street of the city was pure gold, as it were transparent glass."

I saw no temple therein: for the Lord God Almighty and the Lamb are the temple of it. And the city had no need of the sun, neither of the moon, to shine in it: for the glory of God did lighten it, and the Lamb is the light thereof. And the nations of them which are saved shall walk in the light of it: and the kings of the earth do bring their glory and honor into it. The gates of it shall not be shut at all by day: for there shall be no night there. And they shall bring the glory and honor of the nations into it. And there shall in no wise enter into it any thing that defiles, neither whatsoever worketh abomination, or maketh a lie: but they which are written in the Lamb's book of life.

And he shewed me a pure river of water of life, clear as crystal, proceeding out of the throne of God and of the Lamb. In the midst of the street of it, and on either side of the river, was there the tree of life, which bare twelve manner of fruits, and yielded her fruit every month: and the leaves of the tree were for the healing of the nations. And there shall be no more curse: but the throne of God and of the Lamb shall be in it; and his servants shall serve him: And they shall see his face; and his name shall be in their foreheads. And there shall be no night there; and they need no candle, neither light of the sun; for the Lord God giveth them light: and they shall reign for ever and ever. And he said unto me, "These sayings are faithful and true: and the Lord God of the holy prophets sent his angel to show unto his servants the things which must shortly be done."

"Behold, I come quickly: blessed is he that keeps the sayings of the prophecy of this book." And he (the angel) saith unto me, "Seal not the sayings of the prophecy of this book: for the time is at hand. He that is unjust, let him be unjust still: and he which is filthy, let him be filthy still: and he that is righteous, let him be righteous still: and he that is holy, let him be holy still."

"And, behold, I come quickly; and my reward is with me, to give every man according as his work shall be. I am Alpha and Omega, the beginning and the end, the first and the last." Blessed are they that do his commandments, that they may have right *to the tree of life, and may enter in through the gates into the city.* **I, Jesus,** *have sent mine angel to testify unto you these things in the churches. I am the root and the offspring of David, and the bright and morning star."*

And the Spirit and the bride say, **Come.** *And let him that hears say,* **"Come.** *And let him that is thirsty come. And whosoever will, let him take the water of life freely."*

For I testify unto every man that hears the words of the prophecy of this book, If any man shall add unto these things, God shall add unto him the plagues that are written in this book: And if any man shall take away from the words of the book of this prophecy, God shall take away his part out of the book of life, and out of the holy city, and from the things which are written in this book.

He which testifies these things saith, **"Surely I come quickly. Amen."** *Even so,* **come, Lord Jesus.** *The grace of our Lord Jesus Christ be with you all. Amen."* **(See Revelation 21 & 22.)**

"Come unto me, all **ye that labor and are heavy laden,** *and I will give you rest. Take my yoke upon you, and learn of me; for I am meek and lowly in heart: and ye shall find rest unto your souls. For my yoke is easy, and my burden is light."* **Matthew 11:28-30.** Christ died for the ungodly not for the righteous. *"You see, at just the right time, when we were still powerless, Christ* **died** *for the* **ungodly."** **Romans 5:6** *For it is by* **grace** *you have been* **saved,** *through* **faith**—*and this is not from yourselves, it is the* **gift** *of God.* **Ephesians 2:8.** God's grace is shown to man, by God (the Father) putting his wrath on God **(the Son).** God, the Son, our Lord Jesus Christ, did all that was required by the Godhead for man to be justified (righteousified). **You cannot add one iota** to what the Lord Jesus Christ did by shedding his own blood for the sin of man. **If you do,** it is no more grace. **It is all by faith in His atonement plus nothing.**

Word for the Author

At the age of ten my family moved to a new town. We had planned to attend a local reformation church the following Sunday, as we were accustomed to, but arriving there late, my father decided we would go to a small Bible church across the street. We also went there again the same night, and never went back to the reformation church. The pastor of the Bible church taught and emphasized on the epistles of Paul. At the age of twenty-five, as a result of a serious automobile accident, I became a paraplegic. For many years I drifted from church to church. But in about 1995, I started watching on a daily basis, "Through the Bible with Les Feldick."* Within a month, I was hooked on watching his Bible teaching program every morning.

Many years ago my partner in the construction business, Ted Lubbers, asked me to write a history of our business. This lead to writing my autobiography which I completed sometime in the late 1980's and updated it in 2013. Following that, I began writing on the New Testament gospels and the epistles of Paul. I asked my friend Bob Bailey, to edit the writings. Bob and I met at a Les Feldick meeting many years ago. Both of us are paraplegics, and we sat in the same aisle, and during a break I went up and started talking to Bob. From them we were fast friends. We would have dinner together once a week when we were both up and well. For the past ten to fifteen years or more each morning we both watch, "Through the Bible with Les Feldick." During those years we both learned the Bible from Les. Even now with me living in Michigan, we call each other once a week.

When I first became a believer, I saw God up in Heaven with a baseball bat in his hands read to bop me every time I sinned. Slowly the bat got smaller, then no bat at all, and I saw God with his arms wide open, running down a dusty road to love me as I am . Now, today when I am in prayer or conversation with him, I know he loves me as I am, and I love Him back. He is my best friend. Oh, what a joy, to know God, s love, and be able to love Him back. When I sin, I tell him because he already knows. God know all about it, my sin has already been accounted for on the cross of Jesus, and I thank Him for taking the wrath for that sin upon His Son. Praise God for his matchless love.

Notes: All Bible quotes are from the King James Version or the New King James Version of the Bible.

Les Feldick is an Oklahoma rancher and has enjoyed that lifestyle for many years. Les and his wife, Iris, have been married since 1953. They have three grown children and eight grandchildren. What Les really likes is teaching the Bible. He has been teaching home-style Bible classes for over 30 years. His teaching is non-denominational, and his students come from diverse denominations and backgrounds. It was through one of these classes that a student helped open the door for his "***Through the Bible***" television program.

Les has never had any formal Bible training. It is through the Holy Spirit that he is able to teach night after night, never using lesson plans or notes, and seemingly, never growing tired. Les teaches in four different cities on a regular basis.

Les starts his classes in Genesis 1:1 and works all the way through the Bible. All the Scriptures quoted are referenced from the King James Version. Les comments that "Once a class has been 'Through the Bible' with me, we generally start over and do it again."

Les Feldick Ministries, 30706 W. Lona Valley Rd., Kinta, OK 74552

Phone: 1-800-369-7856 or (918) 768-3218

www.lesFeldick.org